FAR AWAY PLACES

Vice Admiral Charles Emery Rosendahl
and the Navy's Airship Program

M. Ernest Marshall

SUNBURY
P R E S S
Mechanicsburg, PA USA

Published by Sunbury Press, Inc.
Mechanicsburg, PA USA

SUNBURY
P R E S S

www.sunburypress.com

For information about special discounts for bulk purchases, please contact Sunbury Press Orders Dept. at (855) 338-8359 or orders@sunburypress.com.

To request one of our authors for speaking engagements or book signings, please contact Sunbury Press Publicity Dept. at publicity@sunburypress.com.

FIRST SUNBURY PRESS EDITION: October 2023

Set in Adobe Garamond Pro | Interior design by Crystal Devine | Cover by Lawrence Knorr | Edited by Sarah Peachey.

Publisher's Cataloging-in-Publication Data
Names: Marshall, M. Ernest, author.
Title: Far away places : Vice Admiral Charles Emery Rosendahl and the Navy's airship program / M. Ernest Marshall.
Description: First trade paperback edition. | Mechanicsburg, PA : Sunbury Press, 2023.
Summary: Wrapped in a detailed memoir of Vice Admiral Charles Rosendahl, this book tells the story of the US Navy's adoption of German Zeppelin airship technology, describing both the technological advances and conflicts within the Navy.
Identifiers: ISBN : 979-8-88819-146-0 (hardcover) | ISBN : 979-8-88819-147-7 (ePub).
Subjects: BIOGRAPHY & AUTOBIOGRAPHY / Aviation & Nautical | HISTORY / Military / Naval | History / Military / Aviation & Space.

Product of the United States of America
0 1 1 2 3 5 8 13 21 34 55

For the Love of Books!

This book is dedicated to the men and women of the United States Naval Academy who "serve as the young keepers of the nation's honor on the sea."

[Staff Correspondent, *The Baltimore Sun*, June 3, 1914, p. 2]

"THE AEROPLANE IS TRAGICALLY UNSUITED FOR OCEAN SERVICE."

—DR. HUGO ECKENER

CONTENTS

ACKNOWLEDGMENTS

The author expresses deep gratitude to the people and institutions whose assistance made this manuscript possible. Personnel records for Vice Admiral Charles Emery Rosendahl, Admiral Herbert Victor Wiley, Captain Frank R. McCrary, and Rear Admiral William Alger Moffett were obtained from the National Archives and Records Administration (NARA), National Personnel Records Center, St. Louis, Missouri. Copies of the logbooks of the Navy airships, USS *Shenandoah* (ZR-1), USS *Los Angeles* (ZR-3), USS *Akron* (ZRS-4), and USS *Macon* (ZRS-5) and the proceedings of Navy Courts of Inquiry were obtained from NARA, Washington, D.C. Logbooks, action reports, war diaries, and damage reports of the USS *Minneapolis* (CA-36) were obtained from NARA, College Park, Maryland.

Famed lighter-than-air historian and author William F. Althoff donated transcripts of oral histories that he obtained from numerous lighter-than-air notable persons to The William F. Althoff Oral History Library, Smithsonian Libraries/National Air and Space Museum, Washington, D.C. to make them available to researchers. The author is grateful to Mr. Phil Edwards of the National Air and Space Museum for allowing this collection to be used and referenced during the early stages of its organization.

American Peter Belin was a passenger on board the *Hindenburg* during its last flight from Friedrichshafen, Germany, to Naval Air Station Lakehurst, New Jersey. Belin took photographs during that journey, including a number of images captured during the final approach to landing. These were taken just prior to the tragic destruction of the *Hindenburg*. His images captured the last happy moments of the airship. Peter Belin's images remain in the control of his son, Mr. Harry Lammot Belin. Dr. Cheryl Ganz, Chief Curator (Emerita) of the Smithsonian National Postal Museum and the *Hindenburg* exhibition, served as interlocutor that allowed the author to obtain permission for the reproduction of three of Peter Belin's images here, and, for that, special gratitude is expressed to Mr. Belin and to Dr. Ganz.

Special appreciation is expressed for Ms. Patrizia Nava, MA, CA, Curator of Aviation Archives, Special Collections and Archives Division, History of Aviation Archives, The University of Texas at Dallas. Ms. Nava provided access to the Charles E. Rosendahl Collection and copies of numerous documents and photographs from that collection.

Great appreciation is expressed for Ms. Sarah Peachey of Sunbury Press for her excellent and timely editorial skills—she made this a better book.

THE LONG JOURNEY TO LAKEHURST

Of Swedish descent, Charles Emery Rosendahl was born in Chicago, Illinois, to parents Charles O. and Johanna Rosendahl. Emery, as he was known to family and friends, developed a wanderlust at an early age. His father worked for the vast Santa Fe Railroad system—a job that required a number of residential moves until the family settled finally in Cleburne, Texas, where Emery spent his early youth. With a romantic flare, Emery described his life in the outskirts of this small town "with great, wide-open, flat prairies spreading around it like an ocean."[1]

"Over its horizons day and night, trains came and passed to background music of deep-throated locomotive whistles and the clackety-clack of iron wheels on iron rails. On summer nights an impressionable lad could fall asleep wondering about the rest of the world to which those ribbons of steel led, while the prairie breeze fanned the spark of wanderlust."[2]

He was inspired by reports of life as a midshipman at the Naval Academy, and, having passed the preliminary examinations, his long Navy career began as he entered the Academy on July 9, 1910, appointed from the 12th Congressional District of Texas. Final qualifying examinations were administered in Annapolis, and the one Rosendahl worried about most was the physical examination. He feared he might not meet the Academy's minimum weight requirement.

He checked into the old Maryland Hotel in Annapolis, where it was customary for Academy hopefuls to await their final examinations and the call to report to take the oath, swearing them in as midshipmen. Having passed his examinations, including the physical, Rosendahl forever credited the Naval Academy for opening the door to a fascinating life.

It was customary for midshipmen to acquire nicknames and Rosendahl had several. A favorite pastime among his peers was "calling out his goat," and it took little to elicit a vigorous response. He could be riled easily by calling him "Rabbi" or singing, "Rosie the Cowboy Jew." With practice, he learned to control his reactions to such taunts and his responses evolved into harsh, scornful laughs. His general attitude at the Academy earned him the label of "Rhino." "Rhino is Rosie's most prominent characteristic—not pessimism—just cheerful disgust with everything in general and anything in particular." Yet if a fellow midshipman became dissatisfied with his life at the Academy, he found "a good Rhinofest in Rosie's room made him feel much better."[3] Among his peers he was known as a "boner"—a reference to his scholastic achievement and his aloofness,[4] but of the various monikers applied to him, "Rosie" was the one that stuck, and the one by which friends and colleagues knew him for the remainder of his life.

An important part of the education of future Navy officers was the annual practice cruise. Midshipmen were assigned to ships where they performed various duties designed to teach them the organization and administration of a warship. They endured the living conditions of both officers and enlisted men, and they were evaluated on the performance of their assigned duties as well as their overall progress toward becoming officers.

Rosendahl's first summer cruise was in 1911. The Secretary of the Navy assigned three battleships for the cruise—USS *Indiana* (BB-1), USS *Iowa* (BB-4), and USS *Massachusetts* (BB-2). These ships had been commissioned in the mid- to late-1890s and all were showing their age. Rosendahl was assigned to the coal-burning *Indiana* for what became the most interesting of his summer cruises. The three ships visited Queenstown, Ireland; Bergen, Norway; Kiel, Germany; and Gibraltar. Rosendahl thought this a grand beginning to his "seeing the world," but his next summer cruises were served on active battleships of the Atlantic Fleet which remained in home waters.

After four highly structured years in which every aspect of Academy life was designed to mold midshipmen into the "young keepers of the nation's honor on the sea," "June Week"—later called "Commissioning

Week"—arrived for the Class of 1914. The events of the week included "mimic warfare, amateur dramatics, several sessions of the board of visitors and the regular evening dress parade" which made for "a round of continuous enjoyment and festivity."[5]

Of the 207 men who entered the Academy in 1910, 154 graduated on June 5, with Rosendahl ranking fifty-third among them. He considered his time at the Academy had represented nothing more than "the average midshipman's experience."[6] He felt that almost every young man who entered the Academy did so with serious intent, and they discovered quickly what was required for a career Navy officer—hard work and "an honest integration of one's self into the Naval organization."[7] Navy traditions were instilled into midshipmen from the day they entered the Academy. In later years, Rosendahl wrote of his faith in the power of tradition: "Tradition is the inbred force that sustains an officer when his hour or day of decision arrives, steels his courage, strengthens his judgement to make decisions without hesitation."[8]

Commencement exercises were on Friday of "June Week" with President Woodrow Wilson addressing the graduates and an audience of five thousand in the flag-decked armory. The president encouraged the young officers-soon-to-be to serve humanity as instruments of civilization,[9] not as instruments of aggression.[10] The week ended that night with a Farewell Ball given to the graduates by the rising First Class (Seniors). Rosendahl's father attended the graduation ceremony and it was the source of great pride that his son—a second-generation American—had become an officer in the United States Navy.

As a junior officer, Rosendahl's assignments were typical of new Academy graduates—a series of postings of variable duration. He received orders on June 5, 1914, to report for duty on board the armored cruiser USS *West Virginia* (ACR-5) then in the Pacific where he was commissioned ensign on June 6. This *Pennsylvania*-class armored cruiser was commissioned in 1903 and had seen duty with the Atlantic Fleet and the Asiatic Squadron before her assignment to the Pacific Fleet in 1908. When Rosendahl joined her, she was cruising off the west coast of Mexico, protecting American interests there. Rosendahl's detail was the "black gang," as the engineers force on a coal-burning ship was called.

"Through the ordeal of coal bunkers, firerooms, and engine rooms," he qualified as assistant engineer officer.[11]

Rosendahl's shortest ship assignment lasted only one month but on May 13, 1915, he was ordered to the protected cruiser USS *Cleveland* (CL-19) where he served for sixteen months. Each ship assignment provided a taste of life with the fleet, but his time with the *Cleveland* was his best glimpse yet of life at sea. Available recreation was meager. Many hours were spent swimming over the side of the ship or catching sharks off the forecastle. Occasionally, some of the officers got to play golf on a nine-hole sand course laid out by the Southern Pacific Railroad for its officials at their Mexican headquarters at Empalme.

Available movies were old silent films rented from the Movie Exchange at San Francisco for a dollar a reel per month. The "Keystone Cops" comedies and films showing bathing beauties were among the favorites. In some ports, in exchange for seeing the movies, native musicians came on board to sit on the deck and play marimba music to accompany the films.[12]

Rosendahl was ordered back to the *West Virginia* on September 6, 1916, but on November 11, the name of the ship was changed to the USS *Huntington* to allow the name "West Virginia" to be assigned to the newly authorized battleship, USS *West Virginia* (BB-48). On this tour, he served as deck watch officer and gunnery officer prior to serving as navigator.[13] In June 1917 he was promoted to lieutenant (junior grade) and in August he was given the rank of lieutenant (temporary).

The American Navy did not experience much combat in the Great War, but it conducted what Rosendahl labeled "a tremendous amount of drudgery needed to sustain a great war overseas" as men, munitions, food, and other war materiel had to be kept flowing in enormous quantities to Europe.[14] Consequently, the *Huntington* was assigned to escort duty in the North Atlantic, shepherding transport ships loaded with troops to almost within sight of the coasts of England and France. The winter of 1917–1918 was a cold one, and the waters in their areas of operation were infested with U-boats. When they got close to European shores, escort vessels turned the duty over to the speedy destroyers and headed back to ports on the American East Coast to pick up the next convoy. Nearly three weeks were required to make these round trips and, in order to have the required cruising range, they set sail from U.S. ports with loads of coal in eight-hundred-pound bags stacked high on the deck.[15]

Convoy duty was largely drudgery, but on one trip to Southampton, England, Rosendahl contracted a potentially lethal bout of what was called "the Spanish flu." This occurred during the influenza pandemic of 1918 which, ultimately, resulted in more deaths worldwide than the battlefields of Europe. Lacking any specific treatment, affected people either lived with supportive care or died. Densely populated ships at sea, such as troop carriers, were deadly incubators for the virus, making their crews especially vulnerable. Rosendahl was among the fortunate ones.

Destroyer duty was particularly appealing to young officers. "We in the 'big' ships had nothing but envy for those fast, oil-burning 'tin cans' and their lucky crews."[16] On July 1, 1918, he was dispatched to Quincy, Massachusetts, in connection with the fitting out of a new destroyer with orders to remain on board as engineering officer once she was commissioned. The war was still on but assignment to European waters was not in his cards. Instead, he was sent to San Francisco as engineer officer on board the destroyer USS *McKean* (DD-90), then nearing completion at the Union Iron Works.

When the war ended, Rosendahl and the *McKean* were still on the Pacific Coast. His cruise on the *McKean* cured any desire he may have had for engineering duty. "Almost every joint and valve in that ship leaked oil, water, steam, air, or whatever it was supposed to hold. Repeatedly due to lost fuel suction, our boilers and engines were without steam to propel us and we wallowed in the sea until old-fashioned muscle power on a good old 'handy-billy' pump got fuel flowing again."[17]

In spite of her problems, the *McKean* made it to the Atlantic, where, in May 1919, just three months after her commissioning, she was assigned to a station off Trepassey Bay, Nova Scotia, where she was to make smoke as a visual navigational aid for the Navy's NC (Navy-Curtiss) flying boats that were attempting to cross the Atlantic. Producing heavy smoke through inefficient combustion was not a difficult task for the *McKean*. She had been rebuked many times for doing it unintentionally.[18]

When his tour with the *McKean* ended in the summer of 1919, Rosendahl was sent to the West Coast for a variety of sea duties. The Navy issued a call for twelve young officers to volunteer for a tour of duty in Japan for the purpose of learning the language and culture. This was an opportunity for Rosendahl to distinguish himself and, potentially, launch him on a career path within the service, but the Navy reduced the number of volunteers to two and he was not chosen. He concluded, "Fate had not yet selected me for a specialty."[19]

After a short tour as gunnery officer on board the very old armored cruiser USS *Brooklyn* (ACR-3), Rosendahl got his first command—the USS *Claxton* (DD-140), a *Wickes*-class destroyer attached to a destroyer division under the command of Commander Milo R. Draemel, whom Rosendahl considered to be a "patient, considerate, and enthusiastic" leader. The *Claxton* was a "happy ship," and it was with regret that, in the fall of 1921, Rosendahl received orders to return to the Naval Academy as an instructor in the Department of Engineering and Physics.[20]

Rosendahl had been waiting for something—or someone—to reveal a path to a rewarding career within the Navy. In his private memoir, he referred repeatedly to "Fate" as the force he hoped would guide him. "Fate" finally put a gentle hand on the helm of Rosendahl's career by associating him with a group of men who were driven so passionately by naval aviation that he could not resist being swept up by their enthusiasm.

It was common practice for officers to rotate back to the Academy to participate in the education of midshipmen, but "some 18 months as an instructor at Annapolis didn't help me subdue a restlessness that had crept up and was besetting me."[21] In the Navy's wartime expansion, Rosendahl had held the temporary rank of lieutenant commander but, by the end of 1921, all temporary ranks were revoked, and he reverted to the permanent rank of lieutenant. "It looked quite permanent indeed, for there were no indications of when the 2½ stripes of a Lieutenant Commander would be mine again, except that it was remote."[22]

In the years following the war, Rosendahl was among the many young regular Navy officers who were concerned about the post-war inactivity and the meager prospects for peacetime promotion. All manner of post-war retrenchments took place. The Navy that had come home looked like it would remain home for a long time. Travel—"seeing the world"—held a fascination for everyone who joined the Navy but more important, Rosendahl realized, was the fact that "men learn to master the sea only through going to sea." His assessment of the Navy in the early 1920s was that it faced a "bleak, conservative, austere existence," and he felt that "swinging around an anchor in Chesapeake Bay indefinitely would be a poor substitute for the enchantment of far away places."[23] He sensed a letdown feeling of uncertainty had overtaken many young officers and, because of this, some resigned from the service, and he gave it serious consideration.

Just as there had been nothing remarkable about Rosendahl's time as a midshipman, there had been nothing special about his tours of duty following graduation. He accepted assignments as they came, not knowing where they would take his career. He had observed that many young officers were more or less content "to move along with the current and take whatever fate and chance alone might bring," and he had fallen into the same pattern.[24]

Six years into his service, he had not found the thing that would ignite his passions for the remainder of his Navy career. Nothing he had seen or experienced thus far had diverted his attention from a career in the surface fleet, but things in the Navy were changing.

THE LIGHTER-THAN-AIR PROGRAM
AND ZR-1

It had been predicted since the late 1800s that a war between Japan and the United States for control of the Pacific was inevitable. Even as the Japanese served with the Allies in the First World War, American newspapers occasionally published articles predicting that once the war in Europe ended, the next war would be in the Pacific. Conducting surveillance of the Pacific Ocean would fall, naturally, to the Navy, but this posed a huge problem. Surface ships were too slow, and the Navy had too few of them, to cover 60 million square miles of ocean and over 95,000 miles of American shoreline, and airplanes lacked the range to do the job. The Navy needed a craft capable of meeting the reconnaissance demands.

When World War I erupted, controlled manned flight was barely two decades old, but the exigencies of war accelerated developments. Two types of machines flew the skies over Europe during the war—heavier-than-air (HTA) craft, represented by airplanes, and lighter-than-air (LTA), represented by blimps and dirigibles.

There were three general types of dirigibles. Blimps were pressure ships that were steerable, and the pressure of the gas inside the envelope determined the ship's shape. Rigid airships had a solid framework that surrounded one or more lifting gas cells, and it was the framework with an outer fabric covering that gave the ship its shape. Both Germany and Britain used the flammable hydrogen as the lifting gas. A semi-rigid airship had a partially rigid frame that provided structural integrity while maneuvering, but it was the lifting gas envelope which maintained the ship's shape.

The term Zeppelin referred specifically to those rigid airships produced by the *Luftschiffbau Zeppelin* (Zeppelin Airship) company. Blimps, dirigibles, and Zeppelins were known generically as *airships*.

While Britain produced her own airships, she also purchased an Astra-Torres airship from France and a Parseval from Germany, but Germany refused to sell her technologically superior Zeppelins to foreign powers.

Airships had a number of advantages over airplanes. They had a much greater range—capable of traveling thousands of miles on a single tank of fuel. They could fly higher and remain aloft much longer than airplanes and could carry a larger crew and payload. Airships had the added advantage of being able to hover over areas of interest.

The American Navy had been observing how the Germans and British used their airships during the First World War, and while Germany used her Zeppelins for both reconnaissance and as platforms from which to drop bombs, it was the reconnaissance function with extended range that interested the Navy most. British airships conducted reconnaissance of the North Sea and the English Channel. Blimps became so effective in submarine hunting that if a U-boat was sighted in the English Channel, it had little chance of escaping.

In September 1916, Secretary of the Navy Josephus Daniels elaborated the ways Zeppelin-type airships could be of value to the U.S. They could perform a scouting function, covering a zone along the American coast day and night at a distance of 750 to 1,000 miles which would provide ample warning time of an approaching enemy ship or fleet. Similar patrols could be conducted from an outlying base as an early warning of approaching enemy. Airships could operate directly with the surface fleet as long-range scouts, and they could be used at various stations along both coasts, at bases in the Caribbean, at the Guantanamo supply base, on the Panama Canal, and on insular possessions. Unlike airplanes, they could travel at great speed or go slowly, as required, and they could travel along with the surface fleet, no matter its speed.[1]

In 1917, it was announced that the U.S. was going to have "flocks of blimps to defend coasts."[2] The Navy sent a contingent of officers to Europe to be trained in the operation of airships. Telling Congress that the Navy was developing its own air program aside from the 625-million-dollar military aircraft project of the Defense Council, Daniels asked for an additional 45 million dollars to support naval aeronautics.

In post-war years, opinions varied concerning the promise of LTA flight, especially in the face of advances being made with airplanes, but the Navy had not lost interest. Vice Admiral Sims proclaimed that rigid airships would "comprise a specific element of the fleet of every first-class naval power," and he recommended the U.S. lose no time in their development.[3] While the Navy had operated blimps during the war, it never had any large, rigid Zeppelin-type airships.

In 1919, Congress authorized the Navy to establish a base from which it could build and operate rigid airships,[4] and in 1920, the government acquired 1,469 acres in the Pine Barrens of New Jersey at the site of the former Camp Kendrick—a chemical weapons proofing ground—to become the home of the Navy's LTA program. The 1920 appropriations bill included four million dollars to acquire two rigid airships. One was to be built by the Navy at Naval Air Station (NAS) Lakehurst, designated ZR-1. In the Navy's scheme for designating airships, "Z" stood for "Zeppelin-type," "R" stood for "rigid," and the number indicated the order of production or acquisition.

A second airship, then under construction, was purchased from England for two million dollars. Designated R-38 by the British, she was redesignated ZR-2 by the Navy. On August 24, 1921, on her fourth—and final—test flight, the R-38/ZR-2 broke up over the city of Hull and crashed into the Humber River, killing sixteen of seventeen Americans and twenty-eight of thirty-two British crewmen. A court of inquiry concluded that the ship's destruction was due to structural defects.

While the Navy remained undeterred by the loss of the ZR-2, it needed a replacement ship because the program would be limited severely in what it could achieve with a single airship.

To create an ambitious LTA program, the Navy needed a corps of officers trained in LTA operations, and on December 21, 1922, the Bureau of Navigation—then responsible for personnel matters—issued its Circular Letter No. 64-22 to "All Ships and Stations," seeking volunteers for training in rigid airships. Rosendahl and his close friend Herbert V. Wiley were serving as instructors at the Academy when the circular letter arrived, and both volunteered for the inaugural class. Both men saw the new LTA program as a way to distinguish themselves and find advancement at a time in the inter-war years when such was slow. Rosendahl also regarded this as a way to feed his wanderlust.

In later years, Rosendahl reflected, "A notice on a bulletin board changed the whole course of my life."[5] He kept a copy in his personnel file for the remainder of his career and revisited it periodically as a reminder of that pivotal moment when he finally embarked on the path that would fuel his passions and, eventually, make him the most prominent figure in American LTA flight.

Forty-one men answered the Navy's call for volunteers and nine were selected: Commander Jacob H. Klein, Jr., Lieutenant Commander Maurice R. Pierce, Lieutenant Commander Joseph M. Deem, Lieutenant Commander Lewis Hancock, Lieutenant J. C. Arnold, Lieutenant Earle K. Kinkaid, Lieutenant W. O. Bailey, Lieutenant Herbert V. Wiley, and Lieutenant Charles E. Rosendahl.

In an introduction to his unpublished memoir, Rosendahl wrote, "Obviously, this story is inextricably, but not exclusively entwined with the contemporary history of airships. By pure coincidence of rank and perhaps because of my enthusiastic interest, my seat in the airship development picture always happened to be front row center."[6]

As the nine volunteers filtered into NAS Lakehurst for the first time, they were struck by the startling sight of the huge Hangar No. 1. Completed in 1921, it was America's first rigid airship hangar. The rectangular-shaped building with asbestos siding was an incongruous sight amid the sand dunes. The hangar was 966 feet long, 350 feet wide, and 224 feet high—as high as a twenty-story building. Its floor area was 211,434 square feet. At each end of the hangar were two pairs of massive steel doors mounted on railroad tracks. Each counter-balanced door weighed 1,350 tons and was powered by two 20-horsepower engines. The hangar was large enough to house two large airships side by side, with extra room for a number of blimps.

In the distance, "like a lighthouse on a barren sandy coast," was a 171-foot-high airship mooring mast with a small machinery house at its base.[7] "The wave-like terrain of sand dunes and hummocks provided almost the only seagoing resemblance."[8] "Except for uniforms, insignias, and salty service language, there wasn't much else at Lakehurst that resembled the older branches of the Navy."[9] Barnegat Bay and the Atlantic Ocean were about fifteen miles from Lakehurst. It was not until years later that Lakehurst had any surfaced runways.

———

When the LTA training program opened, NAS Lakehurst was under the command of Frank Robert McCrary, who had assumed the post on November 10, 1922.[10] McCrary was a Navy aviator among the small contingent sent to France in 1917 to receive training in LTA flight. From February 1918 until the end of the war, he served as the commander of U.S. Naval Air Service Stations in Ireland, with headquarters in Queenstown. Because he was trained in both HTA and LTA flights, Admiral William Moffett, the first chief of the Navy's Bureau of Aeronautics, selected McCrary to command Lakehurst and assume command of ZR-1 when she was ready.

Command of NAS Lakehurst was not a job McCrary wanted, but Moffett essentially forced it on him. Rosendahl believed McCrary's airplane training had "wooed and weaned him away from airships," and his heart had never been in command of either ZR-1 or Lakehurst. The matter was no secret because McCrary discussed it openly. A story circulated about his detachment ceremony when leaving an airplane command to go to Lakehurst. After reading his orders before his assembled command, he announced that he was going to the NAS against his wishes and over his protest.[11]

Rosendahl was convinced that McCrary's statement was simply an impulsive manifestation of his frustration at being forced to duty for which he had no desire. Rosendahl felt it "cast an unfavorable shadow over airships in general and all those assembled airship men he was leading. To those of us who had joined airships enthusiastically, the net impression was anything but wholesome or comforting."[12] Nevertheless, McCrary carried out his duties with complete loyalty but with no great enthusiasm.

Rosendahl held McCrary in high esteem. "He was a fine shipmate and golfing companion, and as considerate a captain as could be found."[13] In later years, as Rosendahl reflected on this time, he was sympathetic with McCrary, especially considering leadership issues. "Old or young, mature or otherwise, the axiomatic prime requisite for pioneering leadership is nothing less than bona fide belief in and enthusiasm for the project. It is even plainer that such leadership should never be forced upon anyone. It is a situation manifestly unfair to both the individual and to the pioneering project. . . ."[14]

From the beginning, the trainees were short of two things: a cadre of experienced airship officers to train them and a rigid airship with which to train. Construction of ZR-1 began on June 24, 1922, but she would not be completed until August 1923. Because she was being assembled in Hangar No. 1 at Lakehurst, the trainees had ample opportunity to observe the construction to appreciate the ship's structure and function.

The ground school opened officially on March 15, 1923. To compensate for the lack of experienced LTA officers to train them, some of the trainees were detailed to deliver lectures on subjects of which they had little, if any, knowledge. They were assigned a block of material to study and understand to the best of their ability so that, subsequently, they could lecture the entire group on the matter.

Captain Anton Heinen, a German aviator with extensive experience handling Zeppelins, had been hired by the Navy in an advisory capacity. While Heinen had an excellent command of English, his instructive papers were not always in the American idiom to which the trainees were accustomed. Consequently, Rosendahl drew the assignment of translation, which required him to study each subject more thoroughly than he would have otherwise.[15]

Training was split between classroom instruction (ground school) and LTA flight. Ground school instruction included aviation history, aerostatics, aerodynamics, aerology, airship gases (hydrogen and helium), heavier-than-air indoctrination, maintenance, construction and design, aviation engines, airmanship, parachutes, aerial navigation, aerial gunnery, radio and aircraft communications, airship instruments, and fleet indoctrination.[16] Aerology was loosely synonymous with meteorology, but it dealt with the full extent of the atmosphere to the highest altitudes, while meteorology dealt with studies of the air close to Earth's surface.

Officers were expected to experience flight in several types of LTA craft, including free and kite (tethered) balloons and nonrigid and rigid airships (when one became available). Each officer's flight time was recorded in hours and minutes—Rosendahl had ten "hops" in a kite balloon in a single day for 1 hour and 11 minutes of flight time. While each flight lasted about five or ten minutes, subsequent flights were longer. On May 4, Rosendahl shared a flight in a free balloon with Herbert V. Wiley and Earle H. Kincaid that lasted 3 hours and 25 minutes.[17]

Because all airships were basically balloons, the Navy considered training in balloons mandatory. Each trainee was required to make a minimum of seven flights in free balloons, one of which had to be a night flight and one a solo flight. A student's first solo balloon flight was something he never forgot. "There is an impressive silence, when a dog's bark on earth can be heard, the balloonist is truly on his own with no power to propel him, no rudders to steer him, and no one to consult. There is nothing comparable to a solo balloon flight for teaching one the rudiments of atmospheric structure."[18]

The trainees remained in student status for a minimum of one full year before qualifying as a naval aviator (airship). "For one thing, while airship operations entail nothing mysterious or beyond the average officer's understanding and ability, it does involve day-in-day-out working familiarity with certain laws of nature and science. The Principle of Archimedes and Charles' Law and Boyle's Law are matters with which an airship pilot deals constantly. The mere steering of the craft is a secondary factor."[19]

Weather was a vital determinant in the flight of any airship, and the trainees were required to observe and study the influence of weather on an airship operation throughout a whole year's weather cycle before assuming responsibility for such craft.[20]

Several trainees were given collateral duties outside their student responsibilities. Rosendahl was assigned to the office of the managing constructor to assist in the development of ground handling gear for ZR-1. This placed him in close contact with Heinen, from whom he learned much about airship handling. Rosendahl became involved in the design of many features of the mobile and fixed mooring masts and the mechanization of handling gear.[21]

The design of ZR-1 began in September 1919—the same month construction on NAS Lakehurst was started—and the final design was approved in October 1921. Because this was the Navy's first experience with airship construction, it was decided to borrow from German technology. ZR-1 was modeled after L-49, a Zeppelin captured during the war.

Built in 1917, L-49 was one of the "height climbers" designed to reach altitudes beyond those of airplanes that had become more successful at attacking Zeppelins. The "height climbers" conducted raids from 16,000 to 20,000 feet, putting them beyond the reach of airplanes that had ceilings of 11,000 to 13,000 feet.[22] Building airships that could reach such altitudes rapidly required sacrificing some design features over others. Most notably, the strengths of materials were compromised in favor of making the Zeppelins lighter, with more lift.

ZR-1's frame was built of duralumin, a hard yet lightweight alloy of aluminum with copper, magnesium, and manganese. Copper strengthened the alloy, but it made it more susceptible to corrosion. Consequently, battling corrosion became a never-ending part of maintenance and repair to keep the ship operating safely. The frame was manufactured at the naval aircraft factory, transported to Lakehurst, and assembled in Hangar No. 1.

Construction on the cradle that would hold ZR-1 began on June 27, 1922. The keel would be 700 feet long, and 70 miles of piano wire would be used as struts and braces to the girders, along with 30 miles of duralumin channel sections.[23]

Admiral Moffett gave the press full access to Lakehurst and Hangar No. 1 from the beginning of construction, and media curiosity for every detail of the ship's structure seemed boundless. Richard Beamish of the *Philadelphia Inquirer* reported on progress from the Navy Yard. "Upon parquetry floor of the finishing department of the naval aircraft factory . . . lay a blue metal polygon with twenty-five sides. Workmen fitted bolts into its hundreds of separate parts until the whole became a great, completed ring eighty-five feet in diameter." It was one of the duralumin ribs for the airship.[24] Installed, each frame was numbered beginning in the stern and advancing toward the bow.

The envelope of the dirigible was constructed of aircraft cloth made of long staple, back-spun cotton of one thickness that was treated with a special varnish to make it sun and waterproof.[25]

The cigar-shaped structure of the ship was built in nineteen compartments, each "the shape of a slice of bologna, each slice being 30 feet wide."[26] The helium gas cells were made of the lightest fabric, cemented and covered with "goldbeater's skin," then varnished. Goldbeater's skin was made from small tough sections of the intestines of cattle. This process dated from the Middle Ages when goldsmiths learned they could put gold between two layers of this "skin" and hammer it into fine gold leaf without tearing it. The "skin" was light in texture but very strong. It was ideal for use in LTA craft because it permitted far less diffusion of gas than any substance then known.[27]

Like L-49, ZR-1 was designed originally to use hydrogen as its lifting gas, but the Navy preferred the nonflammable helium. Helium was safer but heavier than hydrogen and had only about 92 percent of the lifting power. The difference in weight would decrease the cruising range of the ship significantly.[28] To compensate for this, a 30-foot section was added to the body of the airship to allow it to carry more helium. ZR-1 became the first rigid airship to use helium.

Filling ZR-1's gas cells to 85 percent required 1,783,000 cubic feet of helium. The finished airship was 688 feet long with a beam of 78 feet, 9 inches, and it stood 93 feet, 2 inches tall. Powered by its five 300-horsepower, eight-cylinder Packard engines, it could reach speeds of about 60 knots, and it had a range of approximately 5,000 miles. When inflated to 95 percent capacity with 2,100,000 cubic feet of helium, the ZR-1 had a lifting capacity of 53,600 pounds.

Before ZR-1 took the air for the first time, Moffett held great promise for this emerging technology both for military and commercial purposes. He promoted a bold plan for the ship to fly over the North Pole—not merely a round-trip dash to the Pole but one of scientific value and exploration, photographically mapping vast stretches of previously unknown territory. Because of its greater range, variability of speed, and ability to hover, Moffett believed that such exploration could be achieved better by airship than airplane and in greater comfort and safety for its crew. By unshipping two of her engines and their cars and replacing their weight with fuel, ZR-1's normal range of 4,000 miles could be extended easily to 5,000 miles in a nonstop flight.[29]

The control car, rigidly attached to the bottom of the keel about 125 feet from her nose, contained an engine and a huge propeller as well as stations for the navigator, steersmen, and radio operators. Another engine car was aft of this in the centerline of the keel, and four more engine cars were stretched along the sides of the ship.

ZR-1's outer skin was stretched as tight as a drumhead from nose to stern, making her as smooth as a piano top. When preparing for flight, the officer in charge needed to know how many men would be on board, and the length and nature of the flight, to be able to calculate the amount of ballast and fuel to take on board.

Gas was taken into the ship through a central gassing hose that led off into each gasbag or ballonet. There were twenty such bags, each holding about 114,000 cubic feet of gas. As the incoming gas increased the lift of the ship, riggers brought on additional water ballast to offset the lift. Trim for the 680-foot airship had to be maintained at all times. After the lifting gas, fuel, and ballast were taken on board, the engineer force had to check and run the engines. Once this was done, the ship was ready for flight. The crew was taken on board as sufficient ballast (water) was discharged to compensate for the actual weight of the men and their clothing. The ship was then ready to be taken from the hangar by the ground crew but, before being taken out, the ship was ballasted about a half a ton light to facilitate its handling on the ground and to ensure there was a positive buoyancy for leaving the ground.

When the stern was clear of the hangar, it was allowed to trail in the wind, putting the ship's bow to the wind. From this position, she was "walked" by the ground crew to the point for takeoff, where it was weighed off again to check for lift and trim. If satisfactory to the commanding officer, the engines were started, the ground crew released the handing lines, and the ship took to the sky.[30] In flight, the airship was controlled much the same as a surface vessel but, in the control car, in addition to the steering coxswain, there was a "height" coxswain who was responsible for controlling the elevators that sent the ship up or down at varying heights.[31]

ZR-1 was launched officially on August 20, 1923, inside her hangar. "Whereas a waterborne vessel is launched by sliding down the building

ways into the water in which it will float, an airship is launched by letting it rise from its building cradles to float in the atmospheric ocean."[32]
Launching required a ground crew of approximately three hundred Marines and sailors to handle the ship.

For weeks leading to September 4, 1923, thousands of visitors were
drawn to NAS Lakehurst to witness the maiden flight of the great airship.[33] Approximately 15,000 people, including newspaper reporters,
newsreel cameramen, a variety of dignitaries, and curious civilians, comprised the crowd. Press coverage was important to Moffett because it kept
the program in the consciousness of the public and members of Congress
who could influence the huge amount of funding required to sustain the
program.

Clinging tightly to long handling lines, the ground crew walked the
ship out of her hangar. The first flight of a rigid airship using helium as
a lifting gas lasted approximately 55 minutes as ZR-1 circled the field
several times, maintaining a one-mile radius. At 1924, Captain McCrary,
in command of the ship, sent a radio message to Moffett stating, "After
twenty minutes' flying all is going well."[34] It was dusk when the ship
landed with batteries of searchlights guiding her to safe anchorage.

An enthusiastic reporter predicted that the initial flight of ZR-1 pre-
saged a realignment of naval forces for future defense of the nation. He
foresaw three levels of naval craft: surface, subsurface, and air, "with rigid
airships like the ZR-1 a thousand miles in advance of the fleet, followed
by aircraft carriers sending aloft fighting, bombing and torpedo aircraft
for the protection of the capital ships and the capital ships in the air."[35]
This journalist's visions were well ahead of the "old guard" admirals of the
surface fleet. The Navy would devote much time in coming years to identify a proper role for airships and their relationship to the surface fleet.

A second successful flight took place on September 6 that lasted two
hours. The first two flights were the culmination of a great deal of planning and work to get Lakehurst operating and ZR-1 flying, and Moffett
was quick to credit McCrary for these achievements, although McCrary's
relationship with the LTA program had been a strained one from the beginning. At Moffett's suggestion, a letter of commendation for McCrary
was forwarded from Secretary of the Navy Edwin Denby.

Additional test flights would be needed before the ship was commissioned, but the press assured the public that "nothing that human ingenuity can devise has been omitted and no tests have been neglected to guarantee that the ZR-1 will be as safe as any aircraft that can be constructed."[36] Commander J. S. Hunsaker, the chief of naval design in the Bureau of Aeronautics, predicted, "The navy will develop not only a new element in marine defense but an entirely new industry and a new phase of commercial aviation."[37] A lot of promise rested on two short test flights, and Moffett was promoting as a certainty the idea of an ambitious polar flight. Members of Congress were divided in their support for a polar expedition because of doubts about the ship's ability to withstand the physical stresses to be encountered in Arctic regions.

Every flight of the ZR-1, regardless of length, was a learning experience for the crew, and the more they flew, the greater their ambition became to test the abilities of their ship. On September 12, 1923, ZR-1 made her longest flight to date as she moved up the Hudson River while millions of people watched from the streets of New York. Throughout the flight, the ship maintained a pace of 50 miles per hour while giving no impression from the sky of haste. "It moved: it did not fly. Its even progress seemed slow, plodding, irrevocable as change. Time moved with the ZR-1 up the Hudson today." Such elegant descriptions only added to the romance that had attached itself to airships.[38] This record of 11 hours and 31 minutes was soon to be beaten as ZR-1 made a round-trip flight to St. Louis for the Pulitzer Cup air races in October 1923.

Moffett pledged that the ZR-1 would be built so safely that no accident could happen to her. While the early flights made good on Moffett's pledge, the 2,000-mile round trip from Lakehurst to St. Louis with the ship in the air for 48 hours would be its most severe test. Aware that safety was a public concern, Anton Heinen and Commander Ralph Weyerbacher of the Bureau of Construction and Repair (Construction Corps) had given assurances that if the ship were to break in two, "she would simply settle to the ground at a speed no greater than that of a parachute."[39] These bold claims would be put to the test at a later date.

The flight to St. Louis departed Lakehurst on October 1 and passed over as many cities as practicable to show the giant ship off to the public.

While encountering a variety of adverse weather conditions, including gale-force winds, the ZR-1 arrived at St. Louis safely. Moffett, who had been in St. Louis for the air races, decided to join ZR-1 for its return flight to Lakehurst to demonstrate to the American people his confidence in the airship. It was his first flight in an airship and the first time in history that a rear admiral's flag flew from a rigid airship.

While the ship was still in the air, Secretary Denby announced that the Navy Department had decided on "Shenandoah" as the name for ZR-1 and that the christening would take place soon after her return to Lakehurst. When she returned on October 3, 1923, Moffett was the first to step from the car. As Weyerbacher emerged, he proclaimed proudly, "We started with six motors humming and we return with the same number running."[40]

During the Pulitzer air races, the National Institute of the Aeronautical Chamber of Commerce distributed papers addressing aspects of aviation. Hunsaker prepared a paper titled, "The Renaissance of Rigid Airships" in which he referenced the R-38 and Roma disasters.[41]

> During 1920-1921 everything happened that could happen and ought not to happen. This succession of unfortunate experiences was combined with a wave of economy in governmental expenditures and airship development was practically abandoned the world over. The British led by closing all airship stations and scattering the construction personnel. The Germans were stopped by the treaty [of Versailles]. The French and Italians left in their hangars the rigid airships obtained from Germany after the armistice.
>
> But the eclipse was not total and, in every country, there were a few individuals who kept the art alive and continued study and research.[42]

In the U.S., those few individuals were the members of the Navy's LTA service based at NAS Lakehurst and led by Admiral Moffett.

Having completed her trials, ZR-1 was ready for christening and commissioning. On October 5, 1923, McCrary received a letter from the Bureau of Navigation ordering him to assume command of ZR-1 once she was christened and commissioned,[43] and he was to retain command of Lakehurst after taking command of the airship.

The ceremonies were scheduled for October 10, 1923.

CHAPTER 3

USS *SHENANDOAH* (ZR-1)

On October 10, 1923, the ZR-1 was both christened and commissioned. Admiral and Mrs. Moffett were present for the ceremony along with Secretary and Mrs. Denby and a host of other dignitaries, among them Rear Admiral Archibald H. Scales, commandant of the Fourth District, Philadelphia; Admiral Long; and New Jersey Governor Silzer.[1]

At 1553, following preliminaries, Mrs. Denby stood on a platform that had been erected in front of the airship's car. She was handed a line attached to a basket containing carrier pigeons, and as she spoke the words, "I christen thee Shenandoah," she pulled the line, releasing the pigeons to fly out of the hangar back to Washington.[2] Translated from the Algonquin, Shenandoah meant "beautiful daughter of the skies."

The order "ship weigh off" was heard throughout the hangar, and the *Shenandoah* was allowed to rise one or two feet from the cradles. A minute later, the ship was secured again on the cradles. The airship was then commissioned as Rear Admiral Scales read the commissioning orders from the Navy Department.[3] Commander McCrary then read his orders from the Bureau of Navigation, detailing him as commanding officer of the *Shenandoah*, and he assumed command immediately. Commander Klein reported for duty as executive officer, followed by the other officers: Lieutenant Commander J. M. Deem, Lieutenant Commander J. P. Norfleet, Lieutenant C. E. Rosendahl, Lieutenant R. J. Miller, Lieutenant E. H. Kincaid, Lieutenant R. F. Tyler, and Lieutenant (j.g.) E. W. Sheppard.[4]

Following a short address by Secretary Denby, the ship's handling lines were manned, and she was walked out of the hangar. She was underway at 1630 with Denby and guests for a short flight and back in her hangar at 1755.[5]

At last, the Navy had its own Zeppelin-type rigid airship, and there was much to accomplish in the coming years. Getting an airship into its hangar in good weather was no small task—one made much more difficult in windy conditions. The British had developed a means for keeping an airship ready for quick dispatch using a mooring mast. Using hinged nose gear, the airship was secured to the top of the mast, riding out in the open with freedom of motion similar to a flag. The ship pivoted in response to changes in wind direction. The Navy borrowed the concept and built a "high mast" at Lakehurst, but it did not take long to realize that the mast was not the solution to all airship handling problems. Ground handling equipment and techniques needed improvement as well.[6] Using the mooring mast was not a simple task, and it was not until November 16, 1923, that a successful mooring was made.[7] With practice, however, mooring became fairly routine.

On October 27, 1923, *Shenandoah* made her longest flight to date—15 hours and 45 minutes. The flight went without incident, but after landing, as the ship was being walked into the hangar, the No. 1 Car struck the ground with slight structural damage but no injuries to personnel.[8] A similar incident occurred on November 20 as the ship was being docked. Crosswinds gusting 16 to 20 miles per hour resulted in injuries to the after car and minor injuries to a crewman. The dirigible was fragile out of proportion to her size.

Whether in flight, moored to the high mast, or being maneuvered by the ground crew, it was essential to keep the ship in proper trim. Maintaining trim required an accurate accounting of the total weight taken on board, including the crew and its clothing. Weight distribution within the ship was equally important, and men were ordered about within the ship to maintain trim.

The *Shenandoah*'s logbook for January 12, 1924, recorded the details of taking her from the hangar to be secured to the high mast. Preparations began at 1600 with the ship inside the hangar. Once the ship was made ready, the crew and ground handlers were mustered at 1645 in preparation for walking her out of the hangar. About an hour later, the ship was walked out to the East Field by the ground crew, who were simultaneously securing her and guiding her with handling lines.

The ship was stopped on the field at 1745, and at 1804 the shore pilot directed the ground crew to move her to the mast. The order "up ship" was given at 1815, and, with it in flight, it was walked by her drag lines to the mast. At 1825, the ship was lightened by releasing 775 pounds of water from Frame 40, 550 pounds from Frame 170, and the 540 pounds of starboard emergency ballast water from Frame 30. At 1849, the mooring cable was connected. From 1908 to 1926, the No. 2 and 3 engines were idled but stopped at 1930, once the ship was secured to the mast.[9]

As the crew worked to perfect its airship handling skills, Moffett continued to promote the idea of a polar flight, and in January 1924, Secretary Denby announced a plan for the flight. The result of a Special Board of Naval Officers headed by Moffett, the plan called for a serious exploration of the North Pole regions and not simply a "dash for the pole."[10] A series of strategically located mooring masts would serve as temporary "bases" for the *Shenandoah* as she flew to the West Coast, then north to Alaska and beyond.

During its trek, a one-million-square-mile area of unknown surface would be photographed from the *Shenandoah*. The airship had not been tested in the type of gale-force winds to be encountered in Arctic regions, and some in the LTA community were concerned about the ability of the ship to withstand such forces. Chief among these detractors was Frank McCrary, the *Shenandoah*'s commander.

When the House Appropriations Committee met on January 12, 1924, to consider the expedition's plan, congressmen were concerned already about the costs as well as the safety of the expedition. Still making preparation for the polar flight, McCrary was presented with an opportunity to test the stresses gale-force winds would have on an airship while moored to a mast.

As early as January 14, 1924, weather advisories warned of strong gales in the Lakehurst area for the sixteenth and seventeenth. Such winds would match closely the Arctic conditions the *Shenandoah* would encounter. McCrary decided to place a small crew on board and leave the ship moored to the high mast for ten days while conducting tests.

As January 16 arrived, the NAS braced itself for the anticipated gale with the ship tethered to the high mast with a skeleton crew. During the

1200–1600 watch, Klein and Rosendahl were on board with Klein in command. McCrary joined them at 1410, and twenty minutes later a moderate rain began to fall. At 1500, the weather intensified, producing a constant rolling motion to the ship, and by 1600, as Rosendahl was relieved to go to dinner, winds were gusting to 63 miles per hour.

At 1800, Kincaid was in command of the ship with Heinen on board.[11] At 1844, with a steady rain falling and winds gusting to 56 knots, the mooring point to the mast broke away and the ship went adrift. Someone at dinner, gazing out a window, exclaimed, "She's gone!" and before Rosendahl could get to the window, the *Shenandoah* had disappeared into the darkness of the storm.[12]

The ship's nose was torn off completely, and, as it flapped from the masthead at the end of the mooring chain, the missing nose section made maneuvering more difficult. The report of the ship tearing loose was loud enough to be heard above the sound of the gale, bringing officers in the mess to their feet. As they rushed out into the storm, looking up, all they could see were feeble rays of searchlights wavering in the rain as the *Shenandoah* had disappeared into the night.[13] She was battling the worst storm in the fifty-two-year history of the New York Weather Bureau.[14]

When the nose of the ship pulled loose, Kincaid, Pierce, and Heinen instinctively dove for the levers to release ballast. After releasing all the water ballast, including the emergency supply, they released three gasoline slip tanks at Frames 80, 155, and 156, respectively, for a total of 339 gallons. Slip tanks were rigged about every third or fourth tank and secured in a manner that allowed them to be released quickly in an emergency to fall away from the ship to increase buoyancy. The crew then threw overboard anything with weight that was of no immediate use.[15]

After a brief period of confusion at being torn away from the mast, discipline was restored quickly and cool heads went about the work of saving the ship. Five thousand pounds of water ballast had been released within five seconds after the breakaway, preventing the ship from crashing to the ground. The ship was within six feet of the ground when it started to rise, but it had swooped so low that its airspeed indicator, which was slung 75 feet below the gondola, was swept away by the ground.

As the water ballast was released, the ship's engines were started. The ship was heavy in the nose and difficult to manage. The upper part of the after fin had buckled, and the bow was torn off. Proper trim was restored after the fuel tanks were released and weight was redistributed within the ship.[16]

The two forward helium cells were destroyed and another was leaking badly. The fabric of the envelope had been torn for about 75 feet back from the prow. Underway in the storm, the crew used the fabric cover of the helium cells to plug the leaking one and to repair the ship's envelope. Orders were barked out through a megaphone, directing the crew to run back and forth along the catwalk that ran the length of the ship to maintain the head and tail of the ship steady. A slip tank amidships had fallen, breaking a central strut and tearing a hole in the envelope. There was nothing between the men running the catwalk at that point and the surface of the earth if they had fallen.

With ballast released, the ship started to gain altitude and her engines gradually made progress against the storm so that at 2000, they were over New Brunswick, New Jersey, with the wind velocity exceeding the *Shenandoah*'s by 16 knots with Engines No. 1 through 5 running at cruising speed.[17]

At this point, the commander's concern was to keep the ship away from the ocean. Because Heinen was the most experienced dirigible operator on board, the American officers tended to heed his advice during the potentially fatal flight. As they drifted over New York City, the storm began to abate, and Heinen had the ship turned into the wind making progress on its return to Lakehurst.[18]

Searchlights at the NAS spotted the *Shenandoah* at 0150. The hole in the ship's nose made maneuvering difficult, and it took three hours to get her down safely as Heinen dropped her altitude by a few hundred feet at a time. Back on the ground, it took three hundred men to walk the ship into the hangar with cheers from the men in the gondola joining those of the ground crew. The *Shenandoah* made her safe landing at 0330 on January 17, 1924.[19]

Back on the ground, Heinen made his way to a telephone to inform his wife that they were all safe—they had not crashed into the Atlantic.

Officers' wives had spent the night at the field, sitting on coils of rope, enduring the wind and rain, as orderlies ran back and forth between them and the wireless station bearing progress reports. Heinen gave full credit to the *Shenandoah*'s crew, stating that he had never seen a crew behave so faultlessly.[20] Special credit was given also to the ship's riggers for their dangerous work repairing the struts and fabric of the ship while in flight.

Asked about the availability of parachutes on board, Heinen replied that the *Shenandoah* did not carry parachutes. He claimed they were dangerous and that the best parachute was the airship—"No flyer ever is killed if he sticks to his airship."[21]

In the hours following their dramatic flight, Heinen realized that the *Shenandoah* had narrowly escaped the fate of the *Dixmude*—the German-built French naval airship that was carried away in a storm on December 20, crashing into the Mediterranean with the loss of fifty men.

Rosendahl regarded the flight of the *Shenandoah* in the gale as a "truly dramatic episode, and one that residents along the path of the crippled craft will long remember either from having seen the struggling ship or from having heard the almost continuous running radio account of this strange adventure."[22]

Missing from the *Shenandoah*'s logbook was the account of radioman Gunner Robertson, who was in the radio shack in the control car at the time of the breakaway. While the airship was undergoing her tests at the mast, her 300-foot radio aerial was being tested for capacity, inductance, and resistance. The radio apparatus had been disconnected and replaced with testing instruments to determine the efficiency of the present aerial in anticipation of installing a newly-designed 1,000-mile set then under construction.

When the ship broke away from the mast, Robertson[23] immediately started tearing loose his test instruments to hook up transmitting and re-ceiving equipment so he could establish communication with the NAS. With professional calm, he avoided transmitting an "SOS" and sent a message that the *Shenandoah* was under control—a message that allayed anxieties among Navy personnel and families at the NAS.[24]

Once in radio communication, Robertson received a call for "NERK," the *Shenandoah*'s call sign. The call came from radio station

WOR in Newark, New Jersey, giving Robertson the first position report, later verified by NAS Lakehurst. This report allowed navigators to know where the gale was driving the ship.

Robertson claimed, "Communication was then good for the remainder of the trip. We kept the base well informed and they gave us weather data." NERK's reports came through especially well because the airways had been cleared for them.

Still enthusiastic about an Arctic expedition, Secretary Denby put a positive spin on the near disaster, asserting that the experience in the storm had proved that mooring facilities alone (without hangars) would be adequate in the most severe weather and, as long as the ship was fueled and provisioned, it would be safe in its natural element—the air. "From all our information, it may be asserted with positive certainty that there is hardly a possibility that this ship will encounter in her Arctic expedition any test so severe as that she has already met successfully."[25]

The Shenandoah's survival in the gale did not reassure everyone that the ship could survive Arctic conditions, but Moffett was unwavering in his resolve that no conditions to be encountered in the Arctic would be as severe as those presented by the gale. Logbooks from a Coast Guard vessel revealed that the greatest wind forces observed in the Arctic for seven years during summer months had been 40 miles per hour. The gale at NAS Lakehurst had reached 68 miles per hour prior to the breakaway.[26]

A Navy court of inquiry estimated that it would take ten weeks to repair the ship at a cost of $78,000.[27]

At the time, none of the officers was willing to discuss plans for the expedition. The result of the nine-hour breakaway ordeal could have been tragically different, and the officers realized that disaster had been averted by the skillful piloting of Heinen, the performance of the cool-headed crew, and a bit of luck. The entire experience served to amplify undercurrents of distrust that had been brewing at the NAS.

There was a general discontent among the officers and men over leadership, with McCrary at the center of it. The Arctic expedition would require the greatest skills, judgment, and airship handling to ensure the success of the mission and the safety of the men, and there was general mistrust in McCrary's ability to do it. The disgruntlement was not a well-maintained secret, and it found its way into newspapers across the country.

The Navy Department needed to replace McCrary with a skipper holding a secure grip on the confidence of the enlisted men.[28] Consequently, the Navy announced that enlisted men for the Arctic flight would be volunteers and that service on the airship would be optional for enlisted men.[29]

The flight in the gale had given rise also to tensions among some of the officers—particularly Heinen and Kincaid, who had differed over how to manage the ship in the storm. The situation represented both a difference of nautical judgment and a clash of egos.

When the House Naval Affairs Committee met on January 19, 1924, it was aware of leadership problems at Lakehurst that threatened the Arctic expedition.[30] The *Shenandoah*'s performance in the gale did nothing to strengthen McCrary's confidence in airships, and he went public with his belief that the ship would be lost if she were sent to the Arctic—an opinion diametrically opposed to those of Moffett and Denby. The lack of a shared vision for LTA flight, and the Arctic expedition in particular, combined with the lack of confidence among the men in McCrary's leadership, forced Moffett to make changes.

McCrary was relieved from both command of NAS Lakehurst and the *Shenandoah*.[31] Klein, the executive officer, was relieved of that position and given command of the NAS. Rosendahl regarded Klein as a "hard-working, excellent administrator with a fine seagoing background and an outstanding service reputation, and full-out enthusiasm for whatever he undertook or was assigned. In naval parlance, he was an 'Aye, Aye sailorman.'"[32]

Command of the *Shenandoah* went to Lieutenant Commander Zachary Lansdowne,[33] who was well liked and had the respect of Rosendahl, who regarded him as "an oldtimer in airships." He had flown on R-34 on the first airship crossing of the Atlantic Ocean in May 1919. "Fresh from Washington, Lansdowne came to Lakehurst armed with concept and plan for a proposed Arctic exploration by the Shenandoah, scheduled for that spring."[34] Mooring masts were to be placed along the proposed route across the continent and up the Pacific Coast to Alaska to serve as operating bases for the airship. Because Rosendahl had been assigned to the development of ground handling from his earliest days at the NAS, it fell to him to assist in preparing masts and servicing facilities.

In the shakeup, McCrary was sent to sea while Commanders Klein and Weyerbacher and Lieutenants Deem and Kincaid were detached. Enlisted personnel were kept intact.

Lansdowne was an excellent choice to replace McCrary. A graduate of the Naval Academy, he had served as an aviator in the First World War, and in 1917, the Navy sent him to England to be trained in the operation of airships. As he took command of the *Shenandoah*, he had more flying time in dirigibles than anyone else in the Navy.[35] Lansdowne had been working on a manual for the safe operation of airships that warned against flying near thunderstorms.[36]

Lansdowne took command of the *Shenandoah* on February 16, 1924. The incident in the gale had occurred before the House Appropriations Committee rendered its decision regarding funding for the Arctic expedition. To many, the ship's ordeal in the storm was testimony to the strength of the vessel and skill of the crew, but to members of the Appropriations Committee, the ship seemed frail in the gale-force winds. To them, the proposed trek would entail massive logistical demands with huge costs and unacceptably high risks. In the end, the project withered on the vine as the committee refused to fund it. Consequently, President Coolidge canceled the project on February 15.[37]

As Rosendahl's experience with airships grew, he confided to himself that they might have been overly ambitious in promoting the Arctic flight when they did because they were not completely ready for it. He recognized as a critical feature the limited usefulness of the "high" mooring masts, both on shore and afloat on an airship tender. They needed more experience before undertaking such a venture.

Moffett was noted for his bold ideas, and the Arctic expedition was one of them. Lansdowne shared his belief in the project. "He was not an incautious, daredevil exponent of spectaculars. Actually, [Lansdowne] was a well-balanced naval officer who never let enthusiasm carry him off a prudent course."[38]

In the wake of the failed polar expedition, the LTA service was left with mooring masts at Fort Worth, Texas; San Diego, California; and

Camp Lewis near Tacoma, Washington. These expeditionary bases opened up opportunities for more training and long-distance flights. To facilitate long flights over the ocean, an airship tender was created. The collier, USS *Patoka* (AO-9), was equipped with a 125-foot mooring mast on her rear deck and storage containers for helium, fuel, and oil at a cost of $100,000.[39]

The *Patoka* was 477 feet long with a beam of 60 feet, displacing 17,070 tons, and capable of 11 knots. She had a complement of 168 men. Additional modifications met the residential needs of the airship crew.

With completion of the ship's repairs and the availability of the *Patoka*, the *Shenandoah* was slated to join the scout fleet in the Atlantic. Lansdowne led the airship to a first in the world of airships when she moored to the *Patoka*'s mast with Rosendahl as the mooring officer. The plan was to use airship tenders as floating bases to extend the range of airships over the oceans. The Navy's plan was to have one tender on each coast, but it was never realized, and the *Patoka* was destined to be the only airship tender in the Navy.

———

The *Shenandoah*'s greatest challenge came in October 1924 when she undertook a round-trip transcontinental flight of 9,000 miles using land-based mooring masts. This record-making cruise, starting from Lakehurst, New Jersey, "twice over the Rockies and twice around three sides of the United States," allowed thousands of Americans to view the great ship as she flew over numerous cities, attracting press coverage along the way.[40]

On September 3, 1924, Rosendahl led the way as he inspected the mooring masts at Fort Worth, Texas; San Diego, California; and Camp Lewis, Washington.[41] The *Shenandoah*'s departure date was October 7, 1924, with renowned journalist Junius B. Wood on board to document the venture for *The National Geographic Magazine*. Wood's coverage began in the morning: "The autumn sun was peeping over the horizon at 5:35 A.M., as the Shenandoah was led out of the big hangar. Every man on the station helped, 300 of them—sailors, marines, Filipino mess boys, and civilians. They came running into the drear, misty morn like ants pulling an immense gray worm out of its nest. The run slackened to a walk when she was safely clear of the shed. Nose to the wind, she was led farther into the field toward the mast, the crew stumbling and slipping in the loose sand. They stopped and waited."[42]

By 0700, the ship was secured to the mast and began to take on water ballast, food, fuel, passengers, and crew. Everything that came on board was weighed and distributed to maintain the ship's trim. As the ship's complement of eleven officers and fourteen crewmen came on board, each went to his duty station, prepared to be ordered to shift his position within the ship to maintain trim. The act of bringing men on board required delicate timing. As each man came to the top of the mast, he was required to ask permission to come on board by way of a small gangway. At times the ship was sufficiently buoyant to take on a man, but at other times, one would be told to "stand by." When the ship grew lighter, the order was given for one more man to step on board. "Weight in fuel took precedence over passenger cargo. If there was enough 'lift' after the required amount of gasoline was on board, the passenger was going; otherwise, no passenger."[43]

As the ship left its hangar and became exposed to the sun, the helium gas began to warm and expand. With each degree of temperature rise in the helium cells, the ship was lifting another three hundred pounds. Too much expansion would result in gas being vented through safety valves and lost. Conversely, significant cloud cover would result in cooling of the gas.

The helium gas cells were never filled to capacity. As the airship gained altitude, the helium expanded, and once it completely filled its cells, it reached what was referred to as "pressure altitude" or "pressure height." If the ship rose beyond this height, the expanding gas would be lost to the environment and could damage the structure of the gas cell. For control and safety, the airship was fitted with valves that automatically released helium if they went above pressure height, and a series of valves could be operated manually if the pilot needed that degree of control on the volume and pressure of the gas.

Trim had to be maintained at all times, even when moored to the mast. Because the mast was only 160 feet high and the ship was 682 feet long, not many degrees' drop was needed before the tail fins would scrape the ground.[44]

Orders were issued from the Bureau of Navigation on October 6 for Rear Admiral Moffett to be included in the *Shenandoah*'s complement for transport to Camp Lewis, Washington. The usual procedure called for Lansdowne to be the next-to-last person to leave the mooring mast and enter the ship and the mooring officer to be the last as he closed the gangway behind him, making it part of the rounded nose. On this occasion, the last to board was Junius Wood, who had been documenting the preparations since early morning.

From his station in the control car, Wood meticulously recorded the procedures that made the *Shenandoah* airborne. He noted that "sailing several thousand feet in the air is comparatively simple. Making a landing and casting off are the difficult parts of airship navigation. It is somewhat like docking a ship, only for the more delicate airship there can be no crunching of fenders or rubbing of piers by steel hulls."[45]

Wood took measure of the ship's commander: "Lansdowne is one of the type who foresees difficulties and does not get excited, but deftly avoids them."[46] As Lansdowne sat in one of the forward windows of the gondola, Lieutenant Commander Lewis Hancock Jr., the executive officer and navigator, was nearby as Lieutenant John B. Lawrence held the steering wheel. Lieutenant A. R. Houghton was officer of the deck and kept hands and eyes on the network of handles that emptied ballast bags, and Chief Petty Officer L. E. Allenly was at the wheel of the "elevators," or horizontal rudders.[47]

With the earth radiating the sun's heat, the ship needed to make its start while it held its handicap of superheat. Personal baggage was limited to six pounds, and the men wore two suits that were lighter in weight, allowing one to be peeled off on warm days. A fur-lined flying suit, mittens, and boots were provided from the ship's stores to be worn on colder days. Wood's typewriter went on board as ship's equipment.

Landings and departures were timed strategically, taking nature into account. Helium was expensive, costing $55 or more per cubic foot. Liberal valving of helium could cost $5,000 to $20,000 for each landing. Consequently, valving off helium to make the ship heavier was frowned

upon. It was common practice for landings to be made at night, when
the ship was cool and heavy, and departures to be scheduled for well after
sunrise when the helium was superheated and light.[48]

The *Shenandoah* left the mast at 1000, making for Fort Worth,
Texas.[49] Her outbound course took her over parts of North and South
Carolina, Georgia, Mississippi, and Louisiana. Wood made note of every
aspect of life on the airship. The ship was not wired for lights. Those in
the navigating and radio rooms, and the running lights, ran on batteries.
Each man carried his own battery-operated light. A cat's walk, only nine
inches wide, ran the 682-foot length of the ship from nose to tail. Wood
found the long keel to be an eerie place in the dark, "with phosphores-
cent figures and letters, which glow from every latticed frame and piece
of emergency gear, with lights which flash in the distance and disappear
and lights which suddenly appear from nowhere, while one fur-padded
form leans at a danger angle and another passes on the ribbon of runway." Night and day, the life of the ship was in the keel—the triangular
tunnel running the length of the ship.[50]

Wood was impressed by the ease with which the men moved along
the catwalk as nimbly as steelworkers. They trotted along the walk, passing each other, and even pausing to wrestle. While half the crew worked,
the other half slept—four hours on and four hours off—day and night.

The *Shenandoah* was secured to the mast at Fort Worth at 2305 on
October 8. The weather was clear but there were thunderstorms to the
north and west. Rosendahl rejoined the ship in Fort Worth as its navigator. The city's reception committee, which had planned a week-long celebration of the ship's arrival, was disappointed to learn that *Shenandoah*
would be there overnight before continuing its journey west.

During the night, the sky above the mast remained clear, but thunderstorms of considerable size and intensity covered the northern sky.
The storms were disappearing in the northeast skies by 0600, and the
ship left its mast at 0946, making for NAS San Diego in California with
Rosendahl as navigator.[51] This leg of the journey was expected to be the
most difficult and unpredictable. The large, rigid airships were best suited
for flying over flat oceans and at low altitudes over coastal regions, but
flying over the plains and mountains of the American West presented

physical conditions to which the ship was unaccustomed, such as heat and winds rising off the desserts, and strong turbulence associated with high mountaintops. This was the first such experience for an American airship and her crew.

The instinctive approach to clearing the mountains was simply to fly over them, but the altitudes required would cause the helium in its cells to expand to 100 percent, and any further expansion would result in the loss of the precious gas from the escape valves. The alternative was to fly as low as possible and negotiate the mountains by flying through their passes. This was the approach chosen, but it presented new challenges in airship handling.

Lansdowne followed the path of the Texas and Pacific Railway to negotiate the mountain passes and cuts.[52] Steering the ship through the passes was made extremely difficult by crosswinds that whipped around mountain peaks. As they approached a mountain pass, every man was on duty.

Half the officers were in the navigating car while others patrolled the keel, watching the gas cells, ready to cut out more ballast if necessary. Every man was alert as split seconds of action could mean success or tragedy. Lansdowne continued to follow his iron roadmap to Tucson, Arizona.

At approximately 1930 on October 10, just before running into a snow squall in the San Gregoria Pass, lights were spotted from Riverside and San Bernardino, California. To bring the ground into sight, the ship dropped from 5,000 to 3,000 feet to get below a large nimbus cloud. The ship became about 6,000 pounds heavy as she accumulated 3,000 to 4,000 pounds of wet snow, but they were through the storm and in clear weather by 1945.[53] They followed the Pacific coastline south to NAS San Diego, where they landed at 2330.

Lansdowne made a ground landing preliminary to mooring to the mast because the ground crew there had no experience with the direct "flying moor." During the landing, the after car bumped the ground, breaking six girder joints and incurring other minor damage. Repairs required a layover of about a week. Fortunately, this was the only accident of the entire cruise.[54]

On October 13, Rosendahl was flown by airplane from San Diego to Camp Lewis, Washington, to inspect the mast there for the next leg of the journey.

> Again as advance agent, I flew from San Diego to Camp Lewis, helmeted, goggled, and fur-suited, in a World War I relic, an open-cockpit DH-4 plane piloted by Lieutenant Ben Wyatt. The jaunt up the Pacific Coast by DH-4 was by far the worst ordeal of the Shenandoah's entire voyage, and I arrived at Camp Lewis deafened, dirty, disheveled, exhausted, and half asphyxiated from the plane's engine exhaust. I remember stopping at a small airport along the coast to refuel our DH-4. When the airport operator learned I was associated with the coming of the Shenandoah, he said he would never fly in anything that didn't have wings. At that point, I'd have been very happy to present him with a winged DH-4. To me the Shenandoah looked like a palatial ocean liner as I rejoined her for the three-part return to Lakehurst.[55]

The *Shenandoah* arrived at Camp Lewis at 1830 on October 18, where Moffett left the ship the next morning to return to the East Coast by rail. On the nineteenth, the *Shenandoah* left her mast at 1205, making for Fort Worth, Texas. Reversing her outbound trek, she arrived at NAS San Diego at 1020 on October 21, dropping her trail ropes to the landing party at 1046. After valving off helium for four and a half minutes, she was still 2,500 to 3,000 pounds light. Thirty-five men were taken on board as extra ballast and she took on 150,000 cubic feet of helium as station personnel made minor repairs.[56]

The crew of the *Shenandoah* was about to learn that there were significant differences in ship handling when approaching the mountains from the west compared to the approach from the east.

The ship left San Diego at 1107 on October 22, 1924, making for Fort Worth.[57] At noon, they were over Sweetwater Lake, California, at 4,500 feet altitude, with the ship approximately 4,000 pounds heavy. They had not yet traveled far enough to have consumed sufficient fuel to lighten the ship, and when they reached Jacumbo, California, at 5,500 feet, they dropped 1,000 pounds of water ballast to lighten the ship. It was the last of their available water ballast and, further on, as the ship became heavy, fuel tanks were dropped to lessen weight.

By 1600 on October 23, they sighted the Southern Pacific Railway that had served as their "iron map" to Fort Worth. An episode occurred on the twenty-third that did not appear in the ship's logbook, but Wood recorded the event. The radioman had been in his shack, experimenting with his equipment, trying to pick up radio stations from near and far. At 1215, the *Shenandoah* was just south of Bisbee, Arizona, where the railroad ended. Because the ship was running heavy, a 710-pound gasoline slip tank was dropped. The radioman had been picking up radio messages from various locations when he suddenly received a fragment of a message that said ". . . in the explosion an automobile burned. Both dead." Visions of the gasoline tank hitting the automobile as it crashed to ground flooded his brain. He worked frantically to locate the station that had transmitted the message but without success until suddenly another message appeared, stating, "Man arrested here confesses to automobile accident." The station transmitting the message was several hundred miles from the airship's course. While bringing great relief, it also illustrated that there could be adverse consequences to dropping the heavy fuel tanks when ballasting.[58]

They were moored to the mast at Fort Worth at 0241 on the twenty-fourth. After refueling, they made for Lakehurst, where their record-breaking trip ended at 2355 on October 25, 1924.

In his memoir, Rosendahl summarized the epic journey:

> Our transcontinental round trip had been as fine a training exercise as could have been prescribed. It involved intimate knowledge of the ship, careful and frugal planning, extended operations away from a main base and hangar, dependence upon expeditionary facilities alone, overland and overwater navigation, conservation of helium gas, study and out-maneuvering of the elements, and operation of the ship almost always to her limits. . . . Now, it seemed, our rigid airship program was really getting into high gear and we were moving ahead.[59]

———

The transcontinental flight proved the *Shenandoah* to be a worthy airship with a very capable crew, but the potential of the Navy's LTA program was limited severely with only one airship. The crash of ZR-2 had left a void in the Navy's plans to acquire two rigid airships. However, through a series of unusual events, the Navy was to acquire a new German-built Zeppelin designated LZ-126 (redesignated ZR-3 by the Navy).

On October 15, as the *Shenandoah* was preparing to make its flight from San Diego to Camp Lewis, Washington, the ZR-3, with a German crew, was delivered to NAS Lakehurst. On her return to Lakehurst, the *Shenandoah* and ZR-3 shared Hangar No. 1.

CHAPTER 4

ZR-3

As of October 1924, there were no plans for the construction of another airship at Lakehurst. The Navy had enough helium to support only one airship, but there was confidence that if another ship were acquired, the government would provide funding for additional helium.

A chain of events was set in motion on June 1, 1919, which ultimately resulted in the Navy acquiring another rigid airship. This came about as a result of the reparations prescribed by the Treaty of Versailles. The ships of the German High Seas Fleet had been interned at Scapa Flow in the Orkney Islands of Scotland, awaiting a decision about how they would be distributed among the allied powers as part of Germany's war reparations. Germany's Zeppelins were part of her navy, and it was expected that they would be distributed among allied nations as well.

Sources varied but it appeared that Germany had built approximately ninety Zeppelins during the war. Former Zeppelin captain Ernst Lehmann claimed that Germany had thirty-four Zeppelins in service with the army and sixty-five with the navy.[1] Of the Zeppelins built during the war, sixteen were intact at war's end. Construction of L-72 had not been completed and it resided intact at the Zeppelin works in Friedrichshafen.[2] The remaining Zeppelins were distributed among airship sheds in Northern Germany in the vicinity of the North Sea and Baltic coasts.[3]

Article 202 of the Treaty of Versailles provided that, once the treaty came into force, Germany would deliver to all the principal and associated powers all "dirigibles able to take the air, being manufactured, repaired or assembled." Until then, Germany was required to maintain the airships at its own expense.[4] A Zeppelin was the one German asset that was of any value to the American Navy, and it was made clear to the other allied nations that she would demand her share of the ships. This would fulfill the Navy's need for a second airship.

On June 21, 1919, Admiral Ludwig von Reuter, commander of the High Seas Fleet, ordered the ships scuttled to keep them out of Allied hands. Fifteen of sixteen capital ships, five of eight cruisers, and thirty-two of fifty destroyers were scuttled. Reuter was celebrated as a hero in Germany.

In late August 1919, a young German naval officer, apparently emulating Reuter's example, sabotaged the greater number of Zeppelins to be turned over to the Allies. It was assumed that the young officer was acting on his own initiative. As usual, the Zeppelins had been suspended in their sheds by cables. The officer ordered the cables to be cut, causing the airships to crash to the ground, crushing the gondolas and engines and resulting in irreparable twisting of the framework.[5] The officer's name, if known, was never given, and he was said to have disappeared.

On September 29, 1919, the supreme council made decisions on the allocation of Zeppelins to the allied powers, but plans were interrupted when the council learned that seven Zeppelins had been destroyed. Consequently, the council decided that aggrieved nations could receive financial compensation for the loss of Zeppelins, but they could retain the right to compensation in kind (i.e., replacement Zeppelins).[6]

The newest Zeppelins, completed just prior to the armistice, were superior to the older ones. They had a greater cruising range, were faster, and could climb to higher altitudes.[7]

The U.S. wanted to lay claims to the super-Zeppelin LZ-114 (L-72). Destined for the German Navy, L-72 was the latest product of the Zeppelin works. She was built to bomb New York City, but the flight, loosely scheduled for mid-November 1918, was thwarted by the armistice.[8] L-72 was in perfect condition hanging in its shed in Friedrichshafen. She was 743 feet, 2 inches long; 78 feet, 5 inches in diameter; with a gas capacity of 2,418,700 cubic feet.

The Germans supported the idea of L-72 going to the U.S. because, in American hands, there was far greater opportunity for commercial airship development. In the end, the ship went to France and was renamed the *Dixmude*.

The U.S. wanted one of the newer, larger Zeppelins as a model of the latest developments in rigid airships. Count Zeppelin had set the standard for airship construction, but the English and Americans had not followed that standard. The latter countries were said to be in over their heads with the airships they were building, and both realized that a Zeppelin model, or a full set of Zeppelin blueprints and specifications, would be of great value. The American Navy's progress with ZR-1 had been progressing "slowly and dubiously, for lack of experience and of knowledge of all the complex engineering principles involved."[9]

Thirsting for first-hand knowledge of Zeppelin manufacturing methods, the Navy sent its expert designer, Commander Jerome C. Hunsaker of the Bureau of Construction and Repair, and Commander Weyerbacher, manager of the Lakehurst dirigible program, to Germany to study the Zeppelin plant and its construction methods.[10]

The terms of the Peace Treaty restricted the Zeppelin firm so severely from manufacturing airships that large parts of it had to close. The scarcity of German labor and capital, along with the weight of war reparations, made the situation worse. To escape the handicaps imposed by the treaty, Zeppelin officials wanted to move the firm to the U.S., where terms of the treaty regarding airships would not apply. The terms of the treaty called for all Zeppelin sheds to be destroyed, but in December 1921, the council of ambassadors granted permission for the U.S. to contract with Germany to construct an L-70-type Zeppelin to be built at Friedrichshafen. This decision was the culmination of diplomatic negotiations that had been ongoing since the previous July.[11]

Germany was allowed to build a single airship for the U.S., with about 2.5 million cubic feet gas capacity.[12] Designated LZ-126 (redesignated ZR-3 by the Navy), it was built in Friedrichshafen because it had the only shed large enough to accommodate it.[13] This class of airship was 743 feet long and 78.4 feet in diameter and carried a crew of thirty men. With its seven 290-horsepower Maybach engines—resulting in a total horsepower of 2,030—it could reach speeds over 80 miles per hour.[14]

The German government accepted responsibility for delivering the ship to Lakehurst with a number of American observers on board believing this act would prove to the world German superiority in LTA construction.[15] Terms of the contract required Germany to provide the U.S. with a 70,000-cubic-meter airship capable of making 70 miles per hour with a lifting capacity to carry twenty passengers in addition to crew. The ship would have a radius sufficient to traverse the Atlantic Ocean to the U.S. with an ample margin of safety even in case of storms or adverse winds. The U.S. assumed no risk for its safe arrival. The ship would make enough trial flights in Germany to ensure her airworthiness and safety.[16]

The Germans were given permission by the Treaty of Versailles to build airships limited to 30,000 cubic meters, but there was no commercial future for such small dirigibles due to their limited range and lifting capacity. Germany was placing all its hopes on the large airship to be built for the U.S.—"the slender thread on which the future of German aviation hangs."[17]

The two largest airships in the world—ZR-1 and ZR-3—were to have the latest radio equipment. NAS Lakehurst was equipped with a high-powered radio station with a new type of radio transmitting antenna without towers. The Navy's radio engineers designed a long, low aerial that was 800 feet long and 120 feet wide. On clear nights, this equipment would allow communication with an aircraft or surface ship 2,000 miles out to sea, and it ensured the ability to pick up the ZR-3 on her maiden trip before she was a third of the way across the Atlantic.[18]

The new equipment also contained a radio compass station to enable airships to determine their positions in the air within a radius of 200 miles and to locate the landing field when returning from a flight, even in darkness or dense fog.[19]

In December 1922, the Bureau of Navigation announced that ZR-1 would be ready by July and ZR-3 would be delivered several months later.[20] When completed, ZR-3 would fly to Berlin for inspection by the American ambassador prior to starting its trek across the Atlantic.[21]

The departure from Germany was delayed due to a number of non-engineering circumstances. Workers at the Zeppelin plant prolonged their work because they knew that completion of the ship meant the end of the Zeppelin industry and their jobs with it.[22] A plot by Bavarian nationalists to commandeer the ship also threatened its completion.[23]

The work that was done was of the highest technical quality. ZR-3 was the 126th airship built by the Zeppelin firm, and officials boasted that they had never lost a ship due to construction defects.[24] Still hopeful for a successful completion, it was announced in November 1923 that Dr. Eckener, now fifty-six years old, would serve as pilot of the ship when her transatlantic flight started—now targeted for the spring of 1924. Journalists described Eckener as a "tall and dignified man who has more the appearance of a college professor than the builder of huge airships. He speaks English, is wrapped up in his work, and smokes an English pipe when off duty outside the Zeppelin sheds."[25]

Finally, in August 1924, ZR-3, "the result of experiments of the most colossal undertaking in aeronautical history," was completed and ready for delivery to Lakehurst.[26] Given the importance of the mission for Germany, the most experienced crew was assembled.

Dr. Eckener had served as an instructor for the Zeppelin works and had commanded LZ-120 during the war. He had run the Zeppelin Airship company since the death of Count Ferdinand von Zeppelin in 1917. Captain Ernst Lehmann, second in command, had served as commander of five different Zeppelins during the war and had made thousands of flights. Hans C. Fleming, navigation officer, was a Zeppelin pilot during the war and held the record for the highest flight after taking his ship to nearly 27,000 feet to dodge British airplanes defending London. William C. Stegle, chief engineer, had been with the Zeppelin works for many years and, as director of construction, was the most active individual at work building ZR-3. Franz E. Wittemann and Walter Scherz were quartermasters. Lieutenant Hans von Schiller had joined the Zeppelin force in 1915 and made thirty-eight night flights over London.

There would be twenty-four officers and men, most of whom spoke English, and all would remain in the U.S. except for Eckener and Schiller.[27]

The Navy made elaborate arrangements for ZR-3's safety during her transatlantic flight, but there was no semblance of ceremony. The airship's delivery was regarded as payment of a war debt, undeserving of ceremony. Because she had not returned from her transcontinental flight, *Shenandoah* would not be on hand to greet the arrival of ZR-3. The two giant rigids would, however, share the same hangar.[28]

Three Americans had been scheduled to make the flight on board ZR-3: Captain George W. Steele, who had been in charge of the American detail at the Zeppelin works; Lieutenant Commander Sidney M. Kraus, who had inspected the airship's engines; and Commander Garland Fulton, who scrutinized the construction work.[29] At the last minute, Klein, commanding officer of NAS Lakehurst, managed to obtain temporary duty orders to make the flight as a fourth.[30]

Barring any great headwinds, the transatlantic flight was expected to take two and a half days. The direct route distance to the East Coast of the U.S. was 3,500 miles. Should adverse weather force the ship to take a southern course across France, past Cape Finisterre, over the Azores to Bermuda, then northward to Lakehurst, the distance would be 4,500 nautical miles. Ironically, the crew selected to bring the airship to the U.S. had been trained during the First World War to bomb New York City.[31]

American support for the transatlantic flight included a system for forecasting weather conditions and transmitting the data to the airship. Surface ships would be stationed in the Atlantic to gather weather information, and a naval radio station within the continental U.S. would transmit the information.

One station ship was positioned at 45 degrees North, 45 degrees West; a second at 55 degrees North, 45 West; and the third at 44 degrees North, 57 degrees West. The latter ship acted as a radio relay ship for the weather information collected by the first two ships. The most northerly of the ships made hourly observations and upper air soundings by pilot balloons every six hours. The information was transmitted four times a day to the second ship in line, which combined the data with observations made on board it. The second ship was known as the primary observation ship, and it accumulated all weather information from the continental U.S. and the observation ship to the north of her. The entire activity was coordinated in the Navy Department in Washington.[32]

The three station ships were the USS *Patoka*, approximately 300 miles south of Cape Farewell, Greenland; the light cruiser USS *Detroit* (CL-8), about 900 miles south of Cape Farewell and approximately 300 miles southeast of Cape Race, Newfoundland, as an observation ship;

and the light cruiser USS *Milwaukee* (CL-5) about 250 miles east of Halifax, acting as a relay ship.[33]

Only Navy shore stations at Bar Harbor, Annapolis, and Washington had permission to communicate with the airship. Radio from the Eiffel Tower in Paris could communicate with the ship until it established radio communication with U.S. Naval Stations.[34]

The ZR-3 was advancing the aeronautical sciences. One journalist wrote, "When the giant airship ZR-3 soars over the Atlantic Ocean and noses her way out of the clouds on the American side a new chapter will have been written on the importance of radio in aviation. For to radio will fall a large part of the responsibility of keeping the air monster on its course and maintaining communication with its officers."[35]

ZR-3 would carry mail from Germany to the U.S., establishing the first transatlantic regular mail flight, and German postal authorities issued a special series of airmail stamps and postcards for the flight.

On the morning of October 11, 1924, all seemed ready for ZR-3 to lift off on its journey. Food, fuel, oil, mail, baggage, and goods had been loaded the previous day. The Americans were each restricted to one suitcase and three blankets.

The Navy station ships had been tossed around in the Atlantic for two weeks, waiting for the flight to lift off. It could have gotten underway on October 11 if the ship had been taken out of the hangar in the cool of the dawn hours instead of two hours later when temperatures were rising rapidly, significantly affecting lifting power. After Eckener had a ton and a half of fuel removed, it was still too heavy, and, for safety reasons, he delayed the flight by another day.[36]

The morning of the twelfth was foggy and the temperature colder— better. At 0625, several hundred men of the ground crew, pulling on long handling lines, brought ZR-3 out of her hangar to be met by a crowd of nearly five thousand cheering people.

At 0635, the "last of the Zeppelins" was off on its epic journey with a German flag trailing from its stern.[37] The crowd's view was brief because, once lines were released, the ship ascended into a dense mist and disappeared, attempting "the greatest dirigible voyage in the history of aeronautics."[38] The flight from Friedrichshafen to the Atlantic Ocean took only nine hours, with an average speed of 60 miles per hour.

Over the ocean, ZR-3 used her radio to communicate with surface ships to verify her location and make necessary course changes. At 2310 on October 13, Lieutenant T. G. W. Settle, in Hangar No.1, intercepted a message sent from the airship to the cruiser *Milwaukee* that reported, "All is well on board ship."[39]

On the morning of the fourteenth, the ship passed the southeast coast of Nova Scotia, crossed the Gulf of Maine, and made for Boston. "It was a sight to swell the bosom of a returning American and one never to be forgotten. Millions of lights. If one looked downwards one could see the buildings, but looking slantwise, nothing but lights."[40] Steele's log ended with that simple sense of wonderment.

Upon arrival at NAS Lakehurst, Lieutenant Herbert V. Wiley commanded the ground crew of several hundred men who would walk the ship into the hangar.[41] The ship's approximate arrival time was noon on October 15. Admiral A. H. Scales, commandant of the Fourth Naval District at Philadelphia, and his staff would be present to greet the ship along with other dignitaries and spouses. The public was allowed onto the field to witness the arrival, but after Wiley's ground crew got the ship into the hangar, the public would be barred until the explosive hydrogen gas had been removed—a process that would take about twenty-four hours.[42]

As soon as ZR-3 was over American soil, she began to receive a flood of congratulatory messages—so many that the radio operator, fatigued from long watches and maximally busy with essential dispatches, was forced to send his own message stating, "Please hold messages of congratulations. Must work with commercial and naval stations only."[43]

ZR-3 first crossed over U.S. soil at 0420, but rather than making for NAS Lakehurst, Eckener chose to make a "demonstration" flight to show off to America the pride of Germany. Seventy-five hours and forty-seven minutes after leaving Friedrichshafen, the ship was over Boston, then on to New York City, where it circled the Woolworth Building at altitudes ranging from 700 to 1,000 feet. Workers in office buildings interrupted their work to lean out of windows for a look at the airship while, below, traffic became hopelessly tangled, but nobody cared.[44]

Eckener took the ship on three complete trips up and down over Manhattan, circled above Brooklyn four times, and saluted the Brooklyn Navy Yard as it climbed over Staten Island.

Finally, at 0930 on October 15, 1924, the ZR-3 arrived at NAS Lakehurst in perfect weather after an eighty-hour transatlantic flight. At precisely 0950, a member of the ground crew caught the first of the descending handling ropes. "This marked the actual landing of the ZR-3, according to the understanding in airship circles."[45] ZR-3 broke the record set five years previously by the British R-34, which had flown from East Fortune, Scotland, to the U.S. in four days and twelve hours. ZR-3 had covered 5,066 miles with no trouble to the engines.

While an atmosphere of excitement continued outside the hangar, preparations were underway inside to deflate the airship. Nine hours were required to cradle the ship properly before starting the process of venting the hydrogen gas. The five motor gondolas and the control car were secured in specially constructed cradles, and ropes made of hemp fiber were used to attach the ends of the ship. Hemp was used in place of steel cables to reduce the chance of friction or sparks that might ignite the hydrogen gas. Because of the dangers inherent in handling hydrogen, no attempt was made to save the gas. The process of venting the gas from the fourteen cells took fifteen hours.[46]

Unnamed military sources had advanced the notion that the value of airships in war had not been demonstrated definitively. Ernst Lehmann, a "quiet-mannered little man, about five-feet-four in height, with blue eyes and a perpetual smile," took issue with the unnamed sources. He had piloted a Zeppelin over London in perfect safety, although he brought it back with four hundred holes in her:

> I was over London in a ship which was bombing the city. The bomb is released, there is an interval of perhaps a half minute, then a sharp blow on the bottom of the pilot cabin, the "bridge" of the dirigible, as if a giant were striking the bottom of the cabin with an iron hammer. That was the upward rush of air from the sound of the explosion. The

uprush of air does not disturb the equilibrium of the ship in the least, not even lifting it, but the sensation is peculiar. . . . The future of the dirigible as a combat or defense unit is assured.[47]

Forbidden by the treaty to be used as a war machine, ZR-3 was classed as a German merchantman, and the first merchandise ever brought from Europe to the U.S. by air arrived on board her, consigned to the Wanamaker Company.[48] About a dozen cases of Christmas toys manufactured in Nuremberg, Germany, arrived on board the ZR-3. The Surveyor of Customs at the Port of Philadelphia drove to Lakehurst to inspect the cargo, collect duty, and turn it over to a Wanamaker Company representative. The first case was expedited to President Coolidge, and the others went to Wanamaker stores in Philadelphia and New York. The promise of transatlantic cargo shipment by air was apparent immediately, as the toys were on display in store windows in Philadelphia three hours after arrival at NAS Lakehurst.[49]

Following a satisfactory ship inspection, Secretary Wilbur shared with the German crew that ZR-3 would be christened "Los Angeles."[50]

By mid-November 1924, the helium supply had improved. Eighteen carloads had arrived at Lakehurst by November 13, representing 1,200,000 cubic feet, with another 400,000 cubic feet to follow. With this and the gas to be transferred from the *Shenandoah,* there was enough helium to fill ZR-3 to near capacity.[51]

As the first American flight of ZR-3 was nearing, the best of German airship expertise was flowing into the U.S. Dr. Karl Arnstein and twelve of his carefully selected engineers traveled to Akron, Ohio, to set up shop.[52]

The Navy announced that November 25 had been selected for the christening of ZR-3 at NAS Anacostia and for her first flight since delivery to the U.S.

USS *LOS ANGELES* (ZR-3)

Because NAS Anacostia lacked a mooring mast, Rosendahl went ahead to organize a ground crew of three hundred men to help land the giant ship and hold her steady during the christening ceremony. On the morning of the ceremony, Commander Klein wanted to arrive in D.C. early enough for the ship to hover over the city and be seen by as many people as possible.

The mile-wide field at Anacostia had been in readiness to receive thousands of people who gathered to see the giant airship. Maneuvering room was narrow and landing made difficult by gusting winds and tree-topped hills. After three attempts failed to land by using the engines to drive the ship down against the lifting power of the helium, Klein valved off precious helium to get the ship down. Handling lines were manned, and the ship was walked to the place designated for the christening ceremony. At the appropriate time, First Lady Coolidge pulled sharply on a line that had been passed out of the ship to her. A trap door high in the ship's bow opened to release a host of message-bearing pigeons that headed homeward. With a bottle of water from the River Jordan, Mrs. Coolidge declared, "I Christen thee Los Angeles"—words inaudible due to the noise surrounding the ship.[1] Mrs. Coolidge then presented the ship with her photograph, inscribed, "To the good ship Los Angeles from her sponsor mother. 'Go forth under the open sky and may the winds of Heaven deal gently with thee.'"[2]

Following the christening, Rear Admiral Hutchinson of the Washington Navy Yard read his orders commissioning the new ship in the Navy. Captain George Steele, Jr., returned from his illness, read his orders. A slender commissioned pennant was dropped and "The Los Angeles was flying her official flags at last."[3]

After President and Mrs. Coolidge, with a host of distinguished guests, passed through the ship on a brief inspection, Admiral Moffett boarded to make the return fight to Lakehurst.

———

A month later, Paul Litchfield, vice president and general manager of the Goodyear Zeppelin Corporation, laid out a blueprint for the Navy's LTA program.[4] He explained the desirability of building an airship of five million cubic feet or more. The *Shenandoah*, with a capacity of 2,115,000 cubic feet of gas, made a 9,000-mile journey around the U.S., while the ZR-3 made a more than 5,000-mile nonstop trip—the longest of any vehicle.[5]

The larger an airship, the higher its efficiency and the higher the proportion of useful lift (freight carrying capacity) in comparison to size. Count Zeppelin's earliest airships could carry but 10 to 20 percent of their weight, while ZR-3 carried between 50 and 60 percent. This meant ZR-3, when inflated under normal conditions, weighed about 45 tons, but it could lift a total of 90 tons. ZR-3 departed Friedrichshafen with 29 tons of gasoline for fuel, but a little less than 22 tons was used on the 5,000-mile journey. A ship twice the size of ZR-3 would not require twice the amount of fuel but would have a considerably larger percentage of space for passengers or cargo.

"A ten million cubic foot ship could carry a proportionately greater pay load than a five million cubic foot ship and could fly around the world in a non-stop flight—could fly it either way—around the equator or around the poles."[6]

Litchfield cautioned against jumping too much in size when building airships because increasing size was associated with unique engineering problems as well as handling issues with the completed ship. Size should be advanced in stages. Further, when building a ship of five or six million cubic feet, it was necessary to know the intended use of the craft—whether for commercial or military use—because architectural considerations would be drastically different.

If a ship were to be built for travel over land features (e.g., between the Atlantic and Pacific Oceans), the ceiling of the ship would be an important factor. If a ship were to travel from California with sufficient fuel to make New York, it would have to carry the maximum weight over the Rocky Mountains. At such altitudes, the air pressure is less and temperatures lower, and both parameters affect the lifting power of the helium. If, however, the ship were intended for coastal patrol or with a surface fleet, it would have different design requirements. "The routes to be followed and the tasks to be done by a Zeppelin ship are primary facts to be studied before the final lines of design can be settled."[7]

The *Shenandoah* was 680 feet long and 78 feet in diameter, whereas the ZR-3 was shorter and fatter—660 feet long and a height of 101.6 feet. This gives a slenderness ratio of 8.7 (i.e., 8.7 times as long as it is in diameter). The ratio for ZR-3 was 7.2. A five-million-cubic-foot ship would be between 860 and 930 feet long with a maximum diameter of 115 to 120 feet and a slenderness ratio of about 7.2.[8]

Litchfield calculated that such a large ship would require engines of 4,000 horsepower to drive it, compared to the 2,000 horsepower for ZR-3. Such engines would allow speeds of 80 to 85 miles per hour. The projected payload was from 50 to 125 passengers, three to 6 tons of mail, and as much as 12 tons of freight over a journey of 6,000 to 8,000 miles.[9]

———

Moffett wanted the *Los Angeles* flying as much as possible, but, due to wintry weather, there were only two flights in December 1924 for a total flying time of less than six hours.

Intended exclusively for peaceful purposes, the *Los Angeles* was promoted as a research vessel, and she was given the opportunity to contribute to scientific research in January 1925. Expecting a total eclipse of the sun on January 24, arrangements were made for the *Los Angeles* to carry aloft a group of scientists, observers, and equipment to document the event. Captain Pollock from the Naval Observatory was in charge of the expedition, and all involved personnel arrived at NAS Lakehurst early in the week to stow gear on board the ship and rehearse the activities to be conducted on the twenty-fourth. Scientific gear included two double long focus astronomical cameras, two motion picture cameras, a spectrograph, and a variety of still cameras. Some officers came prepared to make manual sketches of the corona, while others were detailed as lookouts for comets. The remainder of the payload consisted of forty-two people, eight hundred pounds of food, and sufficient fuel for thirty hours of cruising at full speed.[10]

After a rehearsal flight was canceled due to weather, the scientists and crew rehearsed their duties at their stations with the ship in its hangar.[11] The weather forecast for Saturday, January 23, suggested that winds would be calm enough for the ground crew to walk the ship out of its hangar, but, when the day arrived, Nature did not cooperate. The ship had been made ready and all day on the twenty-third, and throughout the night, the crew ran the engines intermittently to keep them warmed. Originally, the ship was to be in the vicinity of the Nantucket lightship where the studies would be conducted. Rendezvous here at the moment of eclipse required a liftoff by 0300, but by then, winds were averaging 14 miles per hour with gusts of 22 miles per hour.

By then the temperature had fallen to 4° Fahrenheit and the crew boarded wearing fur-lined flying suits, helmets, and boots. Because of the late start, the plan was altered to make the scientific observations in the vicinity of Block Island. The *Los Angeles* started out of her hangar at 0501. The weather was "Bitterly cold, even the ground crew will remember that occasion as they fought their way over the glazed icy surface of the field, tugging whole-heartedly but almost ineffectively as the cross wind threatened to dash the ship against the hangar structure. Timely use of the ship's engine rushed her clear."[12]

After dropping ballast, the ship rose statically to an altitude of 60 feet. All engines were brought to standard speed and the ship rose to 2,000 feet. The *Los Angeles* made Montauk Point at 0802 at an altitude of 4,500 feet, and by 0830 the moon was obscuring about one-third of the sun. As the eclipse progressed, the temperature dropped as the sun became about 75 percent obscured, and numerous clouds were seen to seaward at about 2,000 feet. The eclipse became total at 0913 as the scientific party busied itself taking photographs and making observations. Lieutenant Wiley made the log entry for the 0800–1200 watch recording, "Very wonderful color effects to Northward. Darkness. Stars." The darkness deepened as the moment of totality approached, and the sun could be observed with the naked eye, treating everyone to the sight of Bailey's Beads—small dots around the edge of the disc.[13] The total eclipse ended at 0915.[14] Nature's display had been impressive—a never-to-be-forgotten memory.[15]

Approaching NAS Lakehurst on her return, the *Los Angeles* received a warning from the ground that an area of low barometric pressure was approaching, the weather conditions would not be favorable for mooring to the mast, and they needed to make haste to land in time to get the ship into the hangar safely. A lot of fuel had been burned on the flight, making the ship light and more difficult to land. After two failed attempts to land, helium was released eight times for a total of 5.5 minutes to decrease buoyancy sufficiently to land. The ship landed at 1540 and was in her hangar at 1710.[16]

Winters at Lakehurst were characteristically severe, leading some to wonder why it had been selected as the site for an airship base. January 1925 brought cold temperatures, high winds, snow, and ice—all of which forced the *Los Angeles* to spend most of the month in her hangar undergoing maintenance. With no flights since the January 24 "eclipse" flight, Steele decided that no further flights would be made until February 16.[17] Plans were being made for a flight to Bermuda, where the *Los Angeles* would moor to the mast of the *Patoka*. Just as the "eclipse" flight had demonstrated the utility of the airship for scientific purposes, the flight over the ocean to Bermuda carrying mail would demonstrate the commercial value of airships.

The *Patoka* was sent to Bermuda ahead of the *Los Angeles* on February 17, along with Rosendahl and two enlisted men to ensure a successful mooring.[18] The ship was ready for flight on February 20 with forty-three men on board, including, as guests, Assistant Secretary of the Navy Theodore D. Robinson, Rear Admiral Moffett, Captain Emory Land, Captain Robert L. Gormley, and Lieutenant T. G. W. Settle.

It was hoped that the weather would be favorable for the *Los Angeles* to make a direct flight to Bermuda to demonstrate the ship's speed for carrying mail. Surface steamships made the trip from New York to Bermuda in 40 to 44 hours under normal circumstances, but the Navy hoped to make the trip in the *Los Angeles* in 10 hours.[19]

Plans for the airship to moor to the *Patoka* on the twenty-first were thwarted by heavy rain squalls. There were also concerns about how much load the rain-soaked ship could lift off from the *Patoka* under such circumstances.[20] "And so, to the delight of the insatiable stamp collectors, the Los Angeles dropped the mail and without mooring, pointed for Lakehurst."[21] As they passed over the Governor's Grounds, they dropped 85 pounds of mail.

The ship was back at NAS Lakehurst at 0036 on February 22 with only two hours' fuel remaining. Failure to moor to the *Patoka* did not prevent the flight from being successful because it represented the United States's first transoceanic airmail delivery. Moffett told the press that the *Los Angeles*'s performance had increased his conviction that the dirigible-type aircraft was here to stay.[22]

The next flight to Bermuda departed on the afternoon of April 21, 1925. This transoceanic flight was uneventful, and the ship was moored to the *Patoka* on the twenty-second.[23] The roundtrip transoceanic flights between Lakehurst and Bermuda were proving what airship proponents knew—that LTA craft could find good commercial use in the civilian world for transporting passengers, cargo, and mail and, in all likelihood, generate profits.

On May 1, 1925, while moored to the mast at Lakehurst, the *Los Angeles*, using her high-frequency radio, was in direct communication with the *Patoka*, then at Mayaguez, Puerto Rico—the destination for her next transoceanic flight. She left Lakehurst on May 3 with forty persons on board. At 1040 on May 4, she sighted the steamship *Delfina* on the surface below them on a southerly heading. Horace D. Ashton, a civilian photographer, was on board, and Steele maneuvered the ship to allow him to photograph the steamer. At that moment, there was probably a tacit understanding among the Navy officers present that they had just performed an act of aerial reconnaissance that would be useful for military purposes under other circumstances.

Moored to the *Patoka*'s mast presented issues not present at Lakehurst, where the airship could swing about the high mast freely. At 1820 on May 5, when the airship began to swing toward the *Patoka*, the *Los Angeles* backed full its No. 4 Engine and dropped one emergency ballast tank to avoid hitting the *Patoka*. Ten minutes later, any danger of swing-ing over the tender had been eliminated by the *Patoka*'s use of one of its small powerboats to move the stern to starboard.[24]

Other near misses represented learning experiences that emphasized the need for constant vigilance to protect both the airship and her tender. On May 7, while moored to the mast, the airship encountered unusually gusty weather with strong vertical currents. Strong winds caused the air-ship to swing stern to port, putting her directly over the *Patoka*. When a gust started the stern downward, the emergency ballast bag was pulled to prevent the airship's collision with the cargo mast of the tender. The stern then rose to an angle of 21° before settling as the ship swung clear of the tender.[25] Each such incident strengthened the crew's confidence and handling ability.

The transoceanic flights had given the LTA program favorable media attention, but Moffett wanted more. He resorted to giving airship flights to influential people who could advance his program. Such a high-profile flight took place on May 15, 1925. Officially, the passengers were the guests of Secretary of the Navy Wilbur, but Moffett orchestrated the event. Newspapers described the flight as "a billion dollar junket, unique in the history of aeronautics."[26] The guests for the flight were men with wealth aggregating more than a billion dollars.

The impressive passenger list included dignitaries and notables from various media, manufacturing, and military organizations.[27] Moffett hoped that a successful flight would prompt his guests to influence Con-gress and private investors to fund advances in LTA flight. This ambi-tious undertaking was a signature talent of Admiral Moffett. The guests were not disappointed with their seven-hour, 265-mile flight around the Philadelphia area, traveling over three states.

Moffett loved for the airships to make high-profile "hand-waving" flights whenever possible to keep them in the consciousness of the pub-lic. Moffett's interest was matched by a "great nationwide interest in our airships. The Navy Department received 248 requests from public of-ficials, public and semi-public bodies, and individuals, for a flight of a rigid airship over the Middle West."[28]

A memorandum was issued from the commanding officer of NAS Lakehurst on May 13, 1925, to the chief of naval operation in Washington concerning a trip for the *Los Angeles* to the Midwest.[29] Valuable publicity would be gained from the ship's flying over numerous cities on its way to Minneapolis, Minnesota, to participate in the Norwegian Centennial celebration.[30] There was a romantic aura about the airships, and they seldom flew over a city unnoticed. To complete the planned 1,100-mile trip, it was necessary to land at Minneapolis to refuel. Landing required a trained ground crew, and the commanding officer decided to send Wiley and two enlisted men ahead to assemble and train an improvised crew.

The airship left her mast at 0130 on June 7, making for Minneapolis, but, at 1014, in the vicinity of Cleveland, Ohio, the No. 5 Engine experienced a burned-out connecting rod.[31] A radio message was sent to the Ford Motor Company at 1501, stating, "Account engine trouble abandoning remainder of trip and returning to Lakehurst from Cleveland. Expect to arrive sunrise Monday."[32]

In need of extensive repairs and maintenance, the *Los Angeles* did not fly again in 1925. Rosendahl summarized the extent of the problem:

> While materials used by the Germans in the ZR-3 were the best they then had, they left much to be desired. Structural members and wiring began to show failure. Supposedly gas-tight fabric helium cells developed brittleness and great porosity. In prodigious growth in one generation from 24- to 400 horsepower, the engines had inherited a few strictly 240-H.P. features. Worst of all, we had used a corrosive anti-freeze mixture in our water ballast which had left its warning pockmark signs of corrosive deterioration on parts of the ship's lower structure. Prudence dictated that the L A be laid up for correction of these major flaws.[33]

While waiting for the *Los Angeles* to be made fit again, the baton was passed off to the *Shenandoah*, whose crew was eager to get back into the air. The *Shenandoah*'s gas cells were reinflated with helium from the Los Angeles, and, following short shakedown cruises, she was ready for more challenging assignments with Rosendahl as navigator and mooring officer.

The *Shenandoah* was sent on a public relations mission to Bar Harbor, Maine, for the seventeenth annual state governors conference at the Poland Springs House in Poland Springs, Maine, on June 29, 1925. Governors were given rides in the airship, and the Navy Department, for the first time, granted permission for women to fly, paving the way for a woman governor and the wives of several other governors.

About a month later, the ship was dispatched to conduct gunnery trials of a new anti-aircraft target to be used for target practice from surface ships. The *Shenandoah* towed the giant target while the USS *Texas* (BB-35) fired on it. Rear Admiral Charles F. Hughes was on board *Shenandoah* for part of the exercises, and the *Texas* fired a 13-gun salute in his honor.[34] Rosendahl believed this was probably the first time an admiral had received a gun salute while his flag flew from an airship.[35]

At sunset on July 16, as the ship was approaching the coast on its return to Lakehurst, a storm was encountered of horrifying beauty:

> After sunset, as we approached the coast on our return, there loomed up ahead an imposing cloud barrier making a line squall sweeping across the eastern part of the country. As darkness fell, we began to witness one of the most severe and extensive electrical displays ever to traverse the Atlantic seaboard. Passing Lakehurst, the storm turned into a cloudburst and put the station's entire electrical system, including radio, out of commission for several hours. Here was a startling and emphatic demonstration for the need for alternate ports. Lakehurst was the only port the *Shenandoah* had. There was nothing to do but lie off at sea and await the passing of the storm.
>
> From our safe aerial ringside seat off the coast, we watched this marvelous display extending north and south as far as the eye could see. Thunderbolts and vivid flashes, almost blinding at even our distance, revealed and outlined the towering, turbulent, tumbling thunderheads at the tops of massive clouds that formed almost a solid battle line—a lightning curtain between us and our one port. It was entrancing, gorgeous and extravagantly beautiful, despite its extreme violence. With its apparent subsiding and passing about daybreak, Captain Lansdowne decided to break through and head in to Lakehurst.[36]

The *Shenandoah* penetrated the disintegrating line without difficulty to arrive at the NAS safely.

— -- —

The LTA program had been making good progress with its airship operations. As of August 22, the *Shenandoah* had made 56 flights for a total of 25,835 miles. "A 57th flight awaited us, one of a somewhat different character."[37] The storms encountered on July 16 were harbingers of deadlier things to come as the *Shenandoah* went on a journey to the Midwest, where unpredictable storms of great intensity were commonplace.

THE *SHENANDOAH* DISASTER

The unavailability of the *Los Angeles* did not stem the number of requests for a flyover by an airship. Chambers of Commerce and state fairs were frequent sources of requests, and Moffett—and the men of the LTA service—wanted to satisfy as many as possible.

Days after the *Los Angeles*'s return from her aborted trip to Minneapolis, the Chief of Naval Operations (CNO) directed the *Shenandoah* to make the flight and as soon after July 4 as practicable. The plans were similar to those made previously for the *Los Angeles*, including sending Wiley and two enlisted men ahead to prepare a landing party for refueling at Fort Snelling, near Minneapolis.[1]

Lansdowne recommended postponing the flight until September after the Midwestern thunderstorm period and that he be granted freedom to select the exact date.[2] Consequently, the flight was postponed until late August or early September.[3] Included with the *Shenandoah*'s new orders was the requirement to test the mast constructed by Edsel Ford at Dearborn, said to be the largest in the world.[4]

With an eye on weather and other practical considerations, the plans for the Midwest flight continued to evolve, and, in early August, Lansdowne recommended two flights. The first, to take place in the last week of August, was to test Ford's new mast. The second flight would begin in early September with the purpose of making demonstrations over as many cities as possible. The CNO, however, directed that there be a single flight to begin on September 2. Aware of the volatility of the Midwest weather, orders of August 12 included a prudent directive: "Should the dictates of safety and the weather condition existing make it advisable, the commanding officer of the Shenandoah is authorized to make such modifications in the [itinerary] as he deems necessary, re-membering, however, that this route will be published in the press and that many will be disappointed should the Shenandoah fail to follow the approved schedule."[5] "Both the Atlantic and the Pacific seaboards had seen the Shenandoah, and now the Mid-west would have its turn."[6]

The first leg of the outbound flight from Lakehurst would be to Scott Field, Illinois, near St. Louis, where the ship would land to refuel and service at the Army's airship base there. The ship would then follow a circuitous course to Minneapolis and the Ford airport near Detroit. The course was laid out by Rosendahl as navigator and Hancock as executive officer.

With plans set, the *Shenandoah* departed the NAS at 1452 (EST) on September 2, 1925, equipped for a five- or six-day cruise. Rosendahl recalled the "local weather was excellent and hour convenient, so there was an unusually large gathering of friends and relatives at the foot of the mast as the 'Daughter of the Stars' slipped her moorings and quietly headed westward."[7]

Departing Lakehurst, Rosendahl was busy with his own tasks and did not pay attention to the weather map, but, just before the flight, Lansdowne had told him they would have good flying weather. The forty-three men on board settled into their watch routines of four hours on and four hours off.

Rosendahl and Hancock had laid out a course that would offer many thousands of people the opportunity to observe the great airship, keeping the vision alive in their minds and in the pages of their newspapers. The secretary of the Iowa State Fair Board received a telegram from Secretary Denby, informing him that Lansdowne was under orders to reach Des Moines no later than 1600 on Friday, September 4. The ship would be delayed only by an accident or unduly cold weather.[8] Minnesotans expected the ship to be over their fairgrounds by 0815 on the fifth.[9]

Unfortunately, the *Shenandoah* never made it to Iowa or Minnesota. The great ship crashed in the early hours of September 3. Wiley and the enlisted men had left the NAS en route to Detroit the same day the ship left. When they arrived at Detroit on the third, they learned of the crash. No longer needed at Detroit, Wiley arranged a military flight from

Dearborn Field to Cumberland, Ohio, and from there, an automobile to the crash site at Caldwell, Ohio.

On the ground, concern for the ship developed in the early morning. She had been reported over Wheeling, West Virginia, at 0145, but a sense of alarm developed when she was not heard from after that despite desperate efforts to establish radio contact. The last word from the ship was a cryptic message picked up by Master Sergeant L. J. O'brien, the chief radio operator at Fort Hayes, Columbus, which stated, "I am losing my seat."[10]

Shortly after that final message from the ship, word arrived at Caldwell, Ohio, that a portion of the ship—about 450 feet long—had crashed in a field about a mile and a half from Ava, Ohio. The control car with commander Lansdowne and the navigating crew landed about fifty feet away. A third section of the ship—the 150-foot-long section containing Rosendahl—drifted through the air as a "free balloon" for about twelve miles before landing near Sharon, about ten to twelve miles from Ava.

News of the crash spread quickly to newspaper offices in Columbus, then throughout the country. Because Moffett had always been open and cooperative with the press, Rosendahl gave the survivors permission to relate their personal experiences to reporters. While Rosendahl and Hall gave good accounts of events, the survivors had had no time to digest what had happened. It was understood that a court of inquiry would be convened to investigate the cause(s) of the crash.

The *Shenandoah* was about two years old when she crashed. During her 13,871 hours of existence, she had logged 37 flights for a total of 740 hours of flying time, covering 25,835 miles.

Navy regulations required the vessel's commanding officer to report the circumstances of a wreck to the secretary of the Navy as soon as possible. Lansdowne and Hancock died in the crash, leaving Rosendahl as the senior surviving officer and, consequently, the officer who prepared the report to the secretary. His letter, dated September 21, 1925, gave a narrative of events from the time the ship left NAS Lakehurst.[11]

She cast off from the mast on Wednesday, September 2, making for Philadelphia at an airspeed of 38 knots and an altitude of 2,000 feet at the beginning of the Midwest flight with 43 persons on board. A ground speed of 30 miles per hour was maintained to comply with the ship's schedule.

From Wheeling, West Virginia, the course was set for Zanesville, Ohio. At 0310 (CST), the ship's position was over Byesville, Ohio, but, from that time until the disaster occurred, she made practically no headway. Several course changes were made, but these resulted in changing only the drift and leeway. At 0345, Cambridge and Byesville were in sight, but no effort was made to locate the ship's position precisely because all hands were devoted to saving the ship in the midst of the storm that engulfed them, and it would have been easy to locate their position once they escaped the weather.

Passage over the mountains was smooth and uneventful. The ship's pressure height was approximately 3,800 feet, and by flying at 3,500 feet, there was sufficient altitude to handle the ship easily. Arriving at Connellsville, the altitude was dropped in increments to 2,500 feet.

At midnight, Rosendahl was relieved of the navigator's watch by Lieutenant Commander Hancock, and he turned in to his bunk in the keel. At about 0330, Rosendahl was called to relieve Hancock. He was told the ship had been taken off her course to avoid a thunderstorm and that the ground speed had been reduced significantly during the previous watch. Their course was then 180 degrees—a change made to avoid the storm—altitude 1,500 feet, and airspeed 38 knots. The ship was then over Byesville with a ground speed of practically zero.

A severe electrical display was seen northward and eastward but at a considerable distance. This was the storm the *Shenandoah* had avoided on the midwatch. The captain changed course to the west to resume a more general direction to their objective—Zanesville.

At 0345, the course was changed to 223 degrees True. The electrical display extended from slightly forward of the starboard beam aft to a little on the starboard quarter, and heavy dark clouds from there to a few points on the port quarter. Because they were making practically no ground speed at 2,500 feet, the captain changed the altitude to 2,100 feet, according to the elevatorman's altimeter. At 0350, the drift was about 20 degrees to the right and, at 0405, it was about 45 degrees to the right with the ship still making practically no headway. Three minutes later, the drift was estimated to be 55 degrees to the right, with Cambridge slightly behind the starboard beam and distant about 8 miles.

When Rosendahl came on for this last watch, he found in the control car: Captain Lansdowne; Lieutenant Commander Hancock, who had remained in the car after being relieved; Lieutenant Houghton, the officer of the deck; Lieutenant Anderson, the aerological officer; Colonel Hall, U.S. Army Air Service; R. T. Joffrey, Aviation Rigger First Class; rudderman E. P. Allen, Aviation Chief Rigger; elevatorman George C. Schnitzer; and radio generator mechanic James A. Moore, Jr.

Lansdowne had been watching the storm they had just avoided. As Rosendahl took drift observations out the control car window, he noticed a streaky cloud forming on the starboard bow. Shortly thereafter, the captain went to the starboard side, saying that the new cloud was either coming toward the ship or building up very rapidly. At about this time, the elevatorman called out that the ship was rising. He was told to check the rise by applying sufficient down elevator, but he kept reporting that the ship was rising, and he could not check her. The engine speed was increased and the ship's inclination, down by the nose, was increased in an attempt to drive her down against the vertical lift which was causing the ship to rise rapidly. The angle exceeded what could be registered on the elevatorman's inclinometer, but Rosendahl read the angle on the inclinometer on the chart board as 18 degrees. To avoid the ship's stalling out, Lansdowne ordered that this angle not be exceeded.

The ship continued to rise, at times by over 2 meters per second, as she approached pressure height. Several course changes were made in an attempt to drive the ship southward, but the rudderman had difficulty making the changes. Lansdowne considered it essential to assist the automatic valves by use of the hand-operated maneuvering valves. Houghton valved by hand while Rosendahl timed the valving with a stopwatch so they could calculate the amount of buoyancy lost by the valving.

Lansdowne ordered the manual valving to cease after five minutes. Because the ship was expected to have excessive momentum as it descended, following its rapid rise, the captain ordered ballast to be dumped. The ship made a rapid descent for about two minutes. Word was sent to the keel by both Houghton and Anderson to stand by to slip fuel tanks as a final salvation to check the ship's descent by ballasting. When the ship leveled off, this state lasted but a short time before it began to rise rapidly again—at a rate faster than the first rapid ascent.

Up in the keel passageway, the men knew instinctively that their ship was in trouble. In darkness, they got dressed and assisted those on watch. The clanging of telegraphs signaled the need for more speed. At the altitudes they were sailing, "anti-knock dope" had to be added to the fuel to achieve the high engine power needed. The great inclination of the ship demanded high output of power from the engines, and during the rapid ascent, the No. 2 Engine stopped due to overheating, followed minutes later by failure of the No. 1 Engine. The *Shenandoah* could ill afford to lose that much power in their battle with the storm. The situation was dire and "beyond the intelligent and resourceful ability of the Chief Engineer, Lieutenant Edgar W. Sheppard and his experienced assistants."[12]

Men patrolling the keel were attentive to the control wires to the rudders, elevators, valves, and telegraphs to be certain they did not jam. Constant attention was given to the helium cells to ensure the valves were operating properly. "With open jackknife in one hand, they felt the bulging gas cells with the other, ready to slash the fabric and release the pressure should it exceed what their trained touch told them was safe."[13]

Needing to reply to a radio request, Chief Radioman Schnitzer calmly entered the control space, wearing his headphones momentarily unplugged, to ask for the ship's latest position. Rosendahl told him their position had not changed much since the last report, but there was too much activity at that moment to allow him to ascertain their position with precision. "With a calm 'Aye, Aye, sir,' he stepped back into the radio compartment and closed the door – for the last time."[14]

The five-minute release of helium had allowed the ship's ascent to stop at about 6,200 feet. Their situation was now reversed—the ship was now "heavy"—and they faced the problem of checking the inevitable descent that could result in a crash. Lansdowne sent Rosendahl into the keel to determine that the men were actually ready to slip fuel tanks.

Getting into the keel required climbing an enclosed wooden ladder that resembled the conning tower of a small submarine. As Rosendahl stepped onto the ladder, the storm tossed the nose of the ship upward suddenly, at an angle greater than anything Rosendahl had experienced in an airship.

As he climbed, he heard the snapping of wooden struts, and it seemed to him that the control car lagged behind the rapidly rising bow. Working his way in darkness into the keel, he headed amidships where most of the fuel slip tanks were. After only a few feet, he heard the terrific sound of crashing metal amidst other indescribable noise. The fabric outer cover along the bottom of the keel had pulled away, and a number of metal cross members at the bottom of the keel were cut loose on one side, all the result of the control car carrying away from the ship. Within a few moments, he heard a loud "thud"—the detached control car striking the ground.

The *Shenandoah* had been lightened by the loss of the control car and engines, but the gas cells were intact, causing the 200-foot-long section of bow to shoot rapidly to approximately 10,000 feet. Men found it difficult to hang on as the section of ship spun rapidly in a horizontal plane. Rosendahl initially thought he was alone, but, as he shouted toward both ends of the ship, he got replies from both. Aft of him were Chief Machinist Halliburton and Machinist Mate Shevlowitz. Halliburton was located at about Frame 135. The ship had broken in two slightly behind there—about Frame 130. Forward of Rosendahl were Lieutenant Mayer, Colonel Hall, and Aviation Chief Rigger McCarthy. Fortunately, their weights were evenly distributed, helping keep them on an even keel. Mayer had access to a valve control wire and could valve from a forward cell. At the other end of the ship were two nests of fuel tanks. Lacking pliers to slip them, they drained their contents from their bottom connections. From this point, it was merely a matter of free ballooning as Rosendahl and Mayer communicated regarding valving and ballasting.

Hall and Anderson had left the control car just after Rosendahl and Anderson reached the keel when the control car carried away, tearing out the runway support from one side, and he suddenly found himself sitting astride a segment of the catwalk, desperately holding on with both hands to wires and assorted structures with nothing but sky beneath him. Mayer lowered a line to Anderson and hauled him to relative safety.

Once things settled down and the men realized what they had with their remnant of airship, they operated it as a free balloon until an opportunity to land presented itself. Through coordinated valving of helium and dropping of gasoline ballast, they were able to make a controlled descent. Their first attempt to land was aborted because the wind was driving them at a ground speed of about 25 miles per hour—too fast for a safe landing. As they decided to remain in the air, their balloon struck a clump of trees on a hillside. One particularly tall tree ripped a gash through the outer cover that ran practically the entire length of their craft. During the incident, McCarthy was knocked out of the balloon. He suffered serious injuries from his fall but recovered subsequently and returned to airship duty.

With the wind near the surface moderating, they prepared for a safe landing against a hillside between a farmhouse and a barn. Landing ropes and mooring lines were deployed, as for a normal landing, and the helium cells were slashed as high up their sides as could be reached, allowing the men to bring their balloon safely to ground. The ship's lines caught in trees and fences which helped bring them down gently. They landed about twelve miles from where the airship had broken up.

The rigid, oddly shaped balloon was nestled on the side of a low hill with the jagged open end about twenty feet off the ground. Rather than risk a jump, Rosendahl had a line thrown up to the men, who then climbed down safely. With the sun rising, the helium remaining in the free balloon began to heat and gain buoyancy, and with a rising wind, it appeared the craft might take flight again. Rosendahl borrowed pistols and shotguns from members of the gathering crowd and shot holes through the ship near the top to release the helium.

The Navy Department was informed that the ship had encountered a line squall—a type of storm greatly feared by airmen—shortly after 0500 near Caldwell, Ohio, while at an altitude of 3,000 feet and that she was struck by lightning at 0530, but no explosions were reported. The idea of a lightning strike developed from eyewitnesses on the ground.

Most of the fourteen dead—including Commander Lansdowne—were in the broken wreckage of the control car.[15] As news of the disaster spread throughout Ohio, roads leading to the crash site "became black with automobiles carrying doctors, undertakers, officials and the morbidly curious to the points where the various portions of the ship fell."[16] Souvenir hunters immediately made off with bits of the ship's envelope, bits of wood, and instruments from inside the ship. Fortunately for future investigation, the ship's barograph was recovered. This instrument, operated by clockwork, recorded the airship's path in altitude. Other pieces of equipment that might have offered silent testimony to the cause of the crash were removed and carried off in quick order.

As the senior officer present, Rosendahl took charge of assembling the dead at Belle Valley. He set up headquarters at the railroad station at Caldwell, Ohio, and within an hour of his landing, he started to receive lists of the casualties. He arranged for the bodies to be returned to Lakehurst, where family members were gathering to receive information updates from Ohio. As the list of dead was received at the NAS, officers and enlisted men broke down and wept.

One of the first things Rosendahl did following the successful landing of his free balloon was arrange for photographs of the airship wreckage. Despite promises made, none of the photographs ever reached him. Rising winds beat the wreckage into tangled masses, but souvenir hunters did even more damage to the remains. In the years that followed, practically every photograph Rosendahl saw of the wreckage had been taken after the wind and souvenir hunters had picked over the scene.

Hall stated confidently that the crash of the *Shenandoah* was in no way attributable to any structural defect in the ship. He claimed that meteorological warnings of the storm could have saved the ship but, due to a lack of meteorological stations in the area, such information was not available to them.

—·—

Despite the early hour of the disaster, there were witnesses on the ground. The farming families of S. O. Davis and Frank Nelson, living near Ava, Ohio, watched the ship struggle for survival against the storm. They heard the sounds of the ship's propellers shortly after 0500 as dawn was breaking. Initially, nothing seemed wrong, but the ship suddenly became motionless in the sky, poised in place for about fifteen minutes. The ship then shot upward rapidly while being buffeted about from one direction to another. In its last moments, the ship darted upward for an estimated 200 feet before settling slowly. Her nose pointed perpendicularly upward just before she broke apart. The nose of the ship drifted away into the darkness, leaving twenty-eight men in the section behind it. Witnesses saw men clinging to the outer structures of the framework. Only one man in this portion of the ship died—Lieutenant E. W. Sheppard.

The dead were scattered widely over a number of farms. In the immediate aftermath, it was known that the following men had been killed in the control cabin: Lieutenant Commander Zachary Lansdowne, Lieutenant Commander Louis Hancock, Jr., Lieutenant J. B. Lawrence, Lieutenant A. R. Houghton, Chief Petty Officer George C. Schnitzer, Machinists Mate James A. Moore, and Chief Rigger Everett P. Allen.[17]

Rosendahl sent a telegraphic report to the Navy Department:

> Mild storm suddenly followed by violent line squall subjected ship to enormous uncontrollable angle strains and rapid vertical assent, resulting in ship's structure breaking in about 7,000 feet at vicinity of frames 130 and 90. Control car very quickly wrenched free in air, undoubtedly precipitating occupants. Forward wing cars wrenched from ship's structure in air.
>
> Forward section ship free ballooned approximately one hour with seven occupants, McCarthy being knocked out of ship by tree in landing. Midship section crashed with three occupants, only Gunner Cole being injured in landing. Injuries not serious. After section crashed but landed 17 occupants safely.
>
> Forward section of ship landed at Sharon, about 10 miles east of other sections, which landed at Ava. Probably eight casualties from keel and three from forward wing cars.
>
> Sections of ship were deflated by hand completely and anchored as well as possible. Deputy sheriffs and American Legion guarding property until arrival of troops from Columbus. Accurate identification of dead completed.[18]

On the afternoon of the crash, Lieutenant Hendley left with the survivors to return to Lakehurst, and Wiley arrived from Detroit to remain on site as long as needed. Rosendahl's telegraphic report to the Navy Department ended by stating that the personal effects of all hands had been salvaged from the ship and that no fires occurred during or after the disaster. He offered his opinion that the value of salvageable material was negligible.

It was reported initially that the ship's logbook was missing—presumably taken by looters. As investigators combed the grounds adjacent to the wreckage, they found a personal logbook belonging to Radioman G. W. Armor. This unofficial record provided a useful glimpse into events as they unfolded.

According to Armor, the first hint of the storm came at 2130 as the *Shenandoah* was passing over Chambersburg, Pennsylvania: "See lightning to the south of us; but the sky is clear, and we can see the earth below without trouble."[19] Lightning was seen again as the ship left Wheeling, West Virginia, at 0215.

"Follow valley to the westward through Ohio and see lightning flashes directly ahead. Take higher elevation and find that visibility is bad." Fifteen minutes later: "Strike strong head winds and see storms both northwest and southwest in the distance. Believe we can ride them without trouble and bear straight westward."

An hour later, things got more intense as Armor recorded, "Storm increasing. . . . Ship pitches heavily. Passes over Lore City, Ohio, and steer toward Cambridge northwest to avoid storm direct ahead."

At 0350: "See Cambridge in the distance and make little headway as strong head winds. Storm worst we have encountered to date." At 0420: "Pass over Byesville. Been battling storm over half an hour and decided to steer south to get out of direct wind. Trouble with radio; will not pick up messages; effort to repair is unsuccessful."

At 0455:

> Members of crew called from gondola pit and sent into runway to aid in keeping ship on even keel. Commander orders car in changing course. All engines working perfectly; unable to get in headway of winds.

Lightning increases in intensity. Hope to ride out storm soon. Unable to get radio to function.

Pleasant City seen in distance, observation station off course 30 miles south.

Order to throw off gasoline tanks given and complied with, but does not aid stability. Radio no better; wind increasing in volume; get chance to—

The sentence was never completed.

Commander Klein convened a preliminary Board of Inquiry in Caldwell, Ohio, on September 4, during which four witnesses reported seeing the *Shenandoah* "buckle and hump" in the middle before separating into two pieces, while a fifth witness reported the ship sagging in the center before separating. Slowly, items looted from the crash site were returned, including the ship's logbook.[20]

Inevitably, rumors circulated predicting the end of the LTA program, but Rosendahl was quick to quell them, claiming, "human hands could not have designed a craft to weather the storm the Shenandoah encountered last night before its fall."[21] He also asserted that human hands could not have guided the ship to safety and that daylight would have made no difference.

Immediately, Rosendahl began collecting anything that could be useful as forensic evidence in the forthcoming Board of Inquiry. The most important item was the barograph, which provided data concerning the airship's final moments.

Referring to the state of manned flight, Secretary Wilber expressed the conviction that the Atlantic and Pacific Oceans were still the best bulwarks of the U.S. and that the time had not come when aircraft could cross vast stretches of ocean with impunity or operate effectively at will under all conditions.

Almost immediately after the crash, the Navy was assailed by people who had not been on board the *Shenandoah* and had no firsthand knowledge of events. Three individuals were of a sufficiently high profile that the Navy could not ignore their claims.

Mrs. Margaret Ross Lansdowne, widow of Zachary Lansdowne, made a statement that became the focus of much attention. She claimed that Navy authorities in Washington were responsible for her bereavement, insisting that her husband had undertaken the trip to the Midwest "under protest."[22] She claimed that he knew the weather situation in the Ohio Valley during this season and he had asked Washington officials to postpone the flight. She claimed that he was strenuously opposed to making the flight at this time. She made a number of other outrageous claims that were debunked subsequently during the court of inquiry hearing, and she eventually retracted her claims.

Another assault came from Heinen, who had been at Lakehurst when the crash occurred. He made the accusation that "eight safety valves were removed from the Shenandoah recently to economize on the rare gas at the expense of safety."[23] "The removal of eight of eighteen safety valves in the gas cells of the ship was the direct cause of the disaster," and "It was to save this precious helium that the men gave their lives foolishly."[24] "Had the ship been filled with hydrogen," he continued, "the disaster might not have happened. The hydrogen would have valved more freely and they wouldn't have been so cautious about saving it, because it is not as scarce as helium or as expensive."[25]

As if he had not said enough, he added, "Now there will be a white-wash board and some camouflage to cover up the real story of the cause which was the foolish action of the crew at the station in changing the valves. Already there have been things said to lay the blame on poor dead Lansdowne."[26] Eventually, Heinen's claims would be debunked, as well as Mrs. Lansdowne's.

The wreckage of the *Shenandoah* was strewn over two counties, landing in cornfields and wooded areas. "Thousands of souvenir hunters swooped down on the tangled rigging with saws and hatchets, ripping and tearing, pilfering and wrecking . . . Stationary cabin furniture had been chopped off and taken away. The silver fabric of the giant bag was cut and carried away in sections, lengths of the superstructure were sawed and hacked away and tied to dusty automobiles."[27] Governor Vic Donahey sent three companies of state militia to the crash site, but when they arrived, they found nothing to guard except the huge motors.

As expected, the secretary of the Navy called for a court of inquiry into the cause of the *Shenandoah* disaster to be convened on September 21, 1925. Rosendahl's letter to the secretary served as the backbone for the proceedings. In a ship as large as the *Shenandoah*, even those in the control car could not have firsthand knowledge of everything unfolding in every part of the vessel. Consequently, all the officers and surviving crewmen were questioned to put the finest details into the timeline of events. Other witnesses included experts in aerology, stresses of materials, and lighter-than-air flight.

Even before the court convened, Moffett declared publicly that the disaster would not affect policy with regard to the development of naval aviation.[28] On September 9, 1925, sensing a need to convince the public quickly that its LTA program was alive and moving forward, the Navy announced its plans for a new airship that would be twice the capacity of the *Shenandoah*. The plans for this ship had been prepared just prior to the crash of the *Shenandoah*, and they represented a number of improvements.

While the *Shenandoah* had eliminated the hazards associated with hydrogen by using helium, there were ongoing experiments to determine how much hydrogen could be used to dilute the helium without making it combustible. Further, while the dangers of fire associated with hydrogen had been eliminated, there remained the danger of fire in the fuel tanks that were strung along the keel. The new plans called for the use of lightweight diesel engines that burned heavy fuel oil under pressure instead of gasoline. Finally, the new ship would have twice the gas capacity of the *Shenandoah*—5 million cubic feet—which, its designers claimed, would make it more economical.[29]

In advance of the court of inquiry hearings, the Navy explained to the public how the mysterious barograph device, which had been mentioned in newspapers, would assist the investigations. Heinen had claimed that the *Shenandoah* did not have enough safety valves, which made it impossible for the ship to allow enough gas to escape rapidly enough when it began to expand at 7,000 feet. This, he claimed, caused the gas cells to swell dangerously.

The Navy suggested that the barograph recordings would resolve this issue. It showed the difference in pressure between the inside and outside of the gas cells. If it was found that the inside pressure went above anything ever experienced by the ship, it would prove Heinen's theory to be correct. If, however, the inside pressure was below what the ship had withstood previously, Heinen's theory would fail.[30]

As the court opened, Rosendahl was given the opportunity to retire from the proceedings if he wished, but he chose to remain to hear all the testimonies. While differing observations and personal accounts of survival would originate from men in different parts of the ship, it was expected that a summary of all accounts would contribute to understanding the cause(s) of the crash. Only two survivors were unavailable for testimony: Lieutenant Anderson, who was on duty in Ohio, making weather observations in connection with the crash, and John F. McCarthy, who was confined still to hospital in Marietta, Ohio. The narratives of the surviving officers and men were complete on the second day of the inquiry, but while they assisted with constructing a timeline of events, they provided little, if any, scientific or technical information to indicate why the ship had broken apart in the storm.

Board members traveled to the sites of the crash on September 4—Ava, then Caldwell, Ohio—but were disappointed to find that tourists had gone over the wreck the previous day. Thus, any evidence they had expected to find had been destroyed or removed by vandals.

On the evening of September 4, the board sent a wire to the Navy Department informing it that a section of the bow of the ship to Frame 130 was near Sharon on a hillside a considerable distance from the railroad station. Its structure, wiring, and outer cover were practically a total wreck, and all the gas cells from that section were missing. A section of the stern to Frame 102 was located on a hillside about two miles east of Ava. The structure was broken severely, and the cover and gas cells were torn badly. The No. 2 Car was under the wreckage and the No. 3 Car was at the edge of it. Both cars were attached still to the ship's structure. The No. 1 Car, resting on its side, had been located up the hill about 100 feet from the forward end of the stern section. The section containing Frames 10 to 130 was located about a mile from the stern, and it was damaged very badly. The numbers 4 and 5 cars were under the wreckage. The control car fell about 50 feet from Section 102 to 130 and it was a complete wreck. The floor and underplating were the only remaining parts.[31]

The board recommended to the Bureau of Aeronautics that the ship's structure was so damaged that it was of no value except as junk. It was recommended that the *Shenandoah* be stricken from the Navy's list of vessels and the remains be opened to salvage bidders.

Commander Sydney M. Kraus, assembly and repair officer of the *Los Angeles* and member of the investigating board, had made a detailed examination of the remains about twenty-four hours after the accident and concluded that it was probable that there had been a major failure on one or more of the girders in the vicinity of Frame 130, either simultaneous to or shortly after some very strong rotational oscillation of the ship. Such oscillation would have led to failure of certain struts on the control car and its suspensions.

It was Kraus's opinion that the destruction the *Shenandoah* started when she broke into two pieces and the breaking into a third piece did not contribute to the destruction of the ship but was merely a consequence of the initial breaking. The region around Frame 130 had shown a complete severance of the ship due to the breakage of girders and the tearing out and breaking of wires, but it was not a sharp break at any one frame. Kraus could not formulate an opinion as to what girder had failed first.[32]

Kraus also testified that he had examined valves that had remained with their gas cells, and they all appeared to have been functioning normally, although he could not reach the maneuvering valves for examination. He encountered no cells that had burst as a result of internal pressure. Gas valves that were recovered from the wreck functioned normally, but Aviation Chief Rigger James H. Collier testified that while they functioned normally, it was his opinion that there was an inadequate number of valves.

The court held sessions for thirty-one days, during which it examined sixty-five witnesses, including all the survivors of the crash except for the one who remained hospitalized. In the end, it was revealed that the changes to the valves had been recommended by Lansdowne and, ultimately, were approved by the Bureau of Aeronautics as an experimental installation. Following the valve changes, the ship had flown about 186 hours, covering 6,750 statute miles, not including her final flight, without problems.

The court concluded that a more extensive meteorological service—which would require more weather stations and more frequent broadcasting of reports—would have contributed greatly to safe navigation. Once they were in the storm, Lansdowne and the crew employed every maneuver known to bring an airship under control but without success.

The court's final conclusion was, "The disaster is part of the price which must inevitably be paid in the development of any new and hazardous art."[33] The court recommended that no further proceedings be had in the matter of the *Shenandoah* disaster.

After years of reflection, Rosendahl revisited the *Shenandoah* disaster in his memoir:

> In simple language, the Court's opinion as to the final destruction of the Shenandoah was that it was primarily due to high external forces arising from high-velocity air currents which the structural strength of the ship was unable to match. Whether prior damage from internal helium pressure was a determining factor the Court could not definitively determine. There had been high helium pressure near the point where the ship's structure opened up and separated during the storm. Crushing of the structure there might explain why the hull had failed at that point. Many times since the accident I have pondered the probable causes of the loss of the Shenandoah, and the easiest explanation would be interior damage from excessive helium pressure, I must admit. But in light of the testimony and evidence to the contrary, I cannot conclude that such dangerous over-pressure did exist.

It is an inescapable fact, however, that the basic design was obsolete before the ship was ever built, and that her propulsion system
was woefully deficient in power and reliability, even though both
represented the best we then knew or could achieve.[34]

Perhaps the most important lessons from the court were delivered
by Professor Hovgaard in his lengthy and highly technical report that
included recommendations for future airship development:

> It is recommended to adopt a smaller finesse ratio: length to diam-
> eter than used in the Shenandoah.
> The ratio is 8.6 in the Shenandoah and 7.25 in the Los Angeles,
> but wind-tunnel tests have shown that forms of a much smaller ratio
> can be produced having much less resistance to propulsion. Even a
> ratio as low as 4½ can be adopted with advantage as far as resistance
> is concerned. . . . It has been found that the insertion of a cylindrical
> portion is unfavorable to resistance.
> Ships of relatively short length and great diameter are less sus-
> ceptible to the effects of gusts. . . . On the whole, short full ships are
> superior to long slender ships of the same volume, in their power to
> resist aerodynamic forces.[35]

Hovgaard recommended that future ships adopt the arrangement
of automatic and hand valves, which were originally installed in the
Shenandoah. He also recommended building ships of a moderately larger
size (e.g., 5 million cubic feet displacement for use in war and for long-
distance commercial travel). The rationale was that such ships could be
given greater speed and cruising radius.[36]

At the end of the court proceedings, Rosendahl proclaimed, "Although we are survivors of one of the worst air disasters that has ever
occurred, we nevertheless have not lost faith in rigid airships."[37]

ROSENDAHL AND THE *GRAF ZEPPELIN*

In 1926, with the *Shenandoah* disaster fresh in memory, the LTA program began to move forward again as Moffett made changes in the command structure. Captain G. W. Steele, Jr., who had been in command of the *Los Angeles* since January 19, 1925, was relieved, and at 0900 on March 15, 1926, Lieutenant Commander Rosendahl reported for duty as the executive officer of the *Los Angeles*.[1] Rosendahl's appointment carried with it the expectation that he would succeed Steele as commander of the ship.

Moffett faced a difficult problem—promoting from within the LTA service or bringing officers in from outside the program who had far less experience with airships. Bringing officers from outside the program would block the advancement of officers who were junior but had more LTA experience and had made a commitment to the airship program. Moffett believed that more senior appointees would "carry more water" (i.e., have more influence) for getting things done within the Navy. The *Shenandoah* crash had left in its wake a growing opposition to the LTA program among some members of Congress, and Moffett needed all the influence he could muster to keep his program alive.

Moffett held Herbert Wiley and Maurice Pierce in high regard but had passed them over for command of the *Los Angeles* in favor of Rosendahl, who assumed command of the ship on May 10, 1926, relieving Steele.[2] Wiley had been the *Los Angeles*'s navigator since April 1925, and he and Rosendahl had logged hundreds of hours of flight time together, making them a strong team. Their team was made stronger on June 8, 1926, when Lieutenant Thomas G. W. Settle reported for duty.[3] Settle was a solid officer of strong character with a positive attitude and the constitution of a pioneering aviator. Captain Edward S. Jackson, an officer with no experience in the LTA service, was given command of NAS Lakehurst.[4]

It had long been the case that advancement in the Navy was tied to time served with the surface fleet. Consequently, officers in the LTA service often requested transfers to fleet duties to keep themselves suited for advancement up the ranks. These requests were usually made with the understanding that the officers wanted to return to airships once a tour at sea was completed. During the lull in activity following the crash of the *Shenandoah*, Wiley requested a transfer to sea duty, specifically to battleship duty, but the loss of lives in the *Shenandoah* tragedy had left the LTA service short of experienced personnel, so Rosendahl disapproved Wiley's request.

Social divides and personality issues that had been fomenting for some time reached the surface by 1926. Klein, who had been a very capable destroyer captain during the First World War, came to be regarded around the NAS as an abrasive personality. He had served as the station's commanding officer until delivery of the ZR-3, when George Steele took command of both the NAS and the *Los Angeles*. Klein became resentful when he was not given command of the *Shenandoah* following McCrary's departure, and he found it unsatisfying to take an administrative job while Lansdowne, who was his junior by date of commission by two years, took command of the airship. Consequently, the relationship between Klein and Lansdowne became unrelentingly contentious.

While the decline in the relationship between Klein and Lansdowne had represented a personal rift between an air station officer and an airship officer, it reflected a wider rift occurring at a more general level. Developing over a number of years, the base had become split into two factions—the airship officers and the base officers. The airship crews considered themselves superior to the station-only, non-flying crews. The station crews were comprised of men not on flight status, thus not receiving the higher flight pay. The pay differential became a source of jealousy among the men and, particularly, their wives.[5]

A general malaise was developing among the personnel of the base and it affected the survivors of the *Shenandoah*. Some men requested transfer or were reassigned to other posts. Klein was reassigned to command of the minesweeper USS *Chewink* (AM-39), but in early 1926, he resigned from the Navy.

On May 10, 1926, the crew of *Los Angeles* was mustered for a simple change of command ceremony in which Captain Steele and Lieutenant Commander Rosendahl read their respective orders, and command of the airship passed officially to Rosendahl.[6] From the time Rosendahl assumed command until the end of 1926, the *Los Angeles* logged nearly 300 hours of flight time and accomplished seven moorings to the mast on the *Patoka*.[7]

Marked by routine flights, 1927 passed uneventfully until a near-disastrous event on August 25. The ground crew was called out at 0355 as the ship was ready for flight. With the crew embarked, the ship was walked out, and mooring operations began at 0517. Between 1200 and 1600, the *Los Angeles* was moored to the mast with the 2,200-pound-tail drag at Frame 25. Light and variable winds caused the ship to swing at irregular intervals and the rudder was used to keep the ship into the wind. Trim was maintained also by using the elevator and adjusting the ballast.[8]

At 1329, the ship's rudder was put hard to the left due to a sudden wind shift, and the stern lifted before the motion in azimuth about the mast could begin. The rudder operated to the left but jammed at 6° to the right. The ship's stern rose rapidly upward and slowly to port. To compensate, attempts were made to get men on board from the mast and to add water ballast. Seven men got on board quickly and hurried aft, but it was impossible to add much water ballast. Consequently, the stern continued to rise until the ship was at an angle of approximately 80°. Unsuccessful attempts were made to cast off from the mooring mast, but around 1335, the stern began to level off in the horizontal. The ship was kept in trim by adding water immediately from the mast.[9]

At 1400, the ground crew returned the ship to the hangar, where a full inspection revealed broken wires at a number of frames, two small holes in Cell No. 10 caused by a broken wire, and several ballast bags slightly out of alignment. The frames between Frame 40 and 47.5 on the starboard side were damaged.[10]

Twenty-five men, including officers Settle and Richardson, were on board when this episode took place. The enlisted men were mostly in the hull except for the "galloping kilos" that rushed into the ship from the mast head to counter the rising stern. There were no injuries. While the entire episode took five minutes or less, it seemed like hours to Settle and Richardson. Because of rapid ballasting and de-ballasting, it was a slow, steady rise and a slow, steady descent.[11]

The incident served to hasten the demise of the high mast and the advent of the stub mast, which allowed the stern of the ship to swing freely in the horizontal while acquiring no vertical motion.[12] Rosendahl was standing at the base of the mooring mast as this unusual event unfolded.

> The explanation of this weird incident is simple. As the normal summer sea breeze with its colder air pushed in from the southeast, it gradually pushed back the high gradient northwesterly wind. Immersed in this colder air, the ship gained a "false" buoyancy until the enclosed helium could cool off to the new low temperature. This started the stern upward, and then the sea breeze gently pushed the ship over until it was headed into it.[13]

A Navy photographer was in the vicinity, photographing parachute jumps, when he noticed the *Los Angeles*'s stern beginning to rise. Recognizing immediately that this was not normal, he took a series of photographs of the odd maneuver.

Rosendahl, as the commanding officer of the *Los Angeles*, labeled the photographs "Confidential" with instructions that they could not be released without his permission. He felt the images could be misleading unless accompanied by explanatory captions. Subsequently, Rosendahl gave copies of the images to an officer friend, and they found their way into the hands of "an enterprising writer" a few years later. Without Rosendahl's permission, they were published in a magazine.[14] Regardless, the photographs of the *Los Angeles* performing a "nose stand" from the high mast remain some of the most iconic images from the Navy's LTA program.

The *Los Angeles* was presented with an experimental challenge in January 1928, which involved a collaborative effort between the airship and the aircraft carrier USS *Saratoga* (CV-3). The aircraft carrier was, of course, a huge landing field for airplanes and some inside the LTA program were drawn to the possibility that the carrier might serve as a landing surface for airships, which would allow the transfer of cargo, personnel, and fuel without the need for land bases.

Permission was granted for the *Los Angeles* to attempt a landing on the *Saratoga* while she was at sea off Newport, Rhode Island. Extra handling lines were put on the *Los Angeles,* and Wiley was dispatched on January 20 to report to the commanding officer of the *Saratoga* to make preparations for a landing crew.[15] Wiley returned to NAS Lakehurst four days later, and on the morning of January 27, with no rehearsals between the *Los Angeles* and the *Saratoga*, the airship set out to attempt a landing on the aircraft carrier.

The conditions for this trial were far from ideal—there were strong gusting winds, and the carrier was pitching heavily in the ground swells—but Rosendahl did not have the luxury of waiting for better conditions. The *Saratoga* was headed for the Pacific and the attempted landing had to be made that day or not at all.

The *Los Angeles* was over Newport Harbor by 1200, maneuvering in the vicinity of the *Saratoga* that was still anchored in the harbor below. As the *Saratoga* got underway at 1220, the airship began to drop altitude and at 1415 went to landing stations. With no special equipment and but a single trial approach, the airship came astern of the carrier. The *Los Angeles* made her landing approach about 100 yards off the port beam of the carrier. Winds were then about 10 knots and very gusty, and the *Saratoga* was rolling and pitching moderately below the airship. The *Los Angeles* then valved off gas from all the maneuvering valves for a minute and a half and, at 1453, started its landing approach, dropping 225 feet and maneuvering at various speeds to overtake the carrier that was making 15 knots. This maneuver would have been far less complicated on a calm day with flat seas, but as it was, the gusting winds, combined with the pitching and rolling of the aircraft carrier, made for a situation that was more difficult, unpredictable, and dangerous.

The *Los Angeles* was over the carrier's deck at 1524 when a gust of wind carried her from 225 feet to 400 feet altitude. After valving off gas for another 45 seconds, she returned to 225 feet altitude, and two minutes later, she came astern of the carrier and dropped her ropes to the landing crew on the deck, who hauled her down. The maneuver was achieved while the carrier was responding to the sea and the airship was at the mercy of the fluctuations of the wind, their motions seldom synchronous, but Rosendahl felt the experiment was a success.

Even so, the landing crew had difficulty managing the huge airship. As the landing crew was using the lines to pull the airship down, a gust of wind drove the airship down and to starboard, a motion that was checked by the emergency release of 1,000 pounds of ballast. In spite of difficulties, the *Los Angeles* made its landing at 1535, with the landing crew having a difficult time securing the control car. Due to the sudden and unpredictable nature of the winds, Rosendahl deemed it best to cast off from the carrier entirely.

Rosendahl concluded that the experiment had proved the feasibility of landing an airship on the deck of a large surface ship.[16]

Wiley had left the *Los Angeles* earlier to assist the landing crew on the carrier's deck, and due to the sudden departure of the airship, he was left behind as the airship made its way back to Lakehurst.[17] Wiley's orders were changed retroactively by the Bureau of Navigation to reflect his need to remain behind to assist the carrier's personnel.[18]

It had not been an easy task to land a 638-foot-long airship on the deck of an 888-foot-long carrier on a rough sea, but Rosendahl saw promise in the results, and such efforts in the future would be made with much smaller blimps.

The *Los Angeles* left Lakehurst on February 26, 1928, en route to the Panama Canal. Uncharacteristically for Moffett, the news of her departure was kept secret until the ship was underway.[19] With Rosendahl in command, the *Los Angeles* embarked on the first attempted nonstop voyage to the canal zone. This 2,265-mile trip represented the longest nonstop journey for the airship since her delivery flight from Friedrichshafen, Germany, to the U.S. The flight from NAS Lakehurst to the Canal Zone was completed in 40 hours. She landed at France Field and moored to a stub mast.[20]

After successfully crossing the Panama Canal—the first for an airship—she moored to the *Patoka* before returning to Lakehurst, where she landed in a blinding snowstorm.

———

From the beginning of LTA flight, Germans and Americans had appreciated the potential of LTA craft for commercial, non-military purposes, carrying passengers, cargo, and mail between continents. The Germans, however, were far ahead of the Americans with regard to commercial development. Between 1926 and 1927, the Zeppelin company built another Zeppelin modeled after the LZ-126 and designated LZ-127. She was the largest airship in the world at the time, with a length of 776 feet and a volume of 3,700,000 cubic feet. The goal for LZ-127 was the establishment of a regular commercial transatlantic passenger service.

Of the many improvements this airship had over the *Los Angeles*, the most outstanding were the reversible engines and gas power instead of liquid gasoline. The reversible engines, introduced here for the first time in an airship, offered greater maneuvering and quicker and safer landing than previously.

Adapting her Maybach motors to gas power, known as *blau* gas, was a great advancement. To make a flight to Lakehurst, an airship would carry no less than 30 tons of gasoline. As the motors consume gasoline, the ship becomes lighter and it becomes necessary to valve off hydrogen gas to maintain buoyancy. The *blau* gas, however, had about the same weight as air. Thus, its consumption by the motors did not alter the weight of the airship and did not alter its buoyancy. With *blau* gas, the Zeppelin had a radius of about 7,000 miles without landing to refuel. At that time, no airplane existing had such a radius.

Once LZ-127 completed her test flights, Eckener planned to make a transatlantic flight from Friedrichshafen to Lakehurst. While he had flown the ZR-3 to Lakehurst on a one-way journey, the *Graf* would make the trip back to Germany. For the flight to Lakehurst, Dr. Eckener planned to carry 9 tons of gasoline for emergency purposes since the Maybach motors could be changed quickly from gas to gasoline.

As construction was nearing completion for the LZ-127, Rosendahl received orders on June 26, 1928, to take passage by ocean liner from New York, to Europe, to Friedrichshafen for the purpose of studying airships then under construction there. He was directed, further, to make inspection tours in Cardington and Howden, England, for the same purpose. He was authorized further to make his return trip to the U.S. on board the LZ-127.[21]

LZ-127 was christened *Graf Zeppelin* on July 9, 1928. Although she was the 117th Zeppelin built at Friedrichshafen, she was the first to be christened there. Addressing the future of airships, Eckener proclaimed, "The much-mooted question whether the airship or the airplane will be the commercial aircraft of the future for long distance, and especially for the speedy trans-ocean passenger and mail traffic, will be determined only by experience with the types. . . . I shall take the new zeppelin out in all conditions of weather in the hope of proving to the world the great reliability of this type of aircraft."[22]

Eckener selected Rosendahl, who had accompanied him on the transatlantic flight of the ZR-3, to accompany the first transatlantic flight of the *Graf Zeppelin*. For her first flight, Rosendahl presented the *Graf* with a "diminutive red devil" as a mascot to dangle from a window of the steering compartment.[23] The inaugural flight of the *Graf* was a great success, and the transatlantic flight was scheduled for October 9 with forty crewmembers and twenty passengers, including Rosendahl. The *Graf* would make history by carrying the first paying passengers ($3,000 per ticket) and the first woman—Lady Drummond Hay, an English society woman and writer. Karl H. von Wiegand, a German-born American journalist and frequent traveling companion of Lady Hay, had covered Zeppelin operations during the war and was a knowledgeable observer.

The transatlantic flight was delayed two days due to unfavorable weather, but the ship took the air on the eleventh. At 0635 (EST) on October 13, 1928, the Navy Department received a message from the *Graf* stating that the port horizontal was damaged and the crew was attempting to make repairs. The *Graf* was then 1,100 miles due east of Bermuda and 1,800 miles due east of Charleston, South Carolina. Her speed had been reduced to about 50 knots and she was in rough air. Consequently, the Navy Department ordered all light cruisers stationed at Hampton Roads, Virginia, and the squadron of destroyers stationed at Charleston, South Carolina, to make ready for immediate departure to assist the airship if needed. At 0900, Rosendahl sent a second message stating that the crew had made some repairs and it was not anticipated that the surface vessels would be needed. The ship was then 950 miles from Bermuda and on a heading directly for Lakehurst.[24]

Such damage had never occurred in the history of Zeppelins. The highly skilled crew set about making repairs with the ship in flight at approximately 1,500 feet above the ocean. Four men worked for five hours under highly dangerous conditions to make the repairs. The men ran the catwalk into the tail of the ship, then climbed the girders to the frame that met the fin at that point. Carrying knives and shears, they crawled, one by one, over the spars that comprised the frame of the fin to make repairs. To minimize dangerous motions, Eckener ordered the engines stopped. From their precarious position, they could cut away the hanging pieces of fabric. Eckener's twenty-one-year-old son, Knut, was one of the four men heroically effecting repairs 1,500 feet off the surface of the ocean. Following inspection of the fin, it was obvious that the torn fabric could not be replaced while in flight.

The *Graf* was in a squall with a vital part damaged, making it necessary to reduce speed while maintaining sufficient speed to maneuver the ship in the storm. For the remainder of the flight, Eckener kept the ship below full cruising speed, and while bucking headwinds, they had relatively smooth sailing.[25]

When part of the vital stabilizing fin was torn away, Knut was the first volunteer to crawl out onto the fin to make repairs. With him were Ludewig, one of the wireless operators; helmsman, Samt; and navigation officer Marx. Moments later, when the stern of the ship began to sag under the deluge of rain and wind, Captain Fleming, who was then in command of the bridge, turned to Eckener and told him that they needed to start two engines. The ship at that time was practically standing still with motors essentially idling. Fleming needed more power. This was the moment things became more tense for Dr. Eckener.

Eckener was aware that if he ordered the requested engines to be started, it was very likely that the wind would tear his son and the others off their perch, sending them to their deaths. There was no telephone communication from the bridge to the fin where the men were working—no way to warn them of a surge in power. Again, Fleming urged, "I must have two motors." It became a tense moment—Wiegand watched Eckener aging right before him. Eckener looked out the window, took a deep swallow, and gave the command, "Start the motors."[26]

"[W]hat Eckener lived through in the minutes before word was brought to him that his son, Knut, and the others were safe, only he and his God knew," Wiegand recounted. "I was on the bridge at all hours of the night and day, sometimes sitting with him there, always I found him on his post of duty. Always he took his meals there. Saturday night after the accident, he laid down once, but could not sleep."[27]

Around 2100 on October 14, a report reached the bridge that a part of the upper surface of the fin had carried away. Once again, Knut Eckener led a small crew to effect temporary repairs.

The *Graf Zeppelin* reached the coast of the U.S. shortly before 1000 on October 15, 1928, after a trip of about three days and ten hours, breaking all previous transatlantic records. The record for steamship crossing was held by the Cunard liner *Mauretania* at 4 days, 13 hours, and 41 minutes. In 1919, the British airship, R-34, had made the crossing in 100 hours, followed four years later by the *Los Angeles*'s crossing in 84 hours.[28]

Before landing at Lakehurst, the ship made a demonstration flight over New York City and over the White House. Rosendahl called ahead to the NAS to get materials ready to repair the *Graf*.

Because there were 12-mile-per-hour crosswinds and a large crowd when they landed, it was decided to moor to the stub mast for the night, where the ship could swing gently.[29] Rosendahl told the press that the *Graf Zeppelin* was a good ship, but he did not believe it was a size that would be used eventually for regular transatlantic service. Airships needed to be ever larger until the optimal size was achieved.[30]

The *Graf* had delivered fifteen sacks of mail from Germany, consisting of 28,124 letters and 37,590 postcards. Philatelists competed in bidding for the mail, while potential airship backers were eager to create a transoceanic mail service.

Eckener believed that America and Germany were destined to lead the world in aeronautics, and he paid compliments to Rosendahl: "I have a heart's duty to perform. On our trip to America Commander Rosendahl was one of our best and loyal friends. Now we have among us three splendid American officers who have grown very dear to us." In addition to Rosendahl, who had made the westward trip to America, Eckener included Commander Pierce, Lieutenant Commander Settle, and Lieutenant Bauch, who were about to make the trip eastward to Germany.

Repairs to the *Graf* were completed by October 23, and she was ready for flight and Eckener and Rosendahl were back at Lakehurst the following day to resume their respective commands. The *Graf Zeppelin* lifted off from Lakehurst at 0154 on October 30, 1928, en route to Friedrichshafen with Settle, Pierce, and Bauch on board as observers. Winds from the southwest had been strong most of the day and by late evening they were approaching hurricane-force with heavy rain squalls.[31] The direction of these winds gave a helping hand to the airship, increasing her speed over the Atlantic. The *Graf Zeppelin* landed safely in Friedrichshafen at 1255 (EST) on October 31.

Things were unfolding in 1929 that held great promise for the LTA world. In America, two new airships—ZRS-4 and ZRS-5—were being designed to carry, launch, and recover airplanes similar to aircraft carriers on the sea, although by a different mechanism. The *Los Angeles*, while still active, was already obsolete. She lacked some of the assets the new airships would have, but improvisation allowed her to continue making contributions.

From Germany came word that the *Graf Zeppelin* was planning a double roundtrip between Germany and New York and that the stops between the four ocean crossings would be just long enough for refueling. The trek, scheduled to begin on May 10, was, in effect, final training for a proposed flight around the world from Friedrichshafen with stops in Tokyo, Japan; San Diego, California; and Lakehurst, New Jersey. The

Graf would carry passengers at a cost of $2,000 per person.[32] The multiple crossings of the Atlantic were also a serious test of the feasibility of a regular transatlantic service carrying passengers, cargo, and mail.

Speaking to an organization of WWI veteran flyers in February, Rosendahl announced that the two large airships being built for the Navy would be able to carry five airplanes each and could be launched and recovered by the mother ship. With the airship cruising at 85 to 100 miles per hour, it would be possible to approach within a few miles of the limit of visibility of an enemy fleet, release the airplanes for reconnaissance, and transmit information to the surface fleet regarding an attacking force. Thus, the vulnerability of rigid aircraft from anti-aircraft gunfire would be minimized while knowledge concerning the strength and maneuverability of enemy surface vessels and airplanes could be obtained with minimum risk to the defending personnel and equipment.[33]

Increasing the size of an airplane beyond a certain point decreases its efficiency while increasing the size of an airship raises its efficiency in proportion. "That is why the Graf Zeppelin is half again larger than the Los Angeles . . . and why the new navy dirigibles will be as large as the Graf and the Los Angeles combined."[34] The Navy would soon begin testing its launch and recovery of airplanes with the airship in flight.

Things got busier for the LTA program in 1929 with the installation of additional mooring masts, perfection of the airplane hook-on device and procedure, a search for additional airship bases, and a visit to Lakehurst by the *Graf Zeppelin*, followed by the *Graf*'s around-the-world flight with Rosendahl on board. Rosendahl was relieved of his command of the *Los Angeles* and promoted to commander of the Rigid Airship Training and Experimental Squadron (ComRATES).[35] He assumed his new position on May 9, 1929, with Lieutenant Commander Herbert Wiley taking command of the *Los Angeles*.[36]

The *Graf Zeppelin* was expected to leave Friedrichshafen on May 16, making for Lakehurst, where final preparations would be made for the circumnavigation cruise. The itinerary called for the *Graf* to cross the Atlantic from Lakehurst to Friedrichshafen, then to Tokyo. She would then cross the Pacific Ocean and moor to a mast in California before traversing the U.S. back to Lakehurst. Rosendahl and Zeppelin company representatives agreed that the major significance of the around-the-world cruise—if successful—would be the crossing of the Pacific Ocean, "which will require the keenest aeronautical knowledge and seamanship and will subject the ship to the most rigid tests."[37]

In addition to Dr. Eckener, who would be in command, the *Graf* would carry Captain Ernst Lehmann and a crew of thirty-nine officers and men.[38] Rosendahl was invited as the guest of William Randolph Hearst and his newspapers, who were sponsoring the flight.[39]

The *Graf*'s journey from Lakehurst to Friedrichshafen was a flight of 4,000 miles; from Friedrichshafen to Tokyo was another 6,000 miles; and the flight over the Pacific was 5,900 miles. The last leg, from Los Angeles to Lakehurst, was 2,200 miles.[40]

While awaiting final plans for the *Graf*'s flight to America, Rosendahl, as ComRATES, was named to a board under Moffett to identify a new airship base on the Pacific Coast.[41] San Diego and San Francisco were leading contenders, but early on, the board had not inspected any of the candidate sites.[42] Rosendahl's participation on the board kept him on the West Coast as the *Graf Zeppelin*'s departure date approached.

Following administrative and weather delays, the *Graf* lifted off from Friedrichshafen at 0557 local time on May 16, 1929, on a flight expected to take 65 to 75 hours to reach Lakehurst—an estimated 5,000 to 7,000 miles, depending on the route Eckener chose.[43] The *Graf* had smooth sailing until she neared Gibraltar, where her engines began to fail. With two broken motors, the only safe course was to return to Friedrichshafen to make repairs.

Just thirty-six hours into her flight, in the midst of a gathering dusk, the *Graf Zeppelin* was fighting for her life. Three of her engines were crippled, and the two remaining engines were incapable of battling the strong winds. The ship was being swept eastward from the Rhone Valley toward the foothills of the French Alps. Eckener sent a wireless message that the Zeppelin had "suffered grave damage and was in serious danger."[44] French aviation authorities advised Eckener to make for Cuers Airfield near Toulon, and with some difficulty, he was able to land there at 2055 on the seventeenth with four failed engines—two with broken crankshafts.

Eckener arranged for four new engines to be sent from Friedrichshafen as replacements for the broken ones, and by May 23, the ship was ready to fly back to Friedrichshafen for a full evaluation of the mechanical problem. It was revealed that the problem was not with the motors but with the coupling bolts which were replaced with a new system.[45]

Eckener needed to depart Friedrichshafen for Tokyo before August 15 to avoid typhoons that would threaten the ship's safety. Circumnavigation of a typhoon could delay the flight by several days. Eckener estimated the total flying distance to be approximately 20,000 miles and the actual flying time to be about twelve to fourteen days, barring any accidents or other delays. An additional nine days would be added for refueling. He planned to spend three days in Tokyo before continuing to California on a course that would take them north of Hawaii.[46]

Rosendahl left the base selection board in California to travel by train to Lakehurst to join the *Graf Zeppelin*. Some structural changes had been made to the Zeppelin to improve its safety for the long flight. A sizeable, airtight rubber tubing was attached to the bottom of the passenger gondola that would allow it to float should the ship come down mid-ocean, and protective pneumatic buffers had been attached to the lower surfaces of the five gondolas that contained the motors.[47]

As a procedural matter, the *Graf*'s wireless set would be used for sending messages for only fourteen hours per day; the remaining ten hours would be devoted to weather reports.[48] Eckener considered the flight from Friedrichshafen to Lakehurst to be a trial run.

The official round-the-world tour would start from Lakehurst, traveling east back to Friedrichshafen. Lakehurst was prepared to receive the *Graf* on August 4, 1929. A crowd of 100,000 people was expected to greet the famous Zeppelin. Refueling was scheduled to take about 50 hours.

The *Graf Zeppelin* touched down at NAS Lakehurst at 2053 (EST) on August 4 after a 95-hour, 23-minute flight from Friedrichshafen. This flight time was faster than her previous crossing time of 111 hours, 46 minutes.[49] The Zeppelin was moored to a "stub" mast, and it was not until 1250 on the fifth that the ground crew was able to overcome gusty winds to guide the ship safely into the hangar alongside the *Los Angeles*, whom she dwarfed.

Well rested, well fed, and refueled, the *Graf Zeppelin* and her crew were prepared to depart Lakehurst on August 7. What was called the "Hearst-Eckener" flight around the world would be covered by three very skilled reporters: Sir Hubert Wilkins, Lady Drummond Hay, and Karl H. von Wiegand. Their accounts would appear exclusively in the *San Francisco Examiner* and allied Hearst newspapers.[50]

As the departure date neared, Eckener shared his flight plan more fully. The route selected was a distance of about 22,000 land miles, and he would follow a northern route whenever possible. The most severe conditions encountered were expected during the flight from Friedrich-shafen to Tokyo, due largely to low-hanging clouds over the Russian mountains. This part of the journey was 6,500 miles. Eckener planned to be back in Lakehurst after circling the globe on September 3 or 4.[51]

With favorable weather forecast, Eckener set the departure time for midnight, August 7. Rosendahl and Lieutenant Jack C. Richardson, navigator on the Los Angeles, joined the flight as representatives of the American Navy.[52]

———

The *Graf* lifted off from NAS Lakehurst at 2342 on August 7, heading east toward Friedrichshafen. Eckener was confident he would be receiving weather reports constantly. The only place such reports would not be available would be Siberia, the second leg of the journey. Richardson had commented already to newsmen that that part of the flight would be the most hazardous, because so little was known about weather conditions and prevailing winds there.

After departing Lakehurst, the *Graf* encountered highly favorable winds that were putting her well ahead of schedule. Less than twenty-four hours after leaving the NAS, the ship was more than halfway across the Atlantic with favorable west winds that, at times, pushed her to 70 miles per hour.[53] Weather conditions approaching England were favorable, and the weather bureau felt that conditions were so good they could add 20 to 25 miles per hour to the ship's speed.[54]

Records were being broken. At 0100 on August 10, the Atlantic had been crossed 44 hours after leaving Lakehurst. Eckener invited Lady Hay to the bridge of the *Graf* so she could enjoy the view of London below—her city.[55] Wiegand left the bridge at 0200 as Sir Hubert Wilkins assumed the duties of news watch. When Wiegand awoke later, there was a sense of "thrill in the air," and he ran to the bridge still in his pajamas. Captain Lehmann was in command but Eckener was still there and, grinning broadly, declared, "We are making 172 kilometers—that is around 105 land miles per hour." Eckener had hitched the *Graf* to a 40-mile-per-hour wind that added its force to that of the propellers. Lehmann and navigators Wittman and Pruss could not conceal their pride as they pored over their charts with dividers and paralleled rulers.[56]

Even as they sped over the Atlantic, there was plenty of time for Eckener, Pruss, Wittman, Schiller, Richardson, and Rosendahl to discuss issues related to LTA flight, and to share it with the ever-curious journalists.

Eckener announced that another Zeppelin—bigger and faster than the *Graf*—was to be built at Friedrichshafen in the coming fall. Comparisons were made among the existing and future airships: the *Los Angeles* was 658 feet long with a gas capacity of 2.6 million cubic feet; the *Graf Zeppelin* was 776.2 feet long with a gas capacity of 3.7 million cubic feet; the British R-100, then under construction, would be 709 feet long with a gas capacity of 5.157 million cubic feet; and dwarfing them all would be the Navy's ZRS-4 with a length of 789 feet and gas capacity of 6.5 million cubic feet (to be built).

Eckener shared his plan to build shorter, thicker, speedier dirigibles that would be powered by eight motors instead of five, such as with the *Graf*. He claimed that the increase in motors would advance the ship's speed by 12 miles per hour, thus giving a maximum speed of 88 miles per hour and a cruising speed of 82 miles per hour compared to the *Graf*'s cruising speed of 70 miles per hour.[57] Almost as an afterthought, Eckener added that his new airship would have a smoking lounge.

In open conversation concerning matters surrounding LTA flight, Eckener claimed the location of NAS Lakehurst was meteorologically unfavorable to transoceanic flying and promoted the idea that they—the Germans—would need a hangar somewhere south of Baltimore, and that said hangar would need to be their own, with their own mechanics, attendants, and flying schedule in order to operate economically.[58]

They discussed the safety of an airship using hydrogen as its lifting gas being struck by lightning. Rosendahl stated that lightning striking the *Graf* would have little effect unless the ship's commander was letting off hydrogen while the atmosphere was highly electrically charged. He claimed that there had been many instances of dirigibles being struck by lightning with no adverse effect. He could recall only one incident in which a lightning strike to a dirigible had a disastrous effect, and that happened in Germany when the pilot was letting off hydrogen during an electrical storm.[59]

As if giving a classroom lecture, Rosendahl told the press, "When a dirigible is built and before its covering is applied, between 10,000 and 20,000 volts of electricity are sent through the frame in a darkened hangar to discover whether or not an arc is made. In this way one can tell immediately if the parts of the frame are bonded."[60] Not infrequently, lightning strikes the nose of a dirigible, but the force of the charge is dissipated by the metal frame.

Rosendahl went on to say that the greatest threat to the *Graf* was not lightning but line squalls, such as those that destroyed the *Shenandoah*. "These up and down currents, which cannot always be foreseen, are the worst peril of the dirigible. Much of the territory over which we will pass is uncharted, and the air currents in this area are unknown."[61]

The Graf Zeppelin's transatlantic flight time was record-breaking. Eckener explained that airship navigation over vast stretches was meteorological in nature. The *Graf* made record time, not because Eckener took the shortest way, but because he took advantage of strong southwest winds, which they caught on the opposite rim of a depression coming from Newfoundland.[62]

The *Graf* touched down at Friedrichshafen at 0702 (EST). The ship's flight set three new records: flying from the Statue of Liberty to Lizard Light, the furthest southwest point of England, in 42 hours and 42 minutes; from the Statue of Liberty to the Eiffel Tower in 46 hours, 52 minutes; and, from the Statue of Liberty to Friedrichshafen in 54 hours and 20 minutes.[63]

On the ground in Friedrichshafen, Rosendahl commented that the flight had been a truly wonderful performance and that the navigation had been good, especially in the low visibility that covered half the voyage. Richardson lauded it as the most marvelous flight he had ever made. The significance of the August 10 landing was not lost on Richardson as he commented, "Dr. Eckener deserved this triumph. He worked for many years for just such an achievement and we are happy with him on his birthday."[64] At midnight, Lady Hay presented Eckener with a card signed by all the passengers to celebrate his sixty-first birthday.

Lady Drummond Hay earned the distinction of being the only woman to have flown across the Atlantic in both directions. With the most difficult leg of the journey ahead, there was already much to celebrate.

Within two hours of landing, a small army of mechanics and specialists began a careful inspection of the *Graf* for any maintenance or repair that might be needed before the next leg of her journey. A careful inspection of the ship's hull revealed it to be in perfect order. Machinists gave careful attention to the motors only to find that they were in perfect condition as well. Not a single engine needed to be overhauled or replaced. They simply needed oiling and cleaning. On closer examination, it was discovered that one of the ship's motors had been out of commission for three hours with a broken valve stem. As a precautionary measure, all new valve stems were placed in that motor.[65]

The outer skin of the dirigible had become looser in places, and Eckener had the situation corrected by installing spars from the inside to tighten the cover again.

The fuel formula for the *Graf* was complicated both chemically and logistically. J. C. Davidson, chemical sales manager of the Carbide and Carbon Chemicals Company, catered to the fuel needs of the Zeppelin for this trip. The fuel menu would change once the ship reached Japan. The fuel gas would be comprised of a mixture of Japanese hydrogen and pyrofax from West Virginia. Davidson had arranged for 1 million cubic feet of the fuel-gas mixture to be ready in Japan. The gas would be mixed in an elaborate valve manifold mechanism that had been built in San

Francisco and shipped to Tokyo. A Chemical Corporation engineer had been sent to Japan to have all in readiness for combining the Japanese hydrogen and pyrofax in proportions of two parts pyrofax to one part hydrogen. The resulting mixture would be slightly heavier than air and would contain the proper amount of heat and anti-knock characteristics required by the motors.[66]

Pyrofax was the trade name for highly compressed, purified propane or natural gas. It had been shipped to Japan in 700 steel cylinders of 100 pounds capacity each. The gas was compressed into liquid form for shipment to be released through the mixing apparatus in the form of 700,000 cubic feet of pure natural gas. There would be slightly more than 325,000 cubic feet of hydrogen flowing through the mixing apparatus.

In a difficult process, the fuel gas would have to be pumped at the rate of 100,000 cubic feet per hour, and the total weight, specific gravity of the gas, and its chemical proportions needed to be measured and recorded every minute of the process.[67]

To complicate the process further, the Zeppelin had been fed pure ethane gas at Lakehurst but would get pyrofax and hydrogen in Japan, and pyrofax and natural gas in Los Angeles. Lieutenant "Tex" Settle of the Navy and Lieutenant Karl Lange of the Goodyear Zeppelin Company would be in charge of the operations in Los Angeles.

During the leg of their journey from Siberia to Japan, they would encounter temperature differences that would subject the ship to unusual strains, but the greatest temperature changes would be between Tokyo and Los Angeles.

During his recent trip to China and Japan, Wiegand had made tabulations of the conditions over the Pacific, and he informed Eckener that the ship would have little to fear from the weather conditions along the route selected.[68] Sir Hubert Wilkins, appropriately referred to by Lady Hay as the "ice expert," had predicted that the next leg of their flight would be no colder than the Atlantic, but to be sure, everyone was taking plenty of the warmest clothing they could purchase.[69]

By August 13, Eckener had permission from the Soviet government to fly over their territories, but adverse weather over Russia and the long stretch over the Siberian wastelands caused a flight delay. The next leg of their journey would be the longest and most treacherous, and he wanted the most current weather data before choosing his route. Because he knew little, if anything, about the weather conditions and prevailing winds over the barren stretches of Siberia, and because strong headwinds would increase fuel consumption, he planned to carry a full fuel load.[70]

There was no shortage of hazards for this leg of the trip. Extreme weather conditions included the possibility of typhoons in the China Sea. The Ural Mountains separating eastern Europe from Asia and Siberia posed another threat because a forced landing in that area could go unreported for days or longer.[71]

Dr. Eckener and Lady Hay were hardly strangers and, because she was a journalist, every conversation between them constituted an interview. He told her that, as of then, the weather forecasts were favorable, but he wanted the relatively warm temperatures to cool down a few degrees before he trimmed the ship for a 7,000-mile trip. The warmer the weather, the harder it would be for the ship to rise and, consequently, the less weight it could carry. For each single-degree drop in temperature, the airship would be able to carry an additional 800 pounds. Eckener proclaimed this to be vital. "It also means miles to us, and miles may spell the difference between ice fields and the barren Siberian steppes and the hospitable welcome at our destination."[72] Eckener had an absolute dedication to safety first.

Lady Hay made no attempt to conceal her admiration for Eckener: "What I most admire is the contrasting combination of his tremendous eagerness and pride in the airship's capabilities—his almost boyish enthusiasm—with his cold, unyielding caution and iron-bound restraint against taking the slightest risk. . . . 'Safety first,' he reminded me several times."[73]

In the closing days before his liftoff, Eckener received letters from the governments of each of the countries over which he would fly, offering all-out assistance should the *Graf* encounter any problems. Lehmann considered these offers as "constructive internationalism in the finest sense" because the flight of the *Graf* was bringing countries closer together through its sporting adventure.

Eckener selected August 15 as the departure date. Everything had been considered. Contingency plans included the possibility of illness or injury to Eckener and Lehmann. In this unlikely event, Rosendahl and Richardson could step into their roles, and Commander Nashiro Fujiyoshi, who had navigated the *Graf* in the vicinity of Friedrichshafen, was available.[74]

The *Graf Zeppelin* took off from Friedrichshafen at 0435 (local time) on August 15, 1929, on the longest flight ever attempted by a dirigible.

Lifting off, the *Graf* headed due north across Bavaria and Prussia, then to Leipzig. By mid-morning (local time), the ship was over Berlin, where it was greeted by millions of people in the streets. Turning northeastward from Berlin, the airship reached Danzig, where Eckener decided to continue eastward to make Königsberg. En route to Königsberg, the *Graf* was making 64 miles per hour while using only four of her motors. Barring changes dictated by weather, Eckener had planned to head from Königsberg to Moscow, 1,400 miles from Friedrichshafen, where he would turn east and fly along the Sixtieth Parallel to the Ural Mountains, and from there, he would strike eastward to Yakutsk.[75] From the Ural Mountains to Yakutsk, the airship would cover one of the wildest areas known to man, where the lands were populated by Nomadic semi-barbarous tribes. Rosendahl was finding the trip "extremely interesting from the standpoint of seeing so much wild territory. . . . But to me as an airshipper, the greatest feature was the opportunity to observe airship navigation and operation at the hands of masters."[76]

At 0230 on August 16, the ship was over Vyatka, 600 miles east of Moscow, heading northeast toward the Urals. They passed north of Perm, Russia, at 0700, still tracking toward the Urals. Eckener headed far into the north of Russia before crossing into the Ural Mountains and into Siberia in the direction of the Ob River valley.

Enjoying favorable winds over Siberia, Eckener was able to use only three of his five motors. They were operating well with no signs of strain. The ship was making unusually fast time in her passage over Siberia, moving along at 70 to 75 miles per hour. The country below the ship was rolling but becoming increasingly hilly with thick fir forests. As they flew over 60 miles of Siberia, they saw but twelve human habitations that included several huts and tents and a few reindeer. Dressed in heavy sweaters, leather, and heavy coats, those on board the Zeppelin dined on caviar and champagne as they passed over the wilds of Siberia.[77] It was very cold, but Lady Hay slept very comfortably because of a sleeping kit Rosendahl provided her at Lakehurst.[78]

On August 17, Eckener received cautionary weather reports from Japan that mentioned the possibility of a typhoon.[79] By that evening, the *Graf* was in direct radio communication with the station at Nemuro Hikkaido on the northern island of Yezzo, Japan. At 1600 (local time), Eckener announced that the *Graf* had been in the air for 54 hours, 30 minutes, and had traveled 3,750 miles (6,000 kilometers) from Friedrichshafen.[80] Later that afternoon, the Zeppelin encountered the first storm of the flight. They met a heavy rain squall at 1545, "when a line of low, ink-black clouds loomed before us like an advancing army. There were heavy rains. It grew dark and looked ominous."[81]

Captain Schiller was in command on the bridge when they encountered the storm. Neither the officers nor passengers were at all uneasy with the situation. Lehmann, who had been giving an accordion concert in the lounge, played on without once rising to look out a window. "The Graf flashed into this formidable cloud formation at full cruising speed. We rose; then dropped and quivered. Then the Zeppelin shook itself almost like a dripping dog and was through on the other side in bright sunlight."[82] Subsequently, the temperature rose quickly to 14 degrees. The day and night had been bitterly cold as they traveled on the edge of what Sir Hubert Wilkins said was the coldest region of the world.

At midnight on the seventeenth, the *Graf* was exactly halfway around the globe from Lakehurst. Weather conditions in Tokyo on the morning of the eighteenth were fine. The Japanese government's weather bureau radioed the Zeppelin that there was a calm atmosphere with cloudy skies. The typhoon had passed off Hokkaido.[83]

At 1840 on August 19, 1929, the *Graf* landed at Kasumigaura Air Field near Tokyo, Japan, where a cheering crowd of over 100,000 people greeted her. After first "checking in" at Kasumigaura, the ship proceeded from Tokyo to Yokohama while enjoying the sight of city streets crowded with millions of people eager for a look at the Zeppelin. Wiegand wrote, "Streets and roofs were literally black with people."[84] Eckener, Knut, and all the officers were on the bridge of the ship, Lady Hay was in the navigation room that adjoined the bridge, and passengers were all at the windows of the lounge. They enjoyed the huge crowds below as two squadrons of naval planes escorted the *Graf*. Eckener was touched very deeply by his reception.[85]

With the long trek to Tokyo at a successful end, Eckener suddenly looked and felt very fatigued, but he confided to Wiegand that he planned to leave Tokyo for Los Angeles at dawn on August 22. Commander Rosendahl, Lieutenant Richardson, and Commander Fujiyoshi were amazed at the quick flight time and admired Eckener's command of the airship. They were amazed further that Eckener had deliberately chased down the typhoon to benefit from the pulling winds it brought, thus increasing the ship's speed. He had caught up with the typhoon at midnight, after which it carried them along on its tail.[86]

During the turbulence of the typhoon, most of the passengers were in bed and Eckener "did an unprecedented thing himself, sleeping through the greater part of the roughness he himself anticipated. This must be an infallible sign that the new school air skipper knows what he is doing. . . ."[87]

At breakfast, Eckener commented, "There was nothing to worry about. I never slept better in my life."[88]

On August 20, it was announced that Emperor Hirohito would honor Dr. Eckener, along with eleven officers—including Rosendahl and Richardson—and passengers, at a tea in his detached private palace on the twenty-first.[89] Eckener was hosted at a number of other ceremonies in what quickly became a very busy and crowded itinerary. *The Tokio Asahi* newspaper also hosted an elaborate evening banquet for the ship's crew.

Eckener had planned to depart Tokyo on August 22, but on that morning, the ship's gondola was damaged while being walked out of its hangar, necessitating a twenty-four-hour delay to make repairs.[90]

With an extra day on the ground with nothing scheduled, Eckener and the ship's company got some much-needed rest.

Throughout the night of the twenty-third, strong crosswinds made it hazardous to remove the ship from its hangar, but by mid-day, things improved and, at 1513 (local time), the *Graf Zeppelin* lifted off from the Kasumigaura Naval Base, moving smartly away from Japan at over

100 miles per hour. Early reports indicated some weather disturbances developing along the ship's route, but reports given to Eckener shortly after noon indicated that his course along the Aleutian Islands and down the Pacific Coast to Los Angeles would be clear of any weather disturbances.[91]

The *Graf Zeppelin* reached Los Angeles on August 26 with an official flight time from Japan to the U.S. of 79 hours and 22 minutes. Immediately on arrival Eckener announced that the ship would be ready for departure to Lakehurst at 2300 the same night.

A crowd of 75,000 people had waited through the night to greet the great ship and they cheered wildly at its arrival. Refueling was started immediately after the ship was made fast to the mooring mast. Thanks to the many rehearsals and the supervision of Settle, the landing went smoothly.[92]

Eckener had been ill for two days during the transpacific crossing, and after landing in Los Angeles, he was rushed to a downtown hotel to get some rest before resuming his journey. He was suffering from the stress of the trip, but his health was declared to be good.

Lieutenant Commander Charles E. Rosendahl, referred to by a reporter as the "hero of the Shenandoah disaster," claimed, "This was the finest flight I ever had. I enjoyed every minute of it. We took advantage of every wind we could find which is the reason we changed our course. That and the resultant remarkable speed was one of the chief things which made the flight such an unusual one."[93]

Commander R. Kusaka gave a statement that could have emanated from the heart and mind of Dr. Eckener:

> Four nationalities spent three days in heaven, and in that time went from Japan to America. This remarkable flight made possible by German genius, we feel, changes the map of the world and makes Japan truly a neighbor of the United States. The flight will promote friendship and good will and will bring better understanding between all the nations of the world and the United States, Great Britain, Germany, and Japan especially.[94]

Captain Lehmann—not given to boasting—proclaimed, "The world tour of the Graf Zeppelin demonstrates the superiority of lighter-than-air craft over airplanes for long distance travel under heavy load."[95]

The *Graf* departed Los Angeles 19 hours and 3 minutes after its arrival from Tokyo. This liftoff became the most perilous moment of the entire trip as weight and a temperature inversion caused the tail to strike ground. Damage to the rudder was minimal and no threat to flight.

Heading east, Eckener had to contend with terrain issues that were uncommon for him—namely, the California mountains. To negotiate the San Gorgonio Pass, he needed to attain an altitude of some 9,000 feet. He had lightened his load in Los Angeles, including leaving behind seven members of the crew, who had flown 16,880 miles already, and three Japanese passengers left the ship.[96]

Even with the lightened load, the ship was too heavy to negotiate the mountains. As learned with the *Shenandoah*, the airship would not have consumed enough fuel before confronting the mountains to lessen its weight sufficiently. To circumvent the mountains, Eckener pursued a course along the Mexican border. Just two hours after takeoff, the *Graf* reached a point near the international line at San Diego and headed east.

With about 10,000 people on hand, the *Graf Zeppelin* came into view at NAS Lakehurst at 0652 (EST), August 29, 1929, and at 0712 she touched ground, ending a round-the-world journey of 21 days, 7 hours, and 32 minutes, proving that "the oceanic airways of the world and the sky above broad continents would become the pathways of commerce."[97] Repairs were begun on the damaged rudder immediately and the ship was ready to depart for Germany on the thirty-first, with Lehmann in command.

Once the *Graf* was on the ground, Richardson and Rosendahl were the first to step out. When Eckener alighted, he had a message for the American people:

> I am deeply moved by the reception and cordiality shown on the part of the American people, particularly the warmth of the reception in Los Angeles. I was deeply grateful for the enthusiasm shown by the crowd in Chicago. The enthusiasm was greater than I ever before

witnessed. . . . I am grateful to the United States Government for its
co-operation at all times, and especially to the Navy Department,
whose guest we have always been in America.[98]

Richardson gave reporters some practical comments, saying,

> I am of the opinion that there must be some international coordi-
> nation between nations for the compilation and exchange of me-
> teorological data before lighter than air travel around the world will
> become a commercial possibility.
>
> We crossed over country which no doubt no civilized group of
> men ever had passed. In fact, when people whom we saw on the
> ground sighted us they were astonished and then frightened and
> almost without exception turned and ran away from the ship as if it
> were a monster of which they naturally should be afraid.
>
> It is my belief that lighter-than-aircraft in the future always will
> be used for long-distance travel, particularly over water, but that is
> only possible when we perfect compilation of weather information.[99]

While Lehmann took the *Graf* home to Germany, Eckener, riding a
ground swell of interest in LTA flight stimulated by his great feat, stayed
behind in the U.S. to meet officials in Washington, officials at the Goodyear Zeppelin Company in Akron, and other potential investors.

Eckener was truly grateful for the assistance he had received from the
U.S. Navy during the *Graf*'s transatlantic and round-the-world flights.
He wanted to foster collaboration between Germany and America, and
to promote the idea, he wanted U.S. officers on board every flight of
the Zeppelin so that there might be shared learning. The Navy considered this arrangement invaluable to the design and construction of its
new airships and as the *Graf* sailed back to Germany, eight Navy officers
and one civilian engineer were on board. Secretary Adams gave permission for Lieutenant H. V. Wiley, captain of the *Los Angeles*; Lieutenant
Commander J. M. Shoemaker, the Navy's leading expert on aeronautical
engines; and Lieutenant Roland G. Mayer of the construction corps to
make the flight to Germany.[100]

Eckener had declared the *Graf Zeppelin* to be obsolete in her design. Her geometric dimensions were not proper for successful commercial carriers and she was underpowered. Nevertheless, she was the only really large airship flying at the time, and from her, engineers and crews in a German-American partnership could learn valuable lessons to be incorporated into future airships.

The hangar built at the Goodyear facility in Akron became the largest building in the world unsupported by pillar or post. It was 1,175 feet long, 325 feet wide, and 205 feet high. To make these dimensions relatable, it was said that the finished airship dock would be large enough to house both the Woolworth Building and the Washington Monument lengthwise, or in other words, fourteen football games could be staged in the building simultaneously with space to spare.[101]

To minimize resistance to air currents, the hangar was constructed in the shape of an egg cut in two the long way—in geometric terms, a semi-ellipsoid. The large doors at the ends of the hangar were huge and had to be opened safely and rapidly to allow entry and exit of an airship. The opening was 180 feet high and 240 feet wide at the bottom, with the shape of a parabolic arch.[102]

The new airships, to be built in Akron, were intended primarily for scouting, but given that they carried their own fighting planes and machine guns, it was hoped they would play an important role in fleet operations.[103] With that expectation, Moffett wanted an airship base on the West Coast from which reconnaissance of the Pacific Ocean could be conducted. The surface fleet spent most of its time on the Pacific Coast, and an airship should be familiar with operations over the Pacific area, along the coast, and near the Aleutian Islands.[104]

Congress appropriated $5 million for the base, and following an intensive search, the Navy's general board accepted Secretary Adams's recommendation that Camp Kearny be selected.[105] Subsequently, Rosendahl told the House Committee seeking a West Coast base that Sunnyvale was not only an unrivaled site for a base, but it was the best natural site he had seen anywhere in the world.[106]

The press kept one eye on the base hunt and the other on Akron, writing of the anticipated ZRS-4 and ZRS-5 in expansive terms—"faster, safer, more efficient . . . death-dealing sea scouts with airplanes zooming out of the sides of the bag and machine guns spitting terror from one end of the dirigible to the other."[107]

Visionaries at the Goodyear Zeppelin corporation in Akron were proposing a transpacific airship service with weekly flights to Honolulu, carrying passengers and mail. They watched carefully the progress of the *Graf Zeppelin* over the Pacific Ocean to learn what they could that would assist their plans for a regular Hawaiian service.[108]

CHAPTER 8

USS *AKRON* (ZRS-4)

In October 1928, a contract was awarded to the Goodyear Zeppelin Corporation for the construction of two dirigibles, both of which would surpass the size of the *Los Angeles* or the *Graf Zeppelin*. The two airships were designated the ZRS-4 and ZRS-5. The "S" was added to the designation to denote "scout"—as that was to become their roles in the hands of the Navy. One would cost $2,450,000 and the other $5,375,000.[1]

ZRS-4's design called for a gas volume of 6,500,000 cubic feet—far greater than the 2,470,000 cubic feet of the *Los Angeles*—a length of 785 feet, diameter of 132.9 feet, and a lifting capacity of 403,000 pounds. The result was a craft with a cruising range of 9,180 nautical miles at 50 knots without refueling—over two and a half times the range of the *Los Angeles*. Because the key role of the airship was long-range reconnaissance over the ocean, the greater operating range was crucial.

The ZRS-4 was equipped with an airplane hangar inside her hull, capable of handling five small scout planes, each fitted with a hook-on device on its superior wing. The overall geometry of the ZRS-4 differed significantly from that of the *Los Angeles*. No longer narrow and sleek like the *Shenandoah* or *Los Angeles*, the new airship was fuller and less slender.

Because the lifting gas would be helium instead of hydrogen, the motors would be housed inside the hull, reducing wind resistance and improving safety for the crew. The propellers would be supported on brackets from the hull, driven by the motors through transverse shafts and bevel gears. Uniquely, the propeller axis could be turned to the vertical position to provide upward or downward thrust to assist lifting off or landing.

As before, the hull would consist of longitudinal and transverse duralumin girders with steel wire bracing. The outer envelope would consist of aluminized fabric, drawn taut and smooth. Helium would be contained in eleven separate gas-tight cells. It was predicted that the new design would allow ZRS-4 to endure storms and squalls twice as severe as that encountered by the *Shenandoah*.

The new design also provided three longitudinal corridors and passageways completely around the circumference of each main transverse frame, giving access to all parts of the ship and allowing inspection and repairs to be carried out in flight.[2]

The new ships would be fitted with radio transmitters capable of sending signals to every corner of the world. It was the Navy's goal to provide them with a communication range equal to their cruising radius—over 8,000 miles. Thus, should either ship make transpacific flights, the crew could maintain communication with Lakehurst or Washington the entire way. Engine-driven power units would replace the wind-driven power generators.[3]

On November 7, 1929, over 50,000 people attended the ring-laying ceremony in Akron for the ZRS-4. Visitors and invited guests were welcomed by Paul W. Litchfield, president of the Goodyear Tire and Rubber Company. Dr. Karl Arnstein, designer of the ZRS-4, was greeted with great applause as he was introduced as the most renowned man in his field in the country.[4] Rosendahl was present as ComRATES.

Paul W. Litchfield announced, "Today we start actual construction of the largest airships in the world, so large that this mammoth hangar will house but one of them."[5]

The *Los Angeles* made an appearance over the proceedings, and Wiley dropped a message to those below, offering "best wishes" for the success of the *Akron* project.[6]

Officially, and ceremonially, construction of the new airship began when Admiral Moffett drove a small gold rivet—"no larger than a collar button"—into the highest part of the biggest rib-ring.[7] The small gold rivet had been fashioned in a dentist's laboratory. To drive the rivet, Moffett moved to the front of a platform where President Litchfield extracted the small rivet from a large box and handed it to him with a maul. With a big smile, Moffett drove the rivet home with a single blow, prompting a roar from the crowd. The 133-foot-wide master ring was the first of twenty ring girders forming the ship's skeleton. The ring was so large that, during the ceremony, 1,800 people stood inside it.[8]

Delivering the key speech of the day, Moffett summarized the history of the Navy's LTA program, ending with, "Everything new has its obstacles to surmount and its barriers to jump; it seems to be one of the penalties of progress, and in developing this new art of the air we have had our battles. Dirigible construction is a new art, and we are just now scratching the surface."[9]

The day's ceremonies concluded with a dinner at the Portage Country Club, where Rosendahl was presented with the *Ligue Internationale des Aviateur Diploma d'Honneur* and a gold medal. The trophies had been sent from Paris by Clifford B. Harmon, president of the *Ligue*. They were similar to those presented to Charles Lindbergh the previous year. The presentation to Rosendahl was in recognition of his work with LTA ships.[10] Moffett added, "By winning it, Commander Rosendahl, you have reflected glory and honor upon the United States navy."[11]

Nineteen twenty-nine had been a very busy and productive year for the LTA program, thanks largely—but not exclusively—to Admiral Moffett and his ongoing policy of openness with the press and the public. The program got a rare boost in visibility when Hearst newspapers collaborated with Metro-Goldwyn-Mayer studios to produce an audio-visual documentary for the "big screen" titled, *Around the World via Graf Zeppelin*.[12] Audiences were treated to seeing and hearing Dr. Hugo Eckener, Lieutenant Commander Charles E. Rosendahl, Lady Drummond Hay, and President Hoover. "This is asserted to be one of those rare films that combine information with thrills, and patriotism with suspense. It is the imperishable record of one of the outstanding achievements of the ages."[13]

On June 30, 1930, Rosendahl received orders relieving him as Com-RATES to report to the chief of the Bureau of Aeronautics (BUAER). He was allowed also to travel to Lakehurst three times each month to remain involved in unfinished projects dealing with the mechanical handling of airships, mooring methods, and equipment.[14]

"Flying a desk" in BUAER was not a job Rosendahl wanted, but in late 1930, BUAER was advised that the Bureau of Navigation—then handling personnel matters—was considering him for command of ZRS-4. This was the job Rosendahl wanted most, but it came with a cautionary warning. The Bureau of Navigation was aware that Rosendahl had been on duty in the LTA service since the summer of 1923 and had not served on a surface ship since 1921. The chief of the Bureau of Navigation felt that Rosendahl could be jeopardizing his future by not seeking sea duty on a surface vessel to keep abreast of developments that had been taking place since his long absence from the sea. In a compromise, the Chief of the Bureau offered to shorten the required sea duty from three years to one year.

Rosendahl responded that he believed he could serve the Navy best by taking command of the ZRS-4 before going to sea. With Moffett's backing, that was the way things went. It was on a happy day in April 1931 that Rosendahl "bade a moist farewell to my BUAER desk. . . . and set out on a course that led via Lakehurst to the Goodyear Zeppelin plant in Akron, Ohio."[15] His orders included taking command of ZRS-4 when she was commissioned.[16] Although only thirty-eight years old, Rosendahl was recognized as the country's foremost authority on lighter-than-air flight with 3,333 hours of flight in airships—a record of more hours in the air as commander than any American officer.[17]

When completed, ZRS-4 would be only 15 feet longer than *Graf Zeppelin*, but she would have twice the gas capacity. She would have eight engines with a total of 4,480 horsepower and would travel up to 83 miles per hour. At its cruising speed of 50 miles per hour, she would have a range of 10,580 miles without refueling—enough to fly from New York to San Francisco three times. Helium would be contained in numerous cells, the largest of which would hold 1,000,000 cubic feet of the gas. Useful in combat, her rate of rise would be 2,000 feet per minute while dropping ballast and still traveling at 80 miles per hour. Airplanes could not climb at that rate, and in order to climb at all, they sacrificed much of their forward speed.[18]

ZRS-4 and ZRS-5 would be able to conduct reconnaissance over twenty times more of the ocean's surface than could be covered by a surface cruiser.[19] Not to be overlooked was the ability of the airships to launch and recover airplanes. The storage compartment was about 75 feet long by 60 feet wide, located about one-third of the way back along its length. On the bottom of the ship were collapsible doors covering a T-shaped opening through which the planes could be raised or lowered using a trapeze-like arrangement for taking the planes on board in flight. When the trapeze device was in the lowered position, a biplane equipped with a hook on its superior wing could maneuver into position to "hook on" to the trapeze, thus effecting a "landing," after which the plane would be drawn up into the hangar of the airship through the T opening in its belly.

Secretary Ingalls justified the cost of the airship program:

> The time required for construction of a cruiser is something more than three years; that of the rigid airship less than a year. The original cost of a modern cruiser is approximately $15,000,000; one of these rigids from $2,500,000 to $3,000,000, or one-fifth of the cruiser cost. The operating cost of such cruisers is between $800,000 and $900,000 a year; that of the rigid airship somewhere between $500,000 and $600,000. Aboard the cruiser there must be approximately sixty officers and 550 men—on the rigid airship, twelve officers and sixty men. The top speed of the cruiser is 34 knots—that of the rigid airship 72.8 knots. The cruiser carries on board from two to four planes; the rigid airship five to six.[20]

The christening took place on August 8, 1931, with an estimated 150,000 people witnessing the ceremony. Following the command, "Up, ship!" the airship was allowed to float free of its mooring inside the dock as Mrs. Herbert Hoover pulled a cord freeing forty-eight pigeons from under the ship's prow, and she spoke, "I christen thee USS Akron."[21]

Addressing the crowd, Moffett said that he hoped the ZRS-5 would be enlarged to 7,500,000 feet before her completion. "We do not lead the world in our merchant marine, and, alas, we do not lead the world with our navy, but we do, by construction of this great airship, now take the lead in lighter-than-air."[22]

"Until these two airships [ZRS-4 and ZRS-5] have been in actual service, operating from properly equipped terminals or bases, it cannot be said that airships have had a reasonable 'workout' with the Navy."[23]

To support his arguments, Moffett referenced the experiences of the Germans with their Zeppelins during the First World War, which embraced a total of over 1,100 reconnaissance missions and two hundred attacks conducted with some seventy-eight naval airships. "The bombing attacks made by these airships were spectacular and did some material damage, but it is now generally conceded that this was not a proper function for such airships."[24] The value of Zeppelins was maintaining an almost constant watch over the North Sea, thereby guarding the German Navy against surprise attacks, and there were no losses of airships while on reconnaissance.[25]

The aged *Los Angeles* was about to pass off to the *Akron* the burden of proving the worth of airships to the surface fleet. She was better built and better equipped and would be captained by a visionary skipper in Rosendahl.

———

The flight of the *Akron* was scheduled for September 23, 1931. That morning, the switchboard of the *Akron Beacon Journal* newspaper was swamped with hundreds of telephone calls from people wanting information about the flight. "Questions asked revealed that, although dozens of persons don't know the difference between an airplane and a dirigible, or between the USS Akron and the Graf Zeppelin, they did know something of vast importance was going to happen—and they wanted to know when."[26]

Coverage was provided by both Columbia and National Broadcasting radio corporations, and as expected, Moffett was among the host of celebrities gathered to witness the flight. *Akron* took the air at 1537, and following a smooth flight over the city, she was docked at 2015. The following days involved tests of turning ability and the ship's lift under varying loading conditions and at various altitudes, rates of climb, and other technical issues.[27]

On October 16, in misting rain and steady 13-mile-per-hour winds, the ship lifted off—the strongest wind into which a launch had been taken to date. Four of the eight propellers were pointed downward to help the ship rise quickly after being released from her mooring. Once she rose to a few hundred feet, the other engines were started, and *Akron* headed southwest to begin a 2,000-mile, forty-eight-hour flight.[28] The endurance flight was completed on the morning of the eighteenth, followed by a recommendation that the ship be accepted by the Navy immediately.[29]

On October 21, 1931, having completed her trials successfully, Rosendahl flew the ship in two sweeping farewell circles over the city before making for Lakehurst. Her airplane hangar was tested in flight, although she had not been equipped with airplanes. The T-shaped opening in the hull—50 feet wide and 38 feet deep—was opened in flight and no air blew into the ship's interior.

The USS *Akron* (ZRS-4) was commissioned at Lakehurst on October 27, 1931, and once ceremonies and demonstrations were over, Rosendahl had a weighty task ahead of him for the *Akron*—establishing her role in and proving her worth to the surface fleet.

> After commissioning, we settled down to the task of developing our ship into a worthy member of our naval forces. Every flight had its lessons and differences, none was ever humdrum. We were constantly under pressure to extend our operations, particularly on missions with the Fleet. No one was more anxious [than] we of the ship's company to do just that and have the Fleet's acceptance of airships. But apparently we were the only ones who realized the difficulties involved in working the "bugs" out of a new type of radically new design and of much greater size than any predecessor. No one else seemed to realize the importance of having alternate places to land or reservice in the event we could not get into Lakehurst. We had a battle anytime we wanted the slightest addition or improvement to our facilities, a great contrast with the treatment afforded the airplane.[30]

The *Akron* made her first post-commissioning flight on November 2. It was another "signature" Moffett event with numerous influential persons and press on board to promote the LTA program, and she was accompanied in the air by the *Los Angeles*. As they flew over Washington, both ships dipped noses in salute to the White House and Arlington Cemetery.

Through training and publicity flights, the *Akron* logged more than three hundred hours of flight time by the end of 1931. Vice Admiral Arthur Lee Willard, commander of the Scouting Force (ComScoFor) since 1930, had commanded a number of fleet exercises that demonstrated the value of launching attacks on surface ships from ranges beyond the reach of battleship guns through the use of aircraft carriers. In January 1932, Willard ordered the *Akron* to participate in a fleet exercise with the Scouting Force.

The operations order called for the *Akron* to be off Cape Lookout, North Carolina, by daylight on January 10, 1932 and, from there, to begin scouting in search of an "enemy" fleet. The "enemy" fleet was a group of destroyers en route from Charleston, South Carolina, to Guantanamo Bay, Cuba. Once located, the *Akron* was to keep ComScoFor informed of its position, course, speed, and disposition.

After battling stormy weather on her way south, *Akron* arrived at Cape Lookout, North Carolina, at 0330 on January 10.[31] At 0700, with overcast skies and fair visibility, Rosendahl stationed his battle lookouts and started searching for the "enemy" fleet. Throughout the day on the tenth, they sighted an occasional cruiser or commercial steamer, but there were no signs of an "enemy" fleet.

Rosendahl changed course to the west at 1140 to make navigational calibrations, but they were back on a southerly course by 1240, when the radio room acquired a strong signal from one of the "enemy" destroyers that one of the ships in company was having engine problems.[32] Because the *Akron* had not been equipped with her radio direction finder, she was unable to determine the bearing of the vessel and maintained her southerly course.

While the *Akron* had not spotted any "enemy" ships, two "enemy" destroyers had sighted her. The USS *Dickerson* (DD-157) had sighted the airship at 1350, ten miles to the northwest, and minutes later, she was sighted by the USS *Leary* (DD-158). The *Akron* continued to make course changes in search of the "enemy," and at 0910 on the eleventh, she sighted a squadron of "enemy" destroyers and a cruiser off the starboard bow, fifteen miles distant. The sighting was reported to ComScoFor as the *Akron* continued to track the destroyers while scouting for other "enemy" vessels.[33] At 0952, another squadron of destroyers was sighted off the starboard bow 20 miles distant, and by 1010, it appeared that the two destroyer divisions were converging on the cruiser leader. Rosendahl continued to track until the scouting problem was complete around 1103, and he returned to Lakehurst.[34]

Assessment of the *Akron*'s performance during the exercise was open to interpretation. Admiral Willard claimed that the problem was framed so that the airship should have made contact with the enemy fleet on the tenth. A division of surface cruisers had failed to locate them on the first day of the exercise, and when they made contact on the eleventh, it was seven hours after the *Akron* had sighted them.[35] It was clear to airship advocates that *Akron* had been sent to the exercise before she was ready. She had been sent without her radio direction finding equipment, her trapeze device, and her scout planes.

Rosendahl considered the exercise a qualified success because the airship had located the "enemy" ahead of the surface vessels that were also in the hunt.

———

Dark clouds had hung over the *Akron* from her beginnings with claims of inferior construction materials and methods, possible sabotage attempts, and failure to meet contracted performance requirements. All claims were investigated thoroughly, and no evidence of any harm to the *Akron* was found. The matter seemed to have been resolved in early 1931, but some opponents of the LTA program, and its attendant cost, resurrected the disproven claims in early 1932, and the House Naval Committee decided to investigate.[36]

A nine-member subcommittee was sent to Lakehurst in mid-February 1932 to inspect the airship and report on any defects. Moffett scheduled a flight on the ship for the committee members for February 22. On that morning, with subcommittee members and hundreds of spectators watching, the lower fin of the airship was connected to the stern beam, the flight crew embarked, and the *Akron* was towed, stern first, from the hangar. The towing job was quite erratic, and when the ship was about halfway out of the hangar, the sound of a cable snapping was heard, followed by a report from aft that a major control had broken.[37]

As the bow of the ship crossed the sill of the hangar, she had six degrees of list to starboard. There was a down load at the bow of between 4,000 to 7,000 pounds and a side load of between 3,000 to 5,000 pounds to starboard, and the lower fin carried away from the stern beam, swinging rapidly to starboard. Almost immediately, ballast was dropped aft, but as the ship swung, her lower fin struck the ground severely and there was a hole six feet long in the No. 2 Gas Cell.

The lower fin was placed on a flatcar, and she was hauled by the stern into position on the docking rails. There were no serious injuries, and once the ship was secure in her hangar, subcommittee members were allowed to examine the ship. They made it clear that the accident would not influence their report, and everyone was favorably impressed by the performance of the officers and crew. Rosendahl and Wiley agreed that the damage was not severe, and repairs could be made within about six weeks. In the end, the subcommittee suspended its investigation and gave the airship a good report.

The biggest disappointment for Rosendahl and his crew was that the accident and repairs would interfere with the *Akron*'s participation in the upcoming fleet exercises off California. On February 2, 1932, it was announced that Rosendahl, now thirty-nine years old, after ten continuous years in LTA service, would return to sea duty with Commander A. H. Dresel assuming command of the *Akron*. Rosendahl's deployment to sea duty, however, would not take place until after the *Akron*'s scheduled trip to the West Coast.[38]

On March 28, 1932, Rosendahl left the *Akron* to her repairs as he headed home to Texas for a visit. On his way, he made a quick stopover in Akron, Ohio, to check on the construction progress on the *Macon*. Finding six bays of the framework nearly completed and the tail section due to be raised within days, he left Akron very pleased with the progress.[39]

It was assumed widely that command of the *Macon* would fall to Rosendahl, but he informed Akronites that this would not happen because he expected to be at sea. He was not opposed to the Navy regulation that required sea duty for officers before promotion to full commander, and he expected this tour to last two or three years.

Leaving Akron, Rosendahl continued to Cleburne for a two-week visit with his parents.

On April 19, 1932, the Navy's LTA program received a boost when it was announced that the House Appropriation Committee recommended the expenditure of $1,450,000—the full amount needed to complete work on the *Macon*. This recommendation was interpreted as renewed confidence in LTA flight, especially in light of an $800,000 reduction in the Navy's heavier-than-air appropriations.[40]

The bill included instructions for decommissioning the *Los Angeles* strictly as a measure of economy. No specific recommendations were made for disposal of the ship, but a large part of the $270,000 allocated to the *Los Angeles* could be saved by decommissioning her.[41] Moffett had intended to lay up the *Los Angeles* as soon as the *Macon* entered service. The bill also included funds for the completion of the Sunnyvale, California, LTA facility where the *Macon* was to be stationed.

Rosendahl was at Lakehurst when he received word that his sixty-four-year-old father, Charles Oscar Rosendahl, had died on April 25, 1932, in a hospital in Temple, Texas. The cause of death was not specified.[42] Rosendahl left the same day on five days leave to return home.[43]

The *Akron* was ready to take the air again on April 28 with Wiley in command in Rosendahl's absence. She made a successful shakedown cruise, flying in the vicinity of NAS Lakehurst. Moffett and Arnstein—from his Akron office—were very pleased. Other shakedown flights took place under Wiley's command until Rosendahl's return on May 1, 1932.

The next step was to test the *Akron*'s airplane "hook-on" device. The trapeze apparatus and airplane handling equipment were tested statically inside the hangar on May 2. The airship's bow was elevated approximately 25 feet, and a biplane was hooked onto the trapeze and hoisted into the airship's hangar.[44]

The first in-flight tests took place the following day as Rosendahl steered various courses paralleling the New Jersey coastline preparatory to the hook-on tests.[45] Flying N2Y airplanes, Lieutenants D. W. Harrigan and H. L. Young each completed hook-ons to the trapeze, and following one hook-on by Harrigan, his plane was hoisted successfully into the airship's hangar as designed. These tests represented the first time an airship had captured planes in flight, taken them into her hangar, and launched them into flight again.

Having proved her air worthiness, the *Akron* was ready for her much-anticipated transcontinental trek.

On May 8, 1932, Commander A. H. Dresel reported for temporary duty on board *Akron* as her prospective commanding officer. *Akron* was prepared to make her 3,500-mile trip to the West Coast for the commissioning of the dirigible base at Sunnyvale, California, and to take her place with the fleet then in San Francisco Bay. After lifting off, the ship took on her two small land planes and set out on the course laid by Rosendahl—over Richmond, Virginia; Raleigh, North Carolina; Columbia, South Carolina; and El Paso, Texas.

Over Alabama in the early hours of May 9, the ship encountered gathering clouds but no severe weather. Rosendahl took the ship as low as 1,400 feet at times to fly under cloud layers that presented poor visibility, but the weather began to change as they flew into Texas, where they encountered storms late in the day.

Turbulent and opposing winds were encountered near Beaumont, Texas, and forecasts became increasingly serious with low-pressure areas in northern Mexico, rendering Texas "thick with thunderstorms."[46] *Akron* arrived over San Antonio amid lightning and circling dark clouds. The *Akron* made for Houston, arriving around 1600. From 1759, the weather from the north began to thicken and at 1812 lightning appeared to the west. Rosendahl made course changes to avoid storms, and at 2108 he changed course to follow beacons from San Antonio to Big Springs. Storms became increasingly problematic, and at 2149 there was lightning dead ahead of the ship.

Over San Angelo at 2225, *Akron* circled the city, and at 2310 thunderstorms lay dead ahead and very close aboard. At 2320, a call went down from the ship for a landing crew of five hundred men, and flash-light signals were sent to ground asking the entire city's population to be assembled. Observers commented that, after circling the airport, the airship hung over the city as if it were uncertain whether to proceed into an electrical storm raging west of the city.[47]

The ship was in increasing danger from severe weather with every hour. Electrical storms and high winds along her intended path closed in from three directions after she reached San Angelo and it began to rain. It was suspected that *Akron*'s radios were out of commission due to storms. All government and American airway stations in Texas continued sending weather reports to the ship, but it was unknown if they were received. Airport spotlights turned skyward in an attempt to communicate by blinker code.[48]

About 2,000 people gathered at the San Angelo airport in rain and 15-mile-per-hour winds to watch the ship. Although an emergency ground crew had assembled, airport authorities feared the ship would wreck if it attempted a landing. It was thought impossible to hold the huge ship to the ground even if it landed in windy conditions. Commercial aviators felt the *Akron*'s only hope was to ride out the storm or try to rise above it. Thunderstorms were being reported from Abilene westward to El Paso, with a ceiling of only 1,000 feet. The airship had maintained an altitude of 500 to 800 feet.[49]

The San Angelo airport advised the *Akron* that a landing crew was ready at San Antonio if she could make the 200-mile return trip, but at 2332 they were still over San Angelo with thunderstorms abeam and close aboard. Rosendahl continued to steer various courses and speeds to avoid severe weather, but escaping it seemed impossible. From 0400 to 0800, lightning flashed all around the ship.

At 0515 on the tenth, they encountered intermittent heavy fog. The ground was visible intermittently as they sailed through fog and rain, but over Toyah, in increasingly dense fog, contact with the ground was lost, and Rosendahl reversed course and headed back to Pecos. At 1945, the ship ran into a sandstorm about 4 miles east of El Paso that was producing very turbulent air. Battling thunderstorms, electrical storms, and areas of poor visibility had caused a delay of more than twelve hours in the *Akron*'s travel plan.

In the earliest hours of the eleventh, the ship was steering various courses to conform with mountain passes in the vicinity of Tucson, Arizona, and at about 0800, they were over San Diego, California, where the ground was again obscured by fog. Rosendahl steered various courses, looking for an opening in the fog through which he could discharge the ship's planes. When dropped, the pilots were to proceed to Camp Kearny to assist with the *Akron*'s landing procedure.

Later, Rosendahl would write, "Of all the flights I ever made in the Akron, this one to the Pacific Coast yielded the widest range of experiences, by far."[50]

Certainly, successfully navigating the violent storms of Texas without harm to ship or personnel had been interesting, but interesting took on another connotation as the *Akron* attempted to moor to the mast at Camp Kearny, California. On May 11, thousands of people had gathered to witness the arrival of the *Akron*, but none had expected the tragedy that unfolded.

Approaching Camp Kearny for a mooring, the *Akron*'s trail ropes were dropped at 1055, but the ground crew failed to make contact. Rosendahl made another approach and dropped the main wire at 1125, which was connected to the main wire of the mooring mast.

Three times sailors had seized the landing cables and attempted to walk the airship to the mast, but each time, ground winds forced them to release their holds. On the fourth attempt, the ship became extremely light due to the sun's heat, causing the helium to expand, and the ship was swept upward suddenly. While most of the sailors dropped their handling lines, three men did not release in time and were carried aloft. The three men carried aloft were: Robert Edsall of Elkhart, Indiana; Nigel Henton of Fresno, California; and Charles "Bud" Cowart of Sand Springs, Oklahoma.

Rosendahl and his officers shouted to the ground crew to stand by to let go. Over a minute later, he gave the order to cut the main cable and let go of everything. The mooring officer atop the mast attempted unsuccessfully to sever the cable with bolt cutters. He then slid down a guy wire to the ground where, with an axe, he succeeded in cutting the cable, but the ship's buoyancy carried her aloft along with three men hanging to the line. The main wire was cut because of a terrific strain on the airship, and Rosendahl released helium with the valves wide open at intervals in an attempt to force the ship down with its engines to save the men still clinging to the trail rope.[51] "Not far above the ground, but far enough to be fatal, first one, then a second, loosed his grip and dropped earthward. As though in a hypnotic trance, I could not get my gaze off that awful sight of two falling bodies."[52]

Edsall and Henton had fallen to their deaths from an altitude of about 200 feet. When Cowart saw his mates fall, he hung onto the line with one hand while looping the loose end of the rope around his legs with the other hand, fashioning a "bosun's seat."[53] The *Akron* shot to a height of 1,000 feet with Cowart hanging on below it.

Cowart's quick thinking had saved his life for the moment, but Rosendahl and his crew had to find a way to get Cowart into the airship or land him safely on the surface. Landing him on the ground while dangling below the airship was an unsafe option—it was impossible to judge the exact distance the ship would be from the ground, and they would run the risk of causing serious injury by dragging him along the ground. The only safe solution was to haul him up into the ship.

After securing himself to his line, Cowart went lifeless for a while, and his status was unknown to those in the ship. Speculating that he was unconscious, a volunteer climbed down the rope, hand-over-hand, for a distance of 25 feet to ascertain how secure Cowart was. The volunteer returned to the ship to report that he was secure at the moment.

In the cramped bow of the *Akron*, "the resourceful and imperturbable Lieutenant Roland Mayer worked rapidly and effectively with a small group of men to rig for hauling [Cowart] aboard."[54] A winch was needed, but the only one available that could reel in the 3.5-inch manila line was designed to lay a 7/8-inch cable onto its drum. It took true ingenuity to make it handle the much bulkier manila rope—ingenuity and muscular arms.

For what seemed like an eternity to Rosendahl—and most certainly to Cowart—the airship, at an altitude of about 1,500 feet, cruised in wide circles over the landing field, moving as slowly as control of the ship permitted. In little over an hour, Cowart was brought on board by way of the bow gangway. He was fine and rejected offers of food and water in favor of getting a tour of the ship.

"It was with thankful relief that evening that we disembarked Cowart for public appearances he never dreamed of."[55]

As he looked back in coming years, Rosendahl would always feel that the Camp Kearny visit was the most trying airship operation in which he had ever participated.[56]

A court of inquiry was convened quickly in the matter of the deaths of the two ground crewmen. President of the court was Captain Chester W. Nimitz (later fleet admiral). To Rosendahl, Nimitz's "calm, considerate approach was something I shall always remember. To me, the calming influence of this man was a great consolation. In later years, I saw those same fine characteristics displayed again and again. Chester W. Nimitz is one of the truly great characters who have served the U.S. Navy."[57]

The cause of the deaths was self-evident and no further actions were needed. It was an understatement to say that the tragedy at Camp Kearny was the fault of the inexperienced recruits comprising the ground crew because these young men had never seen an airship before the day they were asked to control it.

There was an occult backstory that Rosendahl kept private until years later when he inserted it into his unpublished memoir.

> There was one particular phase of the story of which San Diego officers could not have been aware, in any case. The trouble actually started well before. In preparation, I had submitted to the Department a list of requirements needed on the Pacific Coast to support and safeguard our contemplated operations. It was a modest list. But at a Departmental conference, I was told firmly to reduce the list radically or the trip would be called off. I yielded, though knowing we would be operating under handicaps with a ship still full of "bugs."[58]

In the end, Rosendahl stated publicly, "I am greatly grieved and shocked over the tragedy which attended the landing of the Akron at Camp Kearney. It is the first time a fatal accident ever has occurred in the landing of a navy dirigible."[59]

So much helium was valved off during the attempts to land that the ship's lift was reduced significantly, and her helium supply was so low that it prevented her from participating in the fleet exercises. There was no helium at Kearny, and the ship had to be lightened to make it to Sunnyvale. Eleven men were flown to Sunnyvale in two amphibian planes provided by NAS San Diego, and the two scout planes flew to Sunnyvale.[60]

As the *Akron* was being refueled, Admiral T. J. Senn and aides arrived to inspect the ship, followed shortly by Rear Admiral H. E. Yarnell and his aides. Inspections finished, the ship unmoored from her mast at 1139 and made for Sunnyvale, where thousands awaited her.

On the twelfth, the battle fleet, commanded by Admiral Frank Schofield, put to sea with over one hundred vessels. It was the largest assemblage of warships ever in the Pacific Ocean. The fleet was to maneuver off the coast until May 18, when it would proceed to its southern anchorage at San Pedro and San Diego. The only ship left behind in San Francisco was the *Patoka*, which was detached from the fleet to provide support to the *Akron*.

Arriving at Sunnyvale on the thirteenth, Rosendahl had difficulty making an immediate landing to their mast. The sun's heat had expanded the ship's helium sufficiently to make her so buoyant that the two-hundred-man ground crew could not handle her. After several unsuccessful attempts, Rosendahl backed off carefully to avoid a repeat of the Camp Kearny disaster. He delayed landing until sundown when the air was cooler, making the ship easier to handle.

On the ground, hoses were connected to the ballast tanks and once the ballast was at capacity, the ship's helium was replenished to bring her cells to 90 percent of their 6,500,000 cubic feet capacity. A margin of 10 percent capacity was maintained to allow for expansion of the gas while in flight.

Temporary grandstands had been erected for speakers, dignitaries, and invited guests for formal ceremonies on the fifteenth under the auspices of the Chamber of Commerce. The Navy was represented by Rosendahl and Rear Admiral William C. Cole, both of whom spoke. The *Akron*'s arrival was a historical event—the first use of the base by an airship—and Rosendahl proclaimed it the best field on the coast for that purpose.[61]

More was needed, however, before the base could become the permanent home of the USS *Macon*. The huge hangar was far from finished, and there were no surfaced roads on the base. "But the Akron's coming proved the base a reality, and it was that fact the San Francisco bay district celebrated today."[62]

Not only was the Sunnyvale base unprepared to serve as home to the *Macon*, she was a poor host to the men of the *Akron*. "We lived in tents when not flying, but that wasn't bad at all. Again, however, we found the mast located in a very unsatisfactory spot. These and many other annoyances were 'family affairs' within the Navy, and couldn't be publicly aired, but they made our West Coast venture pretty much of a nightmare."[63] Rosendahl never shared these feelings publicly. He and Moffett were of the same mind when it came to publicity for the LTA program, and the *Akron*'s appearance at Sunnyvale represented an excellent opportunity for widespread attention to the program.

While at Sunnyvale, awaiting orders from Admiral Schofield concerning the fleet exercises, Rosendahl granted numerous interviews, made public appearances, and participated in radio broadcasts—all intended to promote the LTA service. On the day the *Akron* arrived at Sunnyvale, Rear Admiral W. C. Cole, commandant of the Twelfth Naval District, spoke to the gathered crowd, telling them he visualized a day when commercial LTA craft would offer new means of transportation with this area of California serving as the Pacific Coast center of activity. Cole prophesied that four Navy airships like the *Akron*—or larger—would someday be based at NAS Sunnyvale and that "on the broad plane about it will be centered a trans-Pacific commercial airship activity."[64] He also held hope that the Sunnyvale base would be the beginning of a movement to make the San Francisco Bay the Pacific base of Navy operation.[65]

On May 15, 1932, Rosendahl flew south in an airplane to meet with Admiral Schofield, then on the USS *Pennsylvania* (BB-38) anchored off Long Beach harbor, to discuss any future activities for the *Akron*.[66] They worked out a schedule for press conferences and VIP flights, a mooring to the *Patoka*, and trips to Sacramento, Bakersfield, and Puget Sound.

As the time drew nearer for Rosendahl to leave airships and go to sea, some editorialists turned attention away from the physical strengths of the ships to the skill of their commanders—particularly Rosendahl. Few outside the Navy understood the wisdom of sending an airship officer back to sea duty, but Rosendahl understood the ways of the Navy, and he had made it clear already that he had no objection to a tour at sea.

During their May 15 meeting, Schofield told Rosendahl there would be no opportunity for the *Akron* to operate with the fleet. Later, however, the airship was included in an exercise with the Scouting Force.[67] While the Navy's Pacific Fleet maneuvers were secret, the press suggested that the biggest secret was if, when, and how the world's largest airship would try to locate the fleet. Rosendahl had been informed that the fleet would be operating within an area of 100 square miles.[68]

The fastest vessels of the fleet were the scout cruisers, and their mission was to sight the *Akron* before it found the battleships and other units of the fleet. It was expected that, once the airship spotted fleet vessels, it would launch its planes to attack and drive off the fleet. Countering this were the planes carried by the battleships, which would be on alert to intercept the *Akron*.[69]

The press had been informed that the *Akron* would depart Sunnyvale near sundown on June 1, but her flight plan was unannounced. Rosendahl said he would not decide on his course until departure time. It was known widely that weather was the strongest determinant of an airship's course, and aware of stormy conditions then prevailing along the coast, the press astutely predicted the airship would fly over the San Joaquin Valley. Given its departure time, it was certain that most of the trip would be made in darkness.[70]

The *Akron* departed Sunnyvale at 1740 on June 1 and headed south down the San Joaquin Valley to join the exercises to be conducted off Baja, California.[71] She was to join the Green forces searching for the "enemy" White forces. At 0500 on June 2, Rosendahl posted his lookouts and they began their search for the White fleet, eventually sighted along the western horizon at 1521. The *Akron* maneuvered to follow it.[72]

Rear Admiral William H. Standley, in command of the White force had never been convinced of the value of airships, but to cover his force, he staged something of an ambush for the *Akron*. Wanting to be prepared for whatever the airship might bring against him, he ordered half of his cruisers' Vought O2U seaplanes to be ready on their catapults for a launch within ten minutes' notice. Other planes would follow thirty minutes later. Thus, he had two flights of eight planes to throw at the *Akron*.[73]

Rosendahl did not think the White force would risk launching its seaplanes because the sea was rough, making landing difficult. Being cautious, Standley initially launched only two planes, which Rosendahl did not consider much of a threat.

On June 3, the *Akron* located the enemy cruisers again. Rosendahl positioned the airship between the sun and the surface ships, allowing him to track the fleet for fourteen minutes before he was spotted. Standley launched thirteen planes against the *Akron* within ten minutes of sighting her. Rosendahl took the airship higher into a cloud base where the attacking planes could not maintain their formation, foiling their plan to attack *en masse*.[74]

Consequently, the broken formation of planes swarmed about the airship, diving in simulated aerial combat. At 1535, the *Akron*'s logbook recorded, "Enemy plane attack repelled. No casualties."[75] No explanation for the claim was given, but only actual combat could determine the outcome.

Minutes later, at 1540, two O2Us made a quick dive-bombing run on the *Akron* before breaking off contact. After hiding in clouds for over half an hour, Rosendahl thought he had lost the remainder of the attackers, and he started to track the cruisers again when, at 1622, five O2Us emerged from the clouds to make a series of diving attacks on the *Akron*'s tail.[76]

Interpretation of this simulated combat was left to skilled observers. Opponents of dirigibles felt the *Akron* was an easy target to hit with machine gun fire and artillery, while advocates of the airships claimed that, because she carried non-flammable helium instead of hydrogen, she was not easy to shoot down, able to absorb heavy machine gun fire without destruction.

During these exercises, the *Akron* was deprived of one of her defensive assets—her small landplanes. When the ship left for the exercises,

Rosendahl left the planes on the ground at Sunnyvale. Thus, Standley's planes attacked the *Akron* unopposed. Had the *Akron* launched her planes to do combat with the attacking planes in simulated combat, the results would have been different but still left to interpretation.

Assessment of the *Akron*'s performance was complicated by the fact that no one in the Navy had yet determined the proper role for an airship in relation to the surface fleet. Lessons learned through experience by the Germans with their Zeppelins went unheeded. The *Akron* should have remained at greater distance from the enemy fleet and used her small scout/fighter planes both for protection and to extend the airship's reconnaissance range.

Opinions varied about the *Akron*'s performance. The cruiser commanders viewed her performance favorably, while officers of the Scouting Force believed their aerial attack would have destroyed the airship in actual combat.[77] Admiral Willard believed the *Akron* had performed well as a scout, but he believed the airship's destruction following her first contact was certain, especially if aircraft carriers were involved. He shared the opinion of some within the Navy that the sacrifice of an airship to gain valuable scouting information could be worth it.[78] The press rated the *Akron*'s performance well:

"In spite of clouds, rain squalls, and generally low visibility, the Akron is declared to have accomplished her mission with dispatch and efficiency, finding ships of the scouting force with ease in spite of efforts of planes from the surface craft to technically disable her. Details of her maneuvers with the surface craft, however, are being kept secret."[79]

By the end of the exercises, the airship had put in over sixty hours of operation over the Pacific in her first real test as a fleet scout.[80] The design of the exercise was flawed, however, from the standpoint of how best to utilize the airship.

Rosendahl later wrote, "We in the Akron were satisfied that we had succeeded well in the exercise and imagine our surprise when we got a copy of the report that was sent to Washington and learned the Akron had been strongly criticized."[81] In Admiral Willard's report to the chief of naval operations, he addressed the *Akron*'s vulnerability and registered complaints about the airship's need for nearby hangar facilities. He did not feel he could recommend further expenditures on close airships until they could demonstrate dependability under a range of circumstances.[82]

As an afterthought, Rosendahl added, "But what hurt most was the procession of material troubles. The water recovery apparatus was not holding up. Engines were giving trouble. One thing after another in our new ship needed correction. Our helium supply was meager. The operating spares were not sufficient. It was utter nonsense to expect the Akron to remain on the West Coast 'indefinitely' under such circumstances."[83]

Having the *Akron* remain on the West Coast permanently was precisely what some in the Navy wanted, but following the fleet exercises, the *Akron* needed a level of maintenance and repair that only NAS Lakehurst could provide.

The return to Lakehurst was a transition point in Rosendahl's career. This would be his last flight in command of the *Akron*. A resolution was submitted in the House of Representatives to award the Distinguished Flying Cross to Rosendahl for his significant contributions to the development of aviation.[84] The medal was not immediately forthcoming—he received it fifteen years later.

The *Akron* set out on her return trip to Lakehurst on the morning of June 11, 1932. Early in the flight, Rosendahl received a sign that the eastward flight would not be without complications. At 1425, at an altitude of 1,000 feet, the propeller on the No. 3 Engine carried away, leaving him to make the rest of the flight short one engine.[85]

Flying west to east entailed different technical considerations compared to flight from east to west. As experienced previously by the *Shenandoah*, one of the hurdles was getting the heavy airship over the mountains.

Flying toward the mountains from the west required climbing too soon. When the *Akron* had flown outbound from Lakehurst toward California, she had consumed 20 tons of fuel before climbing into the mountains. In the reverse direction, however, from California to the mountains of Phoenix, Arizona—a distance of only 700 miles—she had burned only 5 tons of fuel and thus was heavy.[86]

When the *Akron* reached Phoenix at 2359, Rosendahl was facing a 3,000-foot climb with his ship too heavy. He sailed around the area for a couple of hours while simultaneously burning fuel and dumping fuel to lighten the ship. At 3,000 feet, he was near pressure height and at risk of valving off precious helium that would be needed over the mountains.[87] Rosendahl decreased the ship's weight by about 4,000 pounds by having Harrigan and Young leave the airship in their scout planes. The pilots were instructed to follow the railroad to El Paso, where they would be picked up again by the *Akron*. When the *Akron* met up with the pilots at Pecos, however, Rosendahl was unwilling to take on the weight again, and he instructed them to fly their small planes back to Lakehurst on their own.[88]

Negotiating the mountains successfully had left Rosendahl with two problems: the ship had lost over a million cubic feet of helium due to automatic valve openings, and he had jettisoned a great deal of fuel in attempts to lighten the ship. He estimated that he had enough fuel to make it back to Lakehurst if he did not encounter severe weather, but not wanting to risk it, he decided to lay over at Parris Island, South Carolina, to refuel.

The layover was complicated by a poorly positioned mooring mast, the mooring circle was under water due to heavy rains, and the fuel ordered for the ship lacked "anti-knock" ingredients. Their departure for Lakehurst was delayed by a day.[89]

This was Rosendahl's last flight in the *Akron* and the last time he would command an airship. Speculation that he would receive command of the *Macon* proved wrong.

Rosendahl recalled, "It was a tremendous relief to get the ship back to Lakehurst and safely in the hangar. It had been a rugged venture, but one which pointed out weaknesses in our thinking on airship matters, as well as specific items to be corrected in the Akron itself, and in the coming sister ship, the Macon. All in all, it was undoubtedly the toughest 'shakedown' cruise that any airship ever went through."[90]

The arduous roundtrip journey had reinforced the notion that the great airships were heavily dependent on their massive hangars for missions of long duration. Further, the airships were far more secure flying over vast expanses of ocean than over land with highly variable terrain and air currents. Unknown to all, however, the *Akron* had flown her last scouting mission with the surface fleet.

It appeared certain that Dresel would assume command of the *Akron*, but Rosendahl met with Moffett to make his case for Wiley being the successor. Wiley had far more experience and greater knowledge, but Dresel had higher rank, and in the end, Moffett stuck to his policy of "rank over experience" and command fell to Dresel. The change of command ceremony took place on June 22, 1932, at Lakehurst.[91]

Following the change of command ceremony, the men of the *Akron*, who had served under Rosendahl, did not allow him to walk away immediately.

> I left Lakehurst with a memory that will always be with me. Upon the conclusion of the ceremonies, the enlisted men of the Akron presented me with a beautiful, custom-made sword. There was never another like it, nor will there ever be. It is the sword I carried for the rest of my active naval service. On the scabbard of this sword, in place of the regulation figures and markings, are an embossed monogram and an engraved replica of the Akron. It may be "non-regulation" in some respects, but to me it is priceless, for etched on the blade is the inscription: "To Lieutenant Commander Charles E. Rosendahl, First Commanding Officer, U. S. S. AKRON, From His Crew June 22nd, 1932."[92]

Rosendahl left the *Akron* with 4,184 "airship hours" in his log.[93]

Later, in a reflective moment, Rosendahl wrote, "But now my bargain was over. I had had the honor of flying the flight trials and of commanding our first really large airship. It was with mixed emotions that I turned over the command and set off to sea. In one way, it would be a relief, but in another I was sure my thoughts would occasionally stray back to Lakehurst and airships."[94]

The press had commented repeatedly that Rosendahl preferred service in the air while Dresel preferred the sea. In reality, both men appreciated the need for sea duty, not simply for promotion but to keep abreast of how the surface fleet operated. The press summarized Dresel's feelings: "Dresel favors the Navy policy of demanding a certain amount of sea duty for officers in specialized posts. 'The Navy can't permit too much specialization,' he says. 'Navy policy is always changing and is never written down. Officers cannot stay away from ships and sea for any great length of time for this reason.'"[95]

Airship command was not the only change taking place in mid-1932. At 0815 on June 30, the crew of the USS *Los Angeles* was mustered at quarters for a decommissioning ceremony. Among the changes taking place, Captain Harry E. Shoemaker was detached from the *Los Angeles* and assigned to the *Akron* as ComRATES. The reading of orders included the chief of naval operations' order of May 13, 1932, directing that the *Los Angeles* be decommissioned no later than June 30, 1932, to be docked in the shed at Lakehurst in custody of the commanding officer of the NAS.[96] Commander Frank C. McCord was assigned to the *Akron* as her prospective commanding officer.[97]

A newspaper published what read like a brief eulogy for the great airship: "The Los Angeles, once proud training ship of countless fliers in the Navy, tonight will rest in its old berth in the hangar, shorn of its engines, precious helium gas, even its name."[98] She was not the finest airship in the Navy, but she was a workhorse and served well as a training and development ship.

When it became clear that Rosendahl would not command the *Macon*, Lieutenant Commander Vincent A. Clarke, Jr. became a probable commander, but he died on August 11, 1932, of "blood poisoning" at age forty-one, following a two-day hospitalization at Mare Island Naval Hospital. Two weeks later, it was announced that Dresel would be the *Macon*'s first commander.[99]

Rosendahl's detachment from command of the *Akron* in June 1932 marked the end of an era that had begun at Lakehurst in April 1923. "It had been a period loaded with adventure and unusual experiences such as fate has never handed out to anyone else."[100] Returning to sea would be a relief from some of the stresses he had been enduring, but he wondered how the next chapter of his career would be written.

He traveled by train to the West Coast to join the *West Virginia*, then in harbor at San Pedro, California. The leisurely train ride offered him a transition period to slow his pace and change his thinking from airships to surface ships. He stopped off at Fort Worth to make the 28-mile trip to Cleburne to visit his mother and sister.

The trip was not without its moments of pleasurable excitement. Traveling westward from Fort Worth, the train stopped in the small town of Ranger to take on passengers. Through his window, he casually watched people on the platform coming and going, and his eye caught an attractive young lady who was bidding goodbye to a couple and their baby. Later, he visited the club car and found the woman sitting there, and his mind immediately wandered away from airships. As he boarded the train after a stop at El Paso, he found the same woman again in his sights, and this time, he spoke to her. That evening, she was his guest for dinner.[101] He did not know it at the time, but he had just dined with the future Mrs. Charles Rosendahl.

His new acquaintance was a "Texas girl" who was returning to California following a visit with her sister and new nephew in Ranger. When the *Akron* flew over that part of Texas a few weeks earlier, local newspapers had given a lot of attention to the airship's trek, both because of the Texas helium with which the ship was inflated and because the ship's captain—Rosendahl—had attended school in Texas and was appointed to the Naval Academy from the Cleburne-Fort Worth congressional district. As Rosendahl remembered the encounter, the young lady's sister had told her of having read the article and that it said he would be on board that train, which elicited the comment that "she wasn't interested in meeting any stiff-necked naval officer."[102] The young woman's first impression of Rosendahl on meeting him was not that of a "stiff-necked naval officer," but she thought he was probably a minister. Rosendahl's first impression of her was that she must be in the movies. She was actually a buyer for a large department store in Texas. "My mind was now indeed 'off airships,' and the Los Angeles area held other fascination for me than the U.S. Pacific Fleet."[103]

Rosendahl reported on board the USS *West Virginia* on July 2, 1932, as first lieutenant. Commissioned December 1, 1923, the *West Virginia* was then one of the latest battleships in the fleet. She was powerful, carrying a battery of 16-inch guns and four airplanes. "From the start she had been the pride of the Navy, and I shall never forget how her cofferdams, voids and doublebottom compartments were kept painted white inside, and immaculately free from rivet weeps, rust and dirt."[104] Rosendahl had responsibility, among other things, for the cleanliness, material upkeep, and maintenance of the ship, except for the engineering department, which belonged to the chief engineer.

The *West Virginia* was then the flagship of the Commander of Battleships, Battle Force, Vice Admiral J. R. P. Pringle, whom Rosendahl described as "a brilliant naval officer."[105] The *West Virginia* was commanded by Captain Walter S. Anderson with Commander Alan G. Kirk as his executive officer—both men having outstanding service reputations and both destined for prominent roles in World War II.

Rosendahl felt the ship's company was excellent throughout, and he concluded, "The Detail Officer in the Navy Department who had sent me to this outstanding combatant ship of the Fleet for my required sea duty had done me a great favor."[106]

He characterized Captain Anderson as a "doer and a driver" who "drove himself as hard as he did the ship and the ship's company, with results to show for it."[107] On first reporting to Anderson, Rosendahl said, "Captain, as you are aware, I have not done sea duty in a surface vessel for several years and may be a bit rusty. The one thing I can promise you is that I will work," to which Anderson replied, "Rosendahl, I know your record and what you have been doing in recent years. I am confident that you and I are going to get along well together, for the most I can ask of anyone is that he try."[108] As it turned out, Rosendahl and Anderson did get along well together.

Rosendahl liked to recall one anecdote relating to Anderson. "He likes to tell the story that I am one of two naval officers he ever advised not to work so hard."[109] Rosendahl learned a lot about the modern Navy afloat in those days and had an altogether happy cruise.

———

On the morning of April 4, 1933, as the *West Virginia* was cruising at sea, a Marine orderly came to Rosendahl and told him that the chief of staff wanted to see him aft on the quarterdeck. As Rosendahl approached, he noticed a serious look on Captain Snyder's face. Snyder told him, "We have a radio flash that the airship Akron is believed to have crashed at sea, but as yet we have no confirmation."[110]

Understandably, Rosendahl was stunned and preferred not to believe what he had just heard. He replied, "Captain, on numerous occasions at Lakehurst we had calls reporting that an airship had crashed, whereas check-up showed that the ship had merely dropped out of sight beyond a hill or into a cloud. That may be the case now."[111] Unfortunately, it was not. Shortly, verification was received that the Akron had been lost in the Atlantic off Barnegat on the New Jersey coast. At the time of the crash, the Akron was under the command of Commander Frank Carey McCord, who had relieved Dresel on January 3, 1933.

The Navy Department sent a message to Rosendahl on board the West Virginia, demanding a statement from him regarding the crash. He knew nothing beyond the fact that the airship was lost, and he preferred not to speculate. He was geographically remote from Lakehurst and not on the frontline of information gathering. Indeed, Navy officials were having difficulty obtaining reports from the crash scene. Eight hours after the crash, officials remained uncertain as to what had happened, as the few reports were fragmentary. Almost immediately, Rosendahl sent a radio message to the commandant of the Eleventh Naval District, stating that "the meagre reports so far available are insufficient to form an opinion as to the cause of the accident." In his judgment, the cause could not be passed "until complete and dispassionate study is made."[112]

He was in a helpless situation so far from Lakehurst, and memories of the crash of the Shenandoah must have flooded his mind as he tried to imagine the horrors of what had happened to the men on the Akron.

Rosendahl knew the entire crew, and many had served with him on the Shenandoah, the Los Angeles, and the Akron, and they had been through a lot together. He sent condolences to the bereaved families. Only three of the seventy-three men on board the Akron that day survived: Lieutenant Commander Herbert V. ("Doc") Wiley, the executive officer and the only officer to survive; Aviation Metalsmith Moody Erwin; and Boatswain's Mate Richard E. Deal. The crash of the Akron was the greatest disaster in aeronautical history to date.

Among the dead was Admiral Moffett, who had gone on board the *Akron* simply to enjoy the flight—a common practice for him. Rear Admiral Ernest J. King succeeded Moffett as chief of the Bureau of Aeronautics, but following Moffett's death, Rosendahl was on point, replacing Moffett as the program's greatest advocate. Rosendahl thought the loss of Moffett was far greater than the loss of the airship itself. His loss to the LTA program was incalculable.

From the inception of the LTA program, Moffett had been in the midst of a struggle inside the Bureau of Aeronautics between airplane advocates and airship advocates. The two opposing forces were vying constantly for government funding to keep their respective programs alive. It was not a level playing field, for the airplane advocates greatly outnumbered the airship advocates.

On the day of the *Akron* disaster, complaints were being aired in Congress about the huge expenditures for airships. Claiming that the U.S. had spent more than 20 million dollars on airships, Chairman Vinson of the House Naval Committee proclaimed that there would be no more big airships built—"we have built three and lost two."[113] He added that he had never been as enthusiastic about airships as some in the Navy.

Dr. Hugo Eckener in Germany was shocked to hear of the *Akron* disaster but commented, "No matter what happens, nothing will shake my complete faith in airships."[114]

On April 4, 1933, Secretary of the Navy Swanson ordered a court of inquiry into the circumstances surrounding the loss of the *Akron*.[115] The court convened at NAS Lakehurst on April 10. In addition to the three survivors, there were witnesses who provided technical testimony. The *Akron*'s flight history spoke for itself. Prior to January 3, 1933, she had made fifty-eight flights for a total of 1,274.3 flying hours.

Wiley, as the only surviving officer, was the first witness. A letter sent by Wiley to the Secretary of the Navy on April 6, reporting the incident, served as the basis for his narrative account.[116] As Wiley was testifying on April 10, word was being relayed from the Coast Guard vessel *Daphne* that the body of Admiral Moffett had been found three miles off Beach Haven, New Jersey, and that positive identification had been made. Examination of the body revealed that the admiral had been struck in the head by a heavy object at the moment of impact of the control car with the water. The death certificate listed the cause of death as "Intracranial Injury (Airship Crash) USS Akron."

As Wiley began his testimony before the court, it became clear quickly that it would be very difficult to piece together the events that led to the crash. With only three survivors from an airship 785 feet long, it was impossible for anyone to know what was happening at every point in the ship at a given time. Wiley's day one testimony produced more confusion than clarity, but after conferring with Deal and Erwin, he came to the conclusion that, as the ship was going down in the storm, the stern struck the water first. Deal recalled that the leading chief petty officer had shouted, "All hands forward!" to the keel personnel, leading to the conclusion that the chief had realized the stern was in the water. Wiley reported that the barometer could have dropped considerably, causing the altimeter to be in error by as much as 250 feet.[117]

On April 18 the fishing boat *Olympia* snagged her trawling nets on what was suspected to be part of the wreckage of the *Akron*. The salvage ship USS *Falcon* (AM-28) and two other ships used grappling hooks to pull pieces to the surface where it was confirmed that they had discovered the remains of the airship. Among the items recovered were a 35-foot section of duralumin, a mass of tangled wires, and a section of fabric on which was printed "Port Station No. 18 forward."[118] The control car and small fragments of the ship were found in a hundred feet of water, but no bodies were found.[119]

Examination of the lower stern fin showed its leading edge to be in good shape with damage limited to its rear underside. This confirmed that the ship, up by the bow, struck the water tail first and was dragged into the ocean.[120] It appeared that the ship was flying at altitudes much lower than anyone on board had realized, and this was likely due to faulty altimeter readings.

Five years later, Rosendahl offered a scientific explanation of the factors that led to the crash of the *Akron*. He was convinced that although the ship was lost during a storm, it was not directly because of the storm but due to a combination of factors, including a lack of sufficient weather information, an inability to ascertain the wind direction and velocity, and a deceptive altimeter which led to a lack of vertical maneuvering room. The tail-first immersion of the ship into the sea at a steep angle, with resultant collapse of part of the tail in the water, led to sudden retardation of the forward motion of the ship and the fatal crashing of the momentum of a 200-ton mass, moving ahead at over 100 miles per hour against the unyielding surface of the sea.[121]

> The present-day instrument used by aircraft to tell their altitude is fundamentally but a form of the aneroid barometer, graduated in linear units rather than units of pressure. For each thousand feet of altitude above sea level, the atmospheric pressure decreases at the rate of about "one inch of mercury." Should it remain on the ground during the passage of a low-pressure area that reduced the barometric pressure 1 inch, the helpless altimeter, actuated as it is simply by atmospheric pressure change, would falsely indicate 1000 feet altitude, although it had actually not been off the ground.
>
> Never was a "non-barometric" altimeter more desperately needed than during the Akron's last journey. When the airship approached the storm center, the lowest recorded surface pressure there was at least 32 one-hundredths of an inch less than when she departed from Lakehurst. Hence, the ship's altimeters indicated an altitude of at least 320 feet greater than the actual height above the surface. Furthermore, under the existent conditions near or at the very storm center, the actual pressure may have been even two- or three-tenths of an inch lower than any recorded value. So it is certain that when the Akron's altimeters read 1,600 feet during the last three minutes of the ship's existence, her actual height could not have been more than 1,280 feet and may possibly have been only 1,000 feet—surely not much maneuvering room at night for an 800 foot ship in rough air.[122]

Following the *Shenandoah* disaster, opponents of the LTA program had predicted the end of airships, but the emergence of the *Akron* kept the program alive. With the loss of the *Akron*, similar predictions were being made, but the *Macon* was in the wings to keep the program alive.

136

FAR AWAY PLACES

Rosendahl had enjoyed a wonderful working relationship with Admiral Moffett as chief of the Bureau of Aeronautics, but he would have to find his way with his new chief—Rear Admiral Ernest J. King. Rosendahl was aware that King had been portrayed at times as "a wholly hard-boiled individual with time only for big projects and principles, and none for individuals or minority matters. I am happy to be able from my own personal contacts with this great naval officer, to dispel that notion."[123] Rosendahl got to know King through numerous interactions when he was in Washington, and he found King to be "sympathetic and open-minded on the subject of airships, and most willing to listen to the airshipper's side of the case."[124]

Rosendahl was called to testify before a Joint Congressional Committee of five senators and five representatives investigating dirigible disasters. Fortunately for the Navy's LTA program, the committee acknowledged that airships had a special utility as scouts and that the Navy should continue to develop them. Recognizing that there had been problems with forecasting and reporting of weather, the committee recommended that four general maps be generated daily instead of the usual two.[125]

Because the Navy's program had lost so many assets and lives—and at great expense—many in the military and within the government realized that the airship era was coming to an end. Rosendahl was not among them—he was a true believer who had invested his entire adult professional career in the LTA program, and he continued to fight for it. For the moment, however, the Navy's hopes of keeping the program alive rested with the *Macon*.

On December 22, 1933, Rosendahl was notified by Admiral Leahy, chief of the Bureau of Navigation, that the bureau planned to reassign him to duty in the Aeronautic Organization about June or July 1934.

ZR-1, constructed inside Hangar No. 1 at NAS Lakehurst, is shown here leaving the hangar for the first time September 4, 1923 (although the print is dated October 1923). (NH 92615)

USS *Shenandoah* (ZR-1) in Hangar No. 1 at NAS Lakehurst. (NH 44092)

Taken during construction, this interior view of the Shenandoah shows the 10-inch-wide catwalk that ran the length of the ship and was used for the crew's movement. Bunks are shown in the foreground. Also visible are fuel and oil tanks. (NH 82266)

Interior view taken during construction shows gasoline fuel tanks, each with a 113-gallon capacity. (NH 82264)

USS *Shenandoah* (ZR-1) moored to the high mast at NAS Lakehurst circa 1924–1925. (NH 98227)

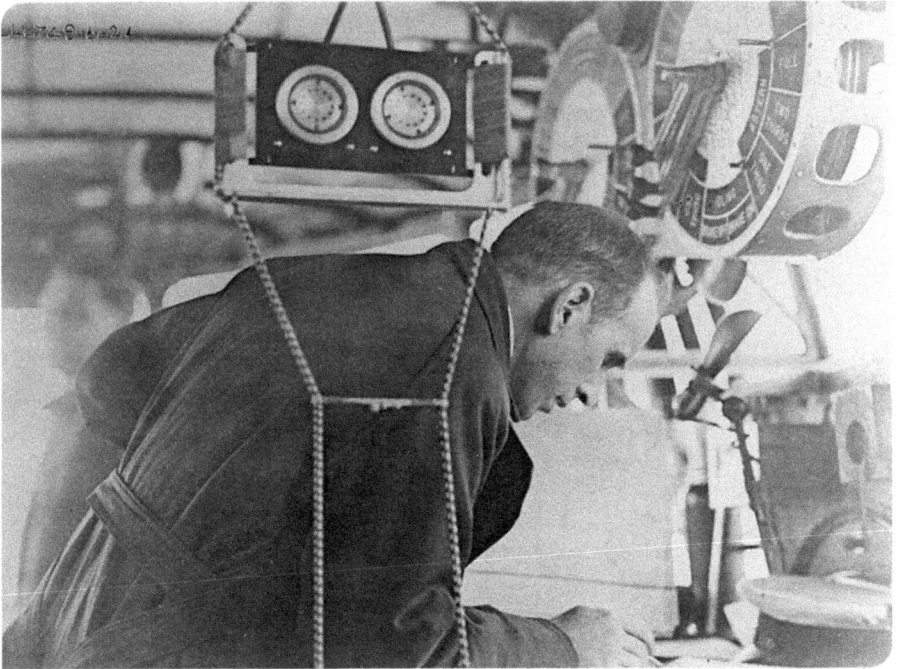

Lieutenant Commander Zachary Lansdowne, commanding officer of USS *Shenandoah*, in the control car, laying out a course. (NH 85128)

Lieutenant Commander Charles E. Rosendahl, circa 1925. (NH 46109)

USS *Shenandoah* (ZR-1) moored to the mast on the airship tender USS *Patoka* (AO-9). Circa 1924–1925. (NH 98222)

Aerial view of the crash of the *Shenandoah* on September 3, 1925, in southern Ohio. Shown here is the after section of the airship surrounded by spectators and their vehicles. (NH 98997)

Aerial view of the bow section of the crashed *Shenandoah*. This section contained Rosendahl and free-ballooned to its landing site. (NH 98998)

LZ-126/ZR-3 is shown entering Hangar No. 1 for the first time following her transatlantic flight from Germany, October 15, 1924. (NH91149)

USS *Los Angeles* (ZR-3) flying over Manhattan, New York City, circa 1924–1932. (NH 944)

USS *Los Angeles* (ZR-3) moored to USS *Patoka* (AO-9) off Panama during Fleet Problem XII, circa February 1931. (NH 73285)

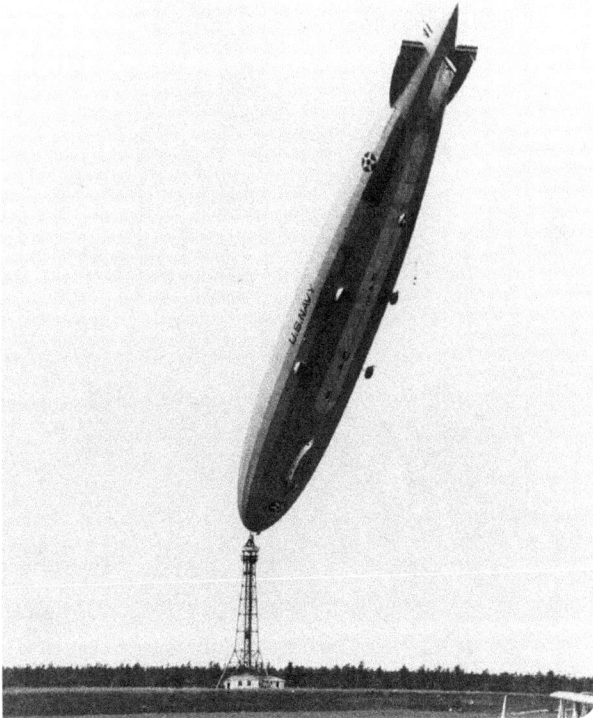

One of the most iconic images from the LTA program shows the out-of-control "nose stand" by the *Los Angeles* on August 25, 1927. (NH 84569)

USS *Los Angeles* (ZR-3) approaching USS *Saratoga* (CV-3) for a landing on her deck, January 27, 1928. (NH 63087)

USS *Los Angeles* (ZR-3) (left) shares Hangar No. 1 at NAS Lakehurst with the hydrogen-filled *Graf Zeppelin* (LZ-127), August 7, 1929. (NH 69168)

USS *Akron* (ZRS-4) moored to stub mast at NAS Lakehurst, June 15, 1932. (UA Archives Goodyear)

On May 11, 1932, the *Akron* was attempting to land at Camp Kearny, California, when a sudden gust of wind took the ship aloft. Three men failed to release the handling line before they were lifted over 200 feet into the air. Charles Cowart was the only one to survive as he found a way to hold onto the line until pulled up into the airship. Nigel Fenton and Robert Edfall fell to their deaths. The first two images from the left show Cowart holding on as he is pulled into the airship; frame at far right shows Cowart following his rescue. The third image from the left shows Fenton and Edfall clinging to the line moments before falling to their deaths. (NH 84169)

Rear Admiral William A. Moffett. This photo was taken a few days before his death in the crash of the *Akron* off Barnegat Light on the coast of New Jersey, April 4, 1933. (NH1208)

USS *Macon* (ZRS-5) in flight with two Curtis F9C-2 "Sparrowhawk" airplanes below her. The airplanes are preparing to "land" on the *Macon* by using the device on their superior wing to hook onto the trapeze device lowered from inside the airship (shown) prior to being hoisted into the ship. (NH 80-G-441983)

Lieutenant D. Ward Harrington has hooked his Curtiss F9C-2 Sparrowhawk onto the trapeze device of the *Macon* in preparation for being hoisted into the hangar of the airship. (NH 80-G-441979)

Hindenburg (LZ-129) moored to the mast at NAS Lakehurst, May 20, 1936. (NH 57945)

Hindenburg's stern protrudes from Hangar No. 1 at NAS Lakehurst. (Rosendahl Box 18 – Fl -003n)

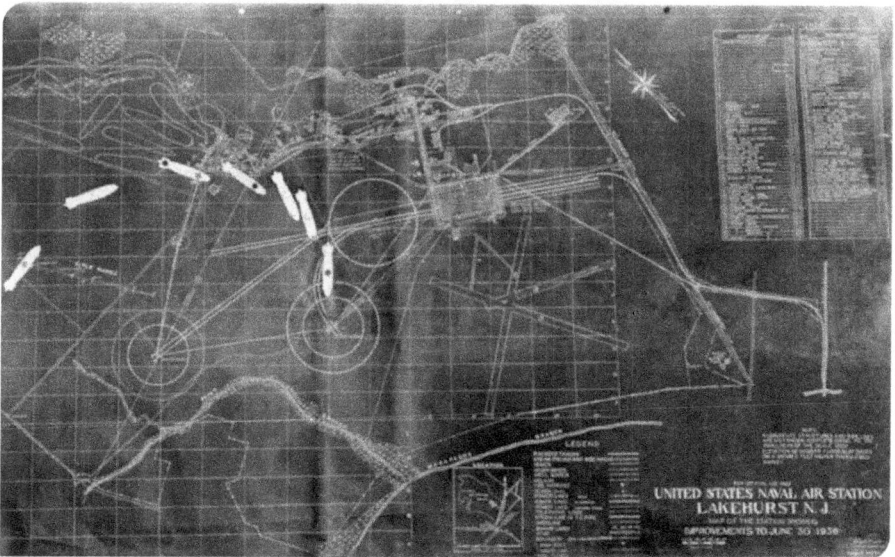

Chart used by the court of inquiry investigating the *Hindenburg* disaster showing the approach of the ship to the mooring mast where the destruction occurred on May 6, 1937. (NH 57957)

Photo of shadow of *Hindenburg* passing over New York city on her way to NAS Lakehurst for the final time. (Photo by Peter Belin; provided courtesy of his son, Harry Lammot Belin.)

Photo of the gigantic Hangar No. 1 at NAS Lakehurst as seen from the *Hindenburg* on her final flight. (Photo by Peter Belin; provided courtesy of his son, Harry Lammot Belin.)

As *Hindenburg* approached the mooring mast, the ground crew is seen gathering at the landing flag in anticipation of manning the handling lines once dropped. (Photo by Peter Belin; provided courtesy of his son, Harry Lammot Belin.)

Hindenburg preparing to land at NAS Lakehurst on May 6, 1937. She was preparing to moor to the stub mast (shown). (NH 57946)

Series of photos showing the fiery end of the Hindenburg. (NH 57965, 57966, 59773, and 57964).

A photographer caught the faces of three people clearly in shock during the fiery demise of the *Hindenburg*. George Grant (far left) had jumped from a window onto the loamy soil only to have another passenger do the same and land on his back. A Navy bluejacket ground crewman (second from left) assisted Grant to his feet and escorted him to the base of the mooring mast where Jean Rosendahl was standing. He entrusted Grant to her while he returned to assist other passengers and crew. (Charles E. Rosendahl collection)

Burned wreckage of *Hindenburg* after the fire had raged for three hours. (NH 57972)

On June 1, 1937, Dr. Hugo Eckener commended the Lakehurst personnel for their actions during the *Hindenburg* disaster. (NH 57958)

Court of inquiry proceedings into the cause of the *Hindenburg* crash met on May 27, 1937, at the NAS Lakehurst and were held as a joint effort of American and German experts. Seated at the far left of the image is Commander Charles Rosendahl; seated at the table in the far right, from right to left, are Ludwig Durr next to Dr. Hugo Eckener. (NH 57961)

German Lieutenant Colonel Joachim Breithaupt placed a wreath at the door of the American Legion Chapel on NAS Lakehurst on May 31, 1937, in memory of those who lost their lives in the crashes of the USS *Akron*, USS *Macon*, and the *Hindenburg*. (NH 57960)

THE NAVY'S LAST GREAT RIGID AIRSHIP

On February 15, 1934, Rosendahl was promoted to the rank of commander,[1] and in March, he was given command of NAS Lakehurst, replacing Lieutenant Commander Jesse Kenworthy. Lieutenant Commander Herbert V. Wiley took command of the USS *Macon*, and Commander Alger H. Dresel was elevated to command of NAS Sunnyvale.[2]

Rosendahl was leaving sea duty a year early to return to aeronautical service—a change in Navy policy supported by Admiral King. A member of the joint congressional committee, who had recommended changes in the Navy policy regarding sea duty for aviators, commented, "I am glad the department has made this move. It will enable Rosendahl, who is one of the foremost experts on lighter-than-air craft to continue his studies and researches in his chosen field. He will have an opportunity to perform much for the service and for the advancement of aircraft."[3]

To the press, there seemed to be some sense of "symmetry" to having Rosendahl and Wiley return to the LTA service simultaneously. With real enthusiasm, Rosendahl proclaimed, "Doc Wiley and I are both coming back with our fighting togs on. . . . Saw Doc and he is in fine shape. You'll see things hum on the Macon when he gets hold."[4]

When he assumed command of NAS Lakehurst, he was still a bachelor, but occupying the large brick quarters assigned to the commanding officer brought with it a taste of domestication. The station commander was not provided with a cook or housekeeper to assist with running his quarters. On his own, he engaged a "capable colored steward named Clarence." Clarence, his wife, and "two cute chubby little daughters" occupied a small guest house that went with Rosendahl's quarters. Rosendahl later recalled that, on the first day of school, the station school bus stopped to pick up Clarence's daughters. As they boarded the bus, the driver asked who they were. "Beaming happily, they replied: 'We're Captain Rosendahl's little girls.' Seems I had acquired part of a family at least, and in a hurry. But that was only part of the story."[5]

While he was commander of the *Akron*, Rosendahl had been presented with a Norwegian wolfhound named Bellau. "Bellau guards the executive mansion where for the first time in his varied career, Rosendahl is able to hang up his fine paintings and etchings and really keep house."[6] He settled into his new quarters surrounded by his keepsakes from his LTA days: dishes that had come over from Friedrichshafen on the *Graf Zeppelin*'s first trip; a pair of binoculars, cut clear in two, which had fallen from the control car of the *Shenandoah* during its fatal crash; a photograph of Rosendahl alongside Henry Ford and Admiral Moffett; a tattered piece of the *Shenandoah*'s flag; a piece of the *Akron*'s duralumin girder; numerous original paintings of airships; and an autographed etching of Count Zeppelin made by Hugo Eckener's brother shortly before the count's death.[7] What had the appearance of a small museum was but a room full of memories for Rosendahl.

Rosendahl returned to Lakehurst filled with a youthful enthusiasm for what lay ahead for the LTA program. He was sought after widely as a speaker on LTA topics, and the press turned to him frequently for stories. He had been in his new role barely a month when the press approached him again about the *Akron* incident—as if time since the crash had given him new insights while the remains of the ship had lain under 80 feet of water for over a year. He chose to repeat the combination of factors that he believed had led to the crash but added no new insights.

Rosendahl used the press to send a hopeful message to his friends in Akron, Ohio. He claimed LTA was not dead, but that development was proceeding slowly but steadily. He suggested that a story was soon to break, which would prove that the Navy Department was not discouraged about the airship situation and still had confidence in its future. Rosendahl had been flying back and forth between Lakehurst and Washington frequently for weeks to press his case for the LTA program, and he was noted to be "jubilant" as he returned to NAS Lakehurst on July 27, as if he had won a victory, but he was not yet free to discuss it.[8]

Approximately one hundred officers were at the NAS in July 1934 engaged in LTA training similar to that of the inaugural class, only now, they occupied a new brick barracks. Several of their number had been sent to Germany to train under Dr. Hugo Eckener.

The man in charge of training at this time was Lieutenant Commander F. W. Reichenderfer, who was considered the Navy's number one aerologist. Described as a quiet, serious-faced man, he laughingly referred to himself as the "principal." Rosendahl and Reichenderfer were considered a great team, and the claim had been made that if the two of them had been on board the *Akron*, the crash would never have happened.[9]

A couple of months later, Rosendahl made an announcement that ended any hopes of getting the *Los Angeles* flight-worthy—she had been deemed unfit for service. Trying to get some use from her, she was being reconditioned for experimental purposes, specifically for making weather tests. Rosendahl planned for the ship to be fastened to a mooring mast, fully manned, to study her reaction to weather under various operating loads. "Her motors will hum, her silvery sides will feel the force of the elements, but 'unfit for service,' she will never again take flight."[10]

NAS Sunnyvale was now the permanent home to the Navy's only remaining large rigid airship—the USS *Macon*—under the command of Dresel until Wiley's tour at sea ended. The *Macon* was not waiting on Wiley, however. She left Sunnyvale on April 20, 1934, on an arduous 54.5-hour cross-country flight to Opa-locka, Florida, to participate in fleet exercises in the Caribbean. Because of the *Akron*'s transcontinental experiences, Dresel was aware of the challenges ahead of him—navigating through mountain passes with strong air currents and sailing over mountains at altitudes unusual for airships.

Even knowing what to expect, the journey proved to be rough on the airship's structure. The *Macon* had lifted off at 0937 and was traversing the San Gorgonio Pass between Capazon and Indio, California, by 1645 when she encountered extremely turbulent air.[11] Moments later, the ship was above pressure height, with all eight engines at standard speed. Dresel pumped 770 pounds of fuel overboard to gain extra buoyancy, followed about two hours later by dumping additional fuel. The ship arrived over Phoenix at 2300, where she circled until daylight on April 21 to negotiate the mountains between Phoenix and Dragoon safely.

Dresel made it past the mountains without difficulty, but at 1140 over Van Horn, Texas, they encountered turbulent air that, by the second day, turned into extremely violent gusts with the *Macon* rising and falling at rates of 24 to 36 feet per second.[12] At 1215, Dresel received a report in the control car that the ship had a broken girder at Frame 17.5 with two others buckled.[13] Chief Boatswain's Mate Robert Davis, who had been near that point when the powerful gust struck the ship, discovered one of the broken diagonal girders and ran forward quickly to summon a repair crew. The damage was attributed to stresses resulting from the violent gusts to the ship around noon. As temporary repairs were completed within half an hour, signs of buckling in other girders started to appear.[14] With the damage she incurred, the *Macon* was fortunate to have made it through Texas without crashing, and with the turbulent weather behind her, she moored at Opa-locka safely at 1916 on April 22, 1934.[15]

From Opa-locka, Dresel sent a message to Garland Fulton describing the ship's damage. Fulton contacted Dr. Arnstein in Akron, Ohio, with the news, and a foreman and several mechanics were dispatched to Florida, where they, in conjunction with the *Macon*'s crew, spent nine days strengthening the temporary repairs that had been made in flight.[16]

The significance of the fleet exercises was played out in the press as much was hanging on the *Macon*'s performance. Headlines read, "Airship's Value to Fleet Will Be Known Soon,"[17] "Macon's Caribbean Flight to Decide Airship Policy: Fleet Maneuver Will Determine If Government Will Construct More Dirigibles,"[18] and "Macon's Worth to Be Studied."[19]

The *Macon* left Opa-locka on the morning of May 5, 1934, to join the fleet in the Caribbean. Following what was becoming standard practice, two F9C airplanes were taken on board once the *Macon* was airborne.

In Exercise M, there were two opposing forces—the Blue fleet and the Gray fleet. The Gray fleet—the enemy—had seized Puerto Rico and the Virgin Islands. The task of the Blue fleet was to traverse the Panama Canal, destroy the Gray fleet, and retake the islands. The *Macon* was assigned to the Blue fleet, and on May 5, after negotiating thunderstorms southeast of Jamaica, she was approximately halfway between the Canal

Zone and Kingston, Jamaica, where she was ordered to begin a search to the northeast.

At 0300 on the sixth, the ship flew over a fleet submarine, and at 0340 she sighted four enemy destroyers, followed at 0504 by the sighting of a battleship off her starboard bow. At 0532, she changed course, maneuvering to avoid a rain squall before resuming her course. After sighting three destroyers at 0657, Dresel launched Trapnell in his fighter landplane for closer scouting. His plane was recovered at 0714. About half an hour later, a heavy cruiser was sighted.[20]

At 0802, Kivette was released in his plane to investigate an enemy cruiser that had been sighted at 0745. He was away from the airship for only 23 minutes. At 0845, two fighter land planes were launched from the *Macon* to scout ahead of the ship. The two planes returned to the *Macon* to refuel at 1005, and five minutes later, the ship was attacked by six airplanes that had been launched from the USS *Lexington* (CV-2),[21] which was spotted a minute later on the port beam, twelve miles distant.

The *Macon* now found herself in the situation many LTA opponents had predicted would bring about her destruction—sighted from surface vessels and attacked by airplanes sent to intercept her. "The carrier pilots had a field day buzzing around the big airship, 'shooting it down.'"[22] Because this was a training exercise and not actual combat with live ammunition, it was up to an umpire to decide if the *Macon* had been shot down. Lieutenant Donald M. Mackey was an umpire on board the *Macon*, and he ruled that the airship had been destroyed.[23] The *Macon* was instructed to continue her operations under the guise of "ZRS-6."

The *Macon* now needed permanent repairs to her girders, and Dresel was eager to return to Sunnyvale. If the fleet exercises in the Caribbean had been intended to establish a definitive role for airships working with the surface fleet, they had failed to do so. The official report of the *Macon*'s performance in the fleet exercises was unfavorable. The *Macon* returned to Sunnyvale on May 18 following an uneventful homeward flight, where she remained grounded for a month while undergoing repairs.

Rosendahl wrote of this time, "The airship situation in the Navy was then, as always, confused. I found myself in the midst of a tense struggle to keep airships alive and get them fair recognition. That meant many extra hours devoted to the cause."[24] The *Macon*'s unsatisfactory performance with the fleet in the Caribbean led to more trouble for the LTA program.

"On the East Coast, the airship picture was confined to Lakehurst, and it too was a bleak one. There we had only a few assorted, obsolete blimps and a mere handful of officers and enlisted men. Our complement of faithful civil service employees had been whittled down to the irreducible minimum. Our appropriated funds were the very least on which the Station could exist. We were constantly plagued by threats that Lakehurst would be closed up completely."[25]

Rosendahl considered Rear Admiral King, chief of the Bureau of Aeronautics, to be one bright spot in the gloomy LTA picture, "[b]ut what he could do for the struggling airship cause was tempered by certain practical considerations." King and Rosendahl were faced with the growing pains of the naval airplane arm, which lacked universal acceptance within the Navy. "On top of that, the negative attitude displayed towards airships in other places in the Navy Department made it doubly hard. Also, whatever the intentions and desires of their own Chief, anti-airship men in the lower echelons of the Bureau could continue to impede lighter-than-air. A difficult situation faced anyone interested in airships."[26]

Rosendahl's chief interest in returning to Lakehurst was to explore opportunities for airships to prove their worth.

> As an officer of the Line, my future did not depend at all on airships. There were plenty of other interesting opportunities for a Line officer, but I was convinced that airships had potentialities. I hoped that during this sojourn at Lakehurst, the Navy would finally make up its mind on the matter. At that point, wholehearted acceptance of airships would have been too much to expect; an honest determination to give the craft a chance would have been enough.[27]

Things were changing in the second half of 1934, both for the *Macon* and for Rosendahl.

The *Macon* had not proved her worth yet to the surface fleet, and many in the Navy felt the airship program was running out of time.

Previously, when one of the great rigids crashed, another one was waiting in the wings to keep the program alive, but now they were down to their last airship. In June 1934, Lieutenant Commander Herbert V. Wiley took over command of the *Macon* from Dresel, who assumed command of NAS Sunnyvale—renamed "Moffett Field."

This change of command was regarded widely throughout the LTA service as a positive move. Wiley was the single most experienced airship officer in the Navy at this point, and he, like Rosendahl, was a true believer in LTA flight and understood that the survival of the entire LTA program rested with him and the *Macon*. He made it a priority to investigate the incident that occurred over Texas that had led to the problem at Frame 17.5 and to examine the state of the repairs that had been made at Opa-locka. Wiley examined the damaged areas of the ship with Lieutenant Calvin Bolster, the ship's construction officer, and it was their assessment that major permanent repairs were needed. Dresel had expressed confidence in the quality of the repairs made in Florida. There had been no evidence of movement in the repaired areas during the return flight to Sunnyvale. Still, he recommended cautiously and wisely "that the entire question of fin strength should be carefully investigated in order that any possibility of failure in this portion of the ship in the future may be prevented."[28]

Captain Frank R. McCrary, assistant chief of the Bureau of Aeronautics, sent Wiley a letter on July 24 addressing the issue surrounding Frame 17.5. He reported that an analysis conducted by the Navy in conjunction with the experts at the Goodyear Zeppelin company had found no explanation for the failure. McCrary told Wiley that there was justification for reinforcing parts of Frame 17.5 along with certain parts of the fins themselves, but in the meantime, the ship's structure was considered strong enough for the *Macon* to fly over the ocean. He said that the work should not interfere with the operating schedule of the airship but should be done when opportunities arose and at the commanding officer's discretion.[29]

King, Rosendahl, and Wiley supported anything which could enhance the *Macon*'s utility to the surface fleet. In this regard, Wiley worked well with his officers, and one of his more creative thinkers was Harold

Miller, one of the landplane pilots. Miller had suggested that, once the planes had been stowed in flight, the landing gear be removed to make room for an accessory fuel tank that would give the small planes thirty extra gallons of fuel, which would increase their flying time by an hour and a half. This worked so well that it became routine practice.

Miller also considered that the practice of sending the pilots out in pairs only burned excessive fuel and exhausted the pilots. Further, the second plane contributed nothing to a scouting run. He and Wiley devised a plan whereby two planes were launched simultaneously, but one flew on one side of the airship while the other flew on the opposite. The idea gained momentum as other pilots and officers contributed to the plan.

The ship's tactical officer developed a plan whereby the ship would hold whatever the course was at a speed of 60 knots. The pilots would double the speed on a 60-degree angle and go up so that the three of them were progressing on a line at all times. They always had a straight line, and anytime they wanted to go back to the ship, no matter what side they were on, the pilot would turn 90 degrees and hold the course and he would intersect. The theory worked well and it created a tremendous 400-mile scouting front.[30]

The *Macon* began experiments with a new radio homing device to guide the planes back to the ship.

With significant improvements to the ship, her airplanes, and her electronic gear, the Navy needed an opportunity to showcase itself. An opportunity arose in the summer of 1934. It was a peaceful demonstration that would closely resemble an actual military scouting exercise. It was known that President Roosevelt would be on vacation on board the heavy cruiser USS *Houston* (CA-30) somewhere in the Pacific Ocean. In a letter to Wiley, King suggested that it could be of use to the program if the president sighted the airship during his journey. The *Houston*'s travel itinerary could be tracked through newspapers.

In his letter, King stated that the position of the president on airship matters would have far-reaching importance from both naval and commercial standpoints, and if he could be brought to the point where he showed interest in airships, it would be very fortunate. King suggested that Wiley arrange the *Macon*'s flight itinerary for July and August to operate in areas where it would likely be sighted from the *Houston*.[31]

The president and several family members embarked on a historic 13,000-mile cruise in July 1934. They sailed from Annapolis, Maryland, and down the Chesapeake Bay on the destroyer USS *Gilmer* (DD-233) to meet the heavy cruiser USS *Houston*. The Roosevelts transferred to the *Houston* for the remainder of their trip as the press corps covered them from the USS *New Orleans* (CA-32). The pair of ships made for Puerto Rico and Haiti prior to entering the Panama Canal, thus making Roosevelt the first U.S. president to traverse the canal while in office.[32]

After the cruisers exited the Panama Canal, they made for Isla de Cocos and then to Clipperton Island. Wiley used the published departure and arrival times for the cruisers to estimate their speed, and he knew they were scheduled to leave the area of Clipperton Island in the afternoon of July 17. Lieutenant "Scotty" Peck, the *Macon*'s navigator, plotted a course that would take the *Macon* to a point 100 miles ahead of the cruisers' estimated position by 1000 on July 19.[33]

Wiley believed that intercepting the ships in the open Pacific Ocean would be a good test of the *Macon*'s scouting abilities in addition to making a favorable impression on the president and the Navy. The act simulated a combat operation because it required the *Macon* to gather intelligence on the locations of the targeted cruisers and to intercept them using that intelligence in combination with the physical and electronic assets available to the airship while tracking an enemy that was unaware it was targeted.

The *Macon* unmoored from the mobile mast at Moffett Field at 0925 on July 18, and at 0950, cruising at an altitude of 1,800 feet, she took on board two landplanes—one piloted by Lieutenant H. B. Miller and the other by Lieutenant (jg) F. N. Kivette. The next day, at 1032 and 1041, respectively, Miller and Kivette were launched in their planes in search of the cruisers. At 1145 they sighted two cruisers off their port beam, 20 miles distant. The planes were now 40 miles ahead of the airship. Five minutes later, they made positive identification of the *Houston* and the *New Orleans*.[34]

The general idea for the *Macon* to intercept the *Houston* was Admiral King's, but Wiley and his officers developed the details of the encounter that unfolded.

The plan created by Wiley and Miller called for two pilots to drop a number of materials to the president. There were two identical water-proof bags—one for each pilot to drop. Each bag contained the latest issue of *Time* magazine, newspapers of the date the ship left Sunnyvale, and a sealed envelope addressed to the *Houston*'s mail clerk containing a note of instruction, eight mail covers, and money for the postage for the covers.[35] Members of the *Macon*'s crew had put about twenty self-addressed letters in the bag. It was well known that Roosevelt was an avid philatelist, and all knew that he would know how to handle the covers that were dropped to him. Among the letters were those to Eleanor Roosevelt, Captain W. B. Woodson of the *Houston*, Herbert Wiley, Harold "Min" Miller, and others.[36]

Each waterproof bag had about two hundred feet of line attached to it and, with difficulty, the pilots held on with one hand as they made their approach before dropping them.[37] Both bags ended up in the ocean. The cruisers went dead in the water, and the *Houston* put over a motor whale-boat to retrieve the bags. When the bags were dropped, the *Macon* was not in sight, but she came into view within half an hour to reboard her planes. Even as the planes were landing, two messages were being received from the *Houston*: "The president compliments you and your planes on your fine performance and excellent navigation [time of transmission] 1210," and "Well done and thank you for the papers. The president 1245."[38]

Wiley had obtained permission from his superiors for the long flight out over the ocean, but he had not informed them of his intentions, and this became a problem for Wiley as reporters filed their stories from the *New Orleans* by radio and the stories hit the streets. The angry, booming voice of ComBatFor filled the *Macon*'s radio room, wanting to know if the reports were true—had the *Macon* made contact with the *Houston* and delivered mail to her, and if so, by whose authority? An immediate reply was demanded. Wiley realized that some within the Navy would regard his achievement as nothing more than a "stunt," and he was worried that the episode could interfere with his scheduled promotion to full commander, due in 1935.

Permissions aside, what Wiley and the *Macon* had done was truly remarkable. They made a plan, gathered intelligence, used deductive reasoning, and executed superb navigation to intercept a ship at sea. Wiley had the full respect of his officers and crew, who understood that he was doing all he could to prove and promote the airship. Not everyone in the Navy saw it that way.

The chief of Naval Operations, Admiral W. H. Standley, demanded a written explanation. Wiley submitted his letter of explanation from Moffett Field on July 25 under the subject of "Operations of U. S. S. Macon, 18-21 July 1934; Contact with U. S. S. Houston." He started by recounting the events of the flight that day and followed with a detailed explanation:

> Since the primary mission of rigid airships is long-range scouting to obtain information and transmit it more quickly than surface vessels can, the commanding officer has been observing published reports of ships at sea with the idea of conducting scouting operations which offer typical war-time missions. Although the problem most generally presented is one of a ship en route from Hawaii to the United States or the Panama Canal, the cruise of the Houston offered the same problem on a reverse course at a sufficient distance to demonstrate the ability of the rigid airship for this use. . . . The reason for making the decision was therefore the presentation of a typical scouting problem, an opportunity to practice scouting problems with airplanes attached to the ship, and a demonstration of the ability to obtain information of a surface force a long distance at sea within twenty-four hours . . . The Commanding Officer believes that such exercises are of inestimable value in developing the efficiency of the airship and demonstrating its worth for naval scouting.[39]

It was unfortunate that the major response from the Navy focused on violations of protocol rather than the remarkable achievement by the *Macon*. This had been the finest example yet of how an airship could perform scouting activities over the open ocean. Rosendahl must have been pleased, although there was never any personal or professional communication between him and Wiley about the matter. There were no adverse sequelae to Wiley's demonstration with the *Macon*.

A month later, Rosendahl and Heinen visited the *Macon* to observe advances being made in scouting procedures. In a training exercise, the airship was to locate and track the cargo transport ship SS *Manini* and the luxury liner SS *Lurline*. Both men were impressed with the efficiency with which the exercise was conducted.

During his October 1934 appearance in California, Rosendahl had the attention of the press because of who he was, and he used the opportunity to advance his support of military and commercial LTA flight. As he was leaving Lakehurst, he told Navy officers that he approved a proposal that the federal government appropriate $17 million for a worldwide commercial air service.[40] A week later, he told the press that commercial air service to the Far East was logical and perfectly safe. In support, he offered the experience of the *Graf Zeppelin* that had been traveling over the Atlantic Ocean between Germany and South America for many months without accident.[41] He urged the government to build four new airships immediately—two for military use and two for transoceanic use by private companies. "I do not believe that the American public will continue to sit by and see only the other nations of the world unfurl their flags over new aerial trade routes."[42]

Dr. Eckener was granted permission to use NAS Lakehurst and the site in Miami for flights by his new giant Zeppelin—LZ-129—when she was completed. In return for the use of the American fields, Eckener would pay all expenses resulting from the landing of his Zeppelin. Lakehurst had been practically abandoned as an airship base since the *Macon* had been shifted to the West Coast.

Rear Admiral H. I. Cone, head of the U.S. shipping board, enthusiastically supported Eckener's plan to establish regular airship service between the U.S. and Europe. Cone declared that America's shipping chances were in the air rather than on the sea. Building a surface ship like the *Queen Mary* in the U.S. would be 50 percent higher than in Europe, and that amount of money would be sufficient to build five airships and airfields to support them.[43] "The thing for us to do," Cone asserted, "is to go into a program of world air traffic with dirigibles. We should put in all the trade routes. It is the only place for us to attain supremacy in international trade."[44]

International airship transit was not without obstacles to overcome. Eckener's visit to the U.S. had a number of goals, among them the acquisition of helium. This raised concerns among the French that Eckener might be seeking it for military purposes.

Sixteen years of peace since the 1918 Armistice had not fully assuaged the fears of a resurgence of the German military machine—including her Zeppelins. "Although the Treaty of Versailles forbids Germany a military air force, the Reich has secretly built up a commercial air service in such a way that more than 2,400 planes could be converted immediately into military aircraft, according to the [Paris newspaper] *Petit Journal*."[45]

"With the Saar situation between France and Germany becoming daily more critical, the French press has been seeking nervously to penetrate the secret of German armaments. *La Liberté* [Swiss-French newspaper] today declared that the real reason behind Dr. Hugo Eckener's request for a helium agreement with the United States for Zeppelin traffic is Germany's desire to get helium for military purposes."[46] The U.S. had a global monopoly on helium supply, and if France had known how difficult it would be to get the U.S. to sell it to foreign powers, she would have had no cause for concern.

Eckener was also seeking a contract with the U.S. for a transcontinental mail service using dirigibles, and the Post Office Department announced that it had a tentative agreement with Eckener for a North Atlantic airmail service to begin in July 1935, coinciding with the LZ-129 being placed in service. Rosendahl predicted that the transatlantic flight would take little more than two days.

Rosendahl was tireless in his efforts as he simultaneously promoted airships for military and commercial development.

———

In November 1934, the *Macon* was called upon to participate in Fleet Exercise Z off the West Coast from the base at Camp Kearny, California. The exercise called for a surface force to sail up the western coast of Mexico from Panama while the opposing force—Orange—was to intercept it.

On November 7, the *Macon* left her mast at 1708, took on her airplanes, and cruised over the Pacific to her initial point assigned for Fleet

Tactical Exercise Z, arriving there at 0355 on the eighth.[47] The main body of the Orange Fleet was sighted at 0445. An hour later, two landplanes piloted by Kivette and Miller, respectively, were launched, and at 0600 the *Macon* started her search according to plan.

At 0905 the *Saratoga* was sighted, distance 30 knots and, at 0944, the *Macon* was attacked by five enemy fighter planes. Two minutes later, Miller and Kivette landed their planes back on board the *Macon*. At 1040, Simpler was launched in his plane, followed at 1055 by Miller in his plane.[48] Wiley continued to conduct tactical scouting in the fleet problem, sending out his landplanes two at a time, rotating the pilots to minimize fatigue.

At 1840 on the eighth, the *Macon* made course to close with the Battle Force, U.S. Fleet, and on the morning of the ninth, they were steering north, up the coast of California, making for San Pedro. As the *Macon* neared the landing field, she released her small land planes to make their way to home base under their own power. The fleet exercises ended at 1610 and the *Macon* was moored to her mast at Sunnyvale in the evening of November 9.[49]

During the exercises, the *Macon* had operated under conditions that closely simulated those of wartime, with her officers and crew on watch continuously from 0500 to 1600, and those on lookout and gun stations took their noon meal at their stations. The *Macon*'s three landplane pilots logged a total of eighteen hours in the air.[50] Admiral Henry V. Butler, ComAirBatFor, complimented the *Macon* and her planes for their excellent job scouting and tracking the aircraft carrier.

The *Macon*'s next exercise came in December 1934. Little was known publicly about this problem. A rigid Naval intelligence shroud of secrecy had masked all movements in this exercise except for mention that the *Macon* would participate.[51] The exercise involved nine battleships, the carriers *Lexington* and *Langley* (CV-1), seven heavy and seven light cruisers, forty-seven destroyers, two or three divisions of submarines, and numerous airplanes.

The *Macon*'s role was to locate the enemy surface fleet, and for the first time, she would carry four airplanes.[52] The *Macon* began her search at 0600 on December 6, 1934, and about an hour into the exercise, she launched her four planes. At 0906, sailing in clear skies at an altitude of 1,200 feet, she sighted an enemy battleship behind her port beam, 20 miles distant.[53] *Macon's* scout planes and onboard lookouts began to sight numerous enemy vessels, and at 1230, she was attacked by six Vought SU-2 dive bombers from the *Lexington* that had emerged out of the sun to make a successful attack on the airship. It was ruled that the *Macon* had been shot down by this attack, but she continued the exercise under the pseudonym ZRS-6, only to be shot down a second time about an hour later.[54]

On the second day of the exercises, December 7, the *Macon* sighted two enemy battleships at 1037. Her search activities appeared to be running smoothly when, at 1325, she received the order to cease the present exercises.[55] The *Macon* and all surface ships were directed to search for two seaplanes from the cruiser *Cincinnati* (CL-6) that had run out of fuel and gone down in the ocean. The *Macon's* response was swift and, at 1542, her scout planes reported that they had located the downed seaplanes and dropped a smoke candle to mark the location. The *Macon* remained on station until the *Portland* (CA-33) arrived at 1635, followed closely by the *Cincinnati, Chicago* (CA-29), and *Indianapolis* (CA-35). The seaplanes and their pilots were retrieved safely.

The *Macon* and her scout planes received a commendation from ComBatFor for the manner in which they had located the *Cincinnati's* seaplanes.

The commendation for successfully locating the downed airplanes was the only bright spot for the *Macon* in these exercises. Admiral Reeves felt that the airship had failed again to perform satisfactorily under conditions where there was a high probability of being attacked by enemy planes.[56]

While the *Macon* was participating in the fleet exercises in the Pacific, Rosendahl was stuck on the East Coast, awaiting the results of the airship's performance. He later wrote, "It was hoped that the Macon's performance in exercises or war games, some of the potentialities of this type of aircraft to the Fleet, would be indicated. But in short order, I learned of the Fleet's very unfavorable report on the Macon's operations. More trouble for airships thereby piled up."[57]

King had become convinced that the airship's utility lay in long-range reconnaissance work, and he slowly made inroads with the general board that the *Macon* should be used only in strategic problems, emphasizing expanding her search radius through her airplanes.[58]

King's beliefs about airship utility matched Rosendahl's perfectly. Rosendahl considered that the airship had special abilities that should be utilized to advantage. "Generally speaking, these [advantages] were long cruising range, speed well in excess of surface speeds, its own airplanes, and the other inherent advantages of an elevated platform."[59]

"Detailed scouting at closer range, or after contact had been made, would generally fall under the heading of Tactical Scouting and be done by types other than the airship."[60]

The Navy's airships had been afforded extremely limited opportunities to demonstrate their intended uses. "When the Macon arrived on the Pacific Coast in mid-October 1933 . . . her performance was to count heavily in determination of the value of the ZRS type. In fact, the fate of rigid airships, rightly or wrongly, then rested upon this one airship."[61] No fleet exercises had been drawn up with the special attributes of the airship in mind—"the Macon was merely injected into a series of exercises previously set up without regard to their suitability for bringing out the correct uses and values of the ZRS."[62]

As December 1934 neared its end, Rosendahl made the single-handed decision to reveal what was likely the most closely guarded secret at NAS Lakehurst. He called his executive officer, Lieutenant Commander J. L. ("Jim") Fisher, into his office and told him he was taking a few days off to get married and would return with his bride on Christmas Eve. Fisher was the only one on the base to know, and he was asked to keep it under his hat. Rosendahl told him, "I want to give the station a surprise."[63]

"My recent seagoing cruise in the Pacific had been a rewarding one for me professionally—and personally. My chance meeting with the young lady whom I had seen on the railroad platform in Ranger, Texas, had blossomed into a real romance. My fellow officers at Lakehurst apparently had not learned of it and still considered me a confirmed bachelor. I had a surprise in store for them."[64]

On December 20, 1934, Rosendahl—now forty-two years old—obtained a license to marry thirty-two-year-old Jean Wilson, a native of

Houston, Texas. They were married two days later in "the Little Church Around the Corner," also known as the Church of the Transfiguration, in New York City.[65]

"The young lady who two years earlier had not cared to meet any stiff-necked naval officer had now become a Navy wife. As we drove to Lakehurst, it seemed to me to be a propitious time to get in some Navy indoctrination. Gathering up my nerve, I said to Jean: 'This may not make much sense to you now, but in time it will. You are the captain's wife, but I am the one who wears the captain's stripes.' And bless her soul, she remembered it."[66]

With the political struggles surrounding airships, and more that lay ahead, it was suggested to Rosendahl on a number of occasions that he abandon airships and transition to heavier-than-aircraft. He usually blew these off as friendly, well-intentioned suggestions, but after a while, he began to wonder if they were intended to distract him from airship matters. "In actively supporting my belief in airships, I was undoubtedly an irritant. In any event, I saw no reason for switching from one specialty to another just because my own was having a tough time. I then felt as I still feel: the heavier-than-air field represents one sufficient specialty, lighter-than-air another. Each branch is of sufficient scope to warrant any serious person's full devotion. My feelings on this subject are strong."[67]

New Year's is typically a time of hope for better things to come. There were two things in 1934 that heralded better times for Rosendahl and the LTA program in 1935. Rosendahl's personal life was enriched by his marriage to Jean on December 22, and on the twenty-ninth, there was the announcement: "American Fleet Plans Greatest Pacific Maneuvers."[68] These fleet exercises, to be held in the spring of 1935, were to be the greatest maneuvers in American history. Admiral Reeves announced that they would encompass the entire northern Pacific Ocean and would range from the Tropic of Cancer to the Aleutian Islands, and from the California coast to Midway Island—an area of more than 5 million square miles—and involve practically every craft in the U.S. Navy, including 177 surface ships, 577 airplanes, the airship *Macon*, and nearly 55,000 officers and men. Nine heavy cruisers of the scouting fleet would be joined by five new ones; there would be 14 battleships, 4 aircraft carriers, 56 destroyers, 9 mine layers, and 39 auxiliary ships.[69]

January 1935 also saw advances for the *Macon*. Improvements had been made that allowed her airplanes to get accurate radio bearings on the airship at distances of up to 185 miles—almost the limit of their operating radius—and clear communications could be made with keyed radio up to 95 miles. The *Macon*'s pilots had practiced night hook-on landings to the point they could be done without difficulty. Wiley and Miller were formulating a plan to conduct a surprise nighttime dive-bombing attack against the *Lexington*. On February 1, for the first time, Wiley shifted complete control of the ship to the auxiliary control station in the leading edge of the lower fin, and it was such a success that he planned to use it more in the future. There was no shortage of new ideas for the *Macon*—only a shortage of time.

Wiley was hoping to showcase the *Macon*'s new abilities during the fleet exercises in February 1935. As planned, workers had been reinforcing the ship's girders as time and flight schedule allowed, but as of early February, no work had been done on the upper parts of Frame 17.5 at the attachment of the upper fin.

The February 1935 exercises would be of extreme importance to the *Macon,* and, thus, to the entire program. The *Macon* lifted off from Sunnyvale at 0710 on February 11, 1935, to join the exercises. She took on her four scout planes once she was airborne as a matter of standard practice and headed out over the Pacific Ocean.[70] Once on board, the landing gear were removed from the small planes and their auxiliary fuel tanks attached. Wiley began his scouting routine at 1023 and launched his scout planes in practiced fashion.

The *Macon* encountered areas of overcast skies, fog, and intermittent rain with 30-knot winds from the moment she crossed the coastline, and they began to sight occasional surface ships.

In the early hours of February 12, the *Macon* was running in clear skies with good visibility but turbulent air. At 0415, lookouts sighted an unidentified cruiser on a westward heading, followed by the sighting of two Coast Guard destroyers at 0805. The *Macon* was doing a good job of scouting with her methodical procedure of launching and recovering her landplanes, searching as wide an area as possible. At midmorning on the twelfth, a *Dobbin*-class destroyer tender was spotted, followed in the early afternoon by the sighting of a submarine on the surface and a submarine tender off the port bow. Thus far, this had been a successful exercise of scouting enemy vessels while remaining undetected. At 1430, the commander in chief of the U.S. Fleet released the *Macon* to return to base at Wiley's discretion.

Wiley wanted to return to Sunnyvale by entering the Santa Clara Valley at Watsonville, 20 miles south, but there was a squall line directly in their path. When Miller returned from a scouting run in his plane, he reported that he had flown over the fleet below and as far as 50 miles ahead of the *Macon*. He had flown through stormy weather but thought it looked worse than it was, and he did not think it would be a problem for the airship.

Campbell relieved the watch as officer of the deck at 1605 and took the ship down to 1,600 feet only to find considerable turbulence beneath the squall. Within the hour, fog banks were rolling in from the west and northwest and obliterating the coastline from view such that only the tallest mountain peaks were visible. Because visibility was closing down ahead, Campbell summoned Wiley, and at about 1615, they encountered another rain squall and the ship took a severe vertical rise.[71] The elevatorman was able to regain control quickly, but the winds became more turbulent as the squall closed on the ship, and things became rougher. Rains hammered the *Macon* and added tons of water weight to her acres of fabric when a sudden blast of wind caused the elevatorman to call out for help controlling his wheel. Within minutes, the ship was out of the squall and on its course along the coast.

At 1705, the Point Sur Light was abeam to starboard, about two and a half miles distant, and a feeling came over the men that they would be warm and dry in their beds soon. There was a small rain squall to starboard as the ceiling started lowering and a light rain fell, but they were in smooth air. Suddenly, the ship was hit by a strong gust of wind that caused papers in the control car to go flying, and the ship was down by the nose at a steep angle and heeling to starboard. Sounds of the ship breaking up were heard from the stern to the bow as the *Macon* headed for the ocean.

Wiley was able to put the ship back in a bow-up attitude and she started ascending rapidly. Very shortly, Wiley was informed that the No. 1 Gas Cell was gone, and he knew immediately that this explained the heaviness in the tail of the ship and the rise by the bow. He ordered ballast to be dropped aft of amidships and for the engines to be slowed, because the ship's speed was generating dynamic lift that contributed to the upward inclination by the bow.

It was becoming increasingly difficult to fly the airship and Wiley was dealing with a situation that required all the experience he could command. He had the problem of preventing the ship from rising too high by slowing the engines and trying to regain trim by keeping the engines going to get desired effect on the elevators. As Wiley later explained, he tried to adjust between two conditions: having enough airspeed to control the ship and trying to get back on an even keel, and not having too much speed so that the ship would not rise to too great an altitude.[72]

Ballast was being dropped aft, but the ship's angle of inclination increased suddenly. Wiley got a call from Chief Boatswain's Mate "Shaky" Davis, informing him that the top fin had carried away, along with the structure on which he had been standing, and word came that the upper rudder controls were gone, but it was believed that they still had control of the lower one. There was a further report that the No. 2 Gas Cell had deflated. Wiley ordered all fuel slip tanks—each weighing 720 pounds—aft of amidships to be dropped. The ship then rose to over 4,600 feet as Wiley received a report that all slip tanks and all ballast aft of amidships had been dropped.

What followed was a series of orders to drop overboard anything of appreciable weight. The lower gas cells in the after part of the ship were cut away and cast overboard, the stern bags were cut away, and preparations were made to drop the four landplanes out of the ship. As the ship was falling, Wiley discovered that it could no longer be steered by the rudder. He decided to use the ship's engines to guide her, but he had difficulty reengaging them because the ship was inclined at an angle of twenty-five degrees. This angle kept the engines from getting water to cool them, with the result that they ran for only a few minutes at a time. When the angle decreased to about ten degrees, the engines could be cut in again. With the engines engaged, the ship rose into the clouds, where they lost sight of the surface of the ocean. Wiley later believed that the damage to the ship had occurred at about 1710 and everything else had unfolded within less than five minutes.

There were high mountains inland, and as the ship was being tossed about by the winds, it was drifting toward shore. Wiley decided to avoid the mountains by landing on the water near the cruisers that he knew were nearby. He sent out an "SOS" and a radio message informing the commander-in-chief that his ship was in distress ten miles southwest of Point Sur.[73] Attempting to steer the ship with its engines, he ordered the engines ahead on the port side and those on the starboard side idled. This maneuver had the desired effect of getting the *Macon* headed back out to sea and away from the mountains. Minutes later, the ship began to drop steadily at an estimated 600 feet per minute.

At an altitude of about 3,000 feet, Wiley realized it would be impossible to get the ship back on an even keel before she struck the water. He warned the engine rooms that they were about to receive a backing signal, and when they did, they were to throw the engines into reverse and abandon their stations. Word was passed to standby to land on the water. When the water became visible at about 2,000 feet, they stopped valving off helium to try to check their fall. Control of the ship was lost completely at 1,500 feet. To make as soft a landing as possible on the water, Wiley ordered, "Ballast forward . . . check her fall," to which came the report that all ballast from Frame 170 had been dropped, and the rate of descent slowed.

When the *Macon* was at about 1,000 feet, Boatswain's Mate First Class Leonard E. Shellberg entered the control car, distributing life jackets, and at 800 feet, Wiley gave the order to stand by to abandon ship. Simultaneously, everyone was ordered to leave the control car. Wiley wanted everyone at a window and prepared to jump just before the ship struck the water. Lieutenant Commander Jesse L. Kenworthy, the executive officer, threw flares overboard to mark the ship's location, and as the ship got closer to the water, he passed flares out to individual men for use once they were in lifeboats. Leaning out a window in the control car, Wiley watched the tail section of the ship as it neared the water, and at the proper moment, he gave the order to "back all engines." When the airspeed gauge registered less than 10 knots, he ordered all engines stopped and announced that the tail was in the water.

Wiley had felt the impact of the tail striking the water while the control car was about 250 feet in the air. Because of his skillful piloting, the landing had been a gentle one as the ship settled softly onto the surface of the ocean. All the men were released from their duty stations as Wiley ordered them to pick a window and jump just before she hit forward.

The men jumped into an icy cold Pacific Ocean, but unlike the crash of the *Akron*, the men were prepared this time to survive. Life rafts were on the water and the men helped each other climb on board, and fought hard to prevent the rafts from drifting away from each other. Each raft was designed to hold seven men, but the one Wiley secured had twelve men on board with water pouring over its gunwales. There were not enough rafts for all the men in the water, so some remained in the water, clinging to the rafts for support.

As the ship crashed, gasoline spilled onto the water, and it was ignited in places, burning from the flares. Gasoline burned inside the airship and, from within, illuminated the red, white, and blue Navy star. Managing the rafts became increasingly difficult as water shipped over the gunwales quite easily, making them heavier, distorting their shape, and making it difficult to row with their small paddles.

The *Macon* had gone down near the surface fleet, and the men struggled to survive long enough for their ships to reach them. After what seemed an eternity for the men in the cold Pacific water, the cruisers USS *Richmond* (CL-9) and *Concord* (CL-10) arrived to take the men on board to safety and warmth. Remarkably, of the eighty-three officers and men, only two were lost.

For six days, the Navy conducted a court of inquiry into the causes of the crash. Calvin M. Bolster, the construction officer, was present during the final moments of the *Macon*, and he testified that he believed the cause of the crash was a structural failure. While it was hard to know the exact location, he suspected it to have been in the diagonal girders in Frame 17.5 as a result of a sudden severe side load on the fin due to the strong wind gusts encountered on the ship's return flight. Among the witnesses, there were some conflicting opinions, but in the end, it was concluded that the upper part of the ship's structure—including the upper fin—had broken up progressively in the area of Frame 17.5, resulting in the loss of the airship.

In the aftermath, Secretary of the Navy Swanson wrote publicly that he would oppose construction of an airship to replace the *Macon*.[74]

———

Rosendahl's personal fortunes were faring somewhat better than the LTA program as a whole. He had been selected for promotion to the rank of commander in the summer of 1934 and passed his written and physical examinations in early 1935, with his promotion becoming final in May. As a married man, the pay increase was welcome, but "More important, the promotion proved I wasn't an outcast, even though I believed in and plugged for airships, and just at that time, airship morale in general needed stimulus, believe me."[75]

CHAPTER 10

THE *HINDENBURG*

After the crash of the *Macon*, a pall fell over Lakehurst as newspapers reported there would be no more government funding for airships.[1] Having the support of most of his admirals, Secretary of the Navy Claude A. Swanson felt that the money required to build an airship the size of the *Macon* could be spent better on constructing surface vessels. Carl Vinson, chairman of the House Naval Affairs Committee, expressed his feelings that the loss of the *Macon* spelled "the death knell" for military lighter-than-aircraft, and he announced his intention to abandon a bill that would appropriate $5 million for new dirigible construction.[2] The cumulative loss of the *Shenandoah*, the *Akron*, and the *Macon* had convinced him that the time had come to abandon experimentation with airships.[3]

Rosendahl was a fighter, and while the loss of the *Macon* was a metaphorical "gut punch" to his plans, he was not yet willing to abandon his dreams for LTA craft. With the *Akron* and the *Macon*, the Navy had been focusing on military applications of airships while the Germans had been enjoying a long and highly successful run with commercial airships. Zeppelins had traveled 600,000 miles and crossed the Atlantic seventy-four times without a single accident.

The track records of the *Akron* and the *Macon* were, themselves, fairly impressive. Each ship had spent nearly 7,000 hours in the air at the time of their crashes.

From the beginning, the Navy had pursued a duality of purpose for airship development—military and commercial—but now, lacking military airships, the Navy turned its attention to the commercial promise of airships. In doing so, the Navy repeatedly cited the successes of the Germans with their Zeppelins.

Rosendahl used his one remaining asset—his voice. A capable speaker, he addressed multiple civic groups, engineering societies, and basically anyone who would listen, trying to stir up interest in LTA flight. Speaking to a Rotary Club in Asbury Park, New Jersey, he said he wanted a five-year plan to give the dirigible a chance to prove itself. "At the end of that time, if the airship has failed to prove its usefulness it can be wiped off the books. Airships have their limitations as has every instrument used in transportation, but I do not believe they can be excelled as a means of long-range scouting, particularly over the water."[4] Unable to ignore military uses altogether, he claimed, "There is an absolute need for airships as coastwise scouting ships. With our great coastal area, we need such ships worse than any other country in the world."[5]

Some key people were attentive to Rosendahl's words, and on July 2, 1935, it was announced that a congressional inquiry into the crash of the *Macon* was promised by Carl Vinson. Rosendahl's speeches had awakened Vinson's attention after months of silence on airships. He had been awaiting the report of the Durand committee of experts concerning the future of airships, and it was expected that the U.S. would depend heavily on the findings of this committee.[6]

Secretary of the Navy Claude Swanson had appointed a committee of eight highly qualified and famous scientists and engineers to study the airship situation. While six of the eight members were in executive session at the Guggenheim Airship Institute, Professor De Forest of the Massachusetts Institute of Technology—a member of the committee—broke the committee's "rule of silence" and issued a statement that "naval refusal to permit reinforcement of the ship's structure at a vital point [area of frame 17.5] was responsible for the Macon's crash."[7] De Forest's statement set off a furor. No one—from Rear Admiral King and the LTA officers, to the officials of the Goodyear Zeppelin company—would offer comment.

Despite the American losses, the Germans were proceeding enthusiastically with their LTA program. Their latest Zeppelin—LZ-129—was due for completion in the fall of 1935, and it was expected to make one or two trips to the U.S. before going into service between Friedrichshafen and Rio de Janeiro.[8]

On the eve of the report of the airship investigating committee, the Navy indicated that it would definitely abandon rigid airship construction, relegating it to civil authorities. It was also announced that a new Zeppelin would make twelve trips between Germany and the U.S. In addition to cargo and mail, the new Zeppelin would carry fifty passengers. The trips were scheduled to begin in the spring of 1936.[9] The Zeppelin company would pay regular commercial rates to the Navy for the use of its mooring facilities at Lakehurst and Miami.[10]

There were visible signs of the Navy's demobilization of its airship facilities. In early October 1935, the Navy transferred its airship base at Sunnyvale, California, to the Army in exchange for war department land. All LTA activities were concentrated at NAS Lakehurst, where there was a class of eight officers undergoing LTA training. Once their training was completed, they would be assigned to other duties and no new classes would be organized. There were only twelve LTA craft left at Lakehurst, and the only rigid airship was the ancient *Los Angeles*, condemned because of her age.[11]

Rosendahl openly criticized what he saw as an "apathetic attitude" toward airships in the U.S. and called for a "fare and adequate program for dirigibles."[12] He asserted that the airship was superior to the airplane for transoceanic travel, and he regretted deeply that Congress had not passed legislation in support of airships as common carriers. Repeatedly, he pointed to the German successes with Zeppelins. Referring to the commercial flights of the *Graf Zeppelin* over the southern Atlantic, he pointed out, "The commercial airship's record for safety is perfect: no other form of transport in the history of the world has had such a record."[13] He ascribed Germany's successes in LTA flight to a "continuity of effort" which had carried through since the First World War.

In January 1936, the long-awaited report of the Durand committee was revealed, and to the surprise of many, it recommended that the Navy continue to acquire and experiment with airships. The report urged that the disasters to the *Akron* and *Macon* not deter the country from making advances in airship development. "On the theory that civilization must advance, the committee recommended that the United States continue the construction and operation of big and small lighter-than-air ships for both civil and military use."[14] Subsequently, it was expected that Secretary Swanson would ask for the construction of a new giant airship to replace the ones that had been lost.

The Durand committee had done a superb, objective, detailed job of studying the elements involved in the crash of the *Macon*, and it suggested that if dirigible construction were to be renewed, the first ship should be used as a "flying laboratory and training ship," rather than being made an adjunct to the fleet right away. The committee also made reference to the advances that had been made in the science of meteorology and weather forecasting and expressed the belief that there should be no further difficulties in avoiding extreme weather hazards, such as the storm that resulted in the crash of the *Akron*.[15]

The *Akron Beacon Journal*, carrying the story, added:

> The *Beacon Journal* traditionally is opposed to vast expenditures for enlargement of the military establishment, and it would be the last agency to suggest a huge building program for dirigibles. But far too much has been invested by the government itself, and too much skill and genius have been centered in Akron, to blindly sacrifice at this point the achievements already to the credit of the dirigible industry in America.[16]

On March 22, 1936, a group of aviation experts recommended to the Senate Air Safety Committee the construction of a fleet of commercial airships and replacements for the *Akron* and *Macon*. Rosendahl urged the committee to "put fear behind and look upon the Zeppelin-type craft as a necessary part of the air transportation and defense system." Pressing his argument, he offered, "For half the cost of a super-liner you can build a whole fleet of airships, build terminals and start a service that will cut transportation time in half. . . . From the standpoint of economics, the airship will prove superior to the airplane by virtue of its lower operating cost per ton mile."[17]

The newfound wave of enthusiasm for LTA craft was about to crest with the announcement that the *Hindenburg*—the epitome of safe, luxurious air travel—was scheduled to arrive at NAS Lakehurst on May 8 or 9, 1936. This demonstration would serve to heighten public and governmental interest in airships.

The May 8 arrival was to be the first of ten scheduled flights by the Zeppelin from her home base at Frankfurt-am-Main to Lakehurst. The tentative dates for the future flights were May 19, June 23, July 4, July 14, August 8, August 18, September 19, September 29, and October 10.[18] Considered a comparatively desolate place since the loss of the *Akron* and *Macon*, Lakehurst was expected to spring to new life with the scheduled Zeppelin visits.

The *Hindenburg* was nearly twice as large as the *Graf Zeppelin* and slightly larger than the *Akron* and *Macon*. She was ten inches longer than the 803-foot hangar but would fit if positioned on a slight angle.[19] The *Hindenburg* was 803 feet, 10 inches long compared to the *Graf Zeppelin*'s 776 feet.

The May 8 arrival was to mark the beginning of a commercial airship service between Europe and North America. "Unofficially, federal agencies will likewise interest themselves in the venture which may either signal the ultimate surrender of this country to German leadership in lighter-than-air transportation or arouse nationalistic spirit to the point of fulfillment of widely urged plans to keep the United States in the running in the matter of dirigible construction, experimentation and development."[20]

The *Hindenburg* would be under the command of Captain Ernst Lehmann, but also on board would be Dr. Hugo Eckener and Lieutenant Commander Scott Peck, who had been in Germany observing the trial flights of the Zeppelin. Rosendahl would supervise the ground crew of ninety trained sailors and two hundred soldiers from nearby Camp Dix. Rosendahl was taking no chances of something going wrong with this landing. When the Zeppelin was reported near the NAS, the ground crew would station itself near the mooring mast several hours before its arrival. Direct radio contact would be established, and when the ship arrived over the station, wind direction and velocity would be given. The motors would be idled as the ship nosed down and handling lines dropped to the ground crew. The *Hindenburg* would be housed in Hangar No. 1 only if weather conditions were completely favorable—otherwise, she would be secured to the mooring mast.[21]

While there would be no formal celebration on arrival, it was note-worthy that Admiral William H. Standley and Rear Admiral Ernest J. King, chief of the Bureau of Aeronautics, would travel from Washington to greet the *Hindenburg*.

The little borough of Lakehurst, located a mile from the NAS, had been a thriving community during the days of the *Los Angeles* and *Akron*. It had depended on the NAS since it was built in 1921, but with the loss of the great airships and the shift of LTA activities to Sunnyvale, the town's economic well-being was weak. Residents hoped that a regular air service by the *Hindenburg* would infuse new life into the town. On May 8, booths selling all sorts of edibles to visitors were erected on vacant lots and along streets and highways.[22]

Newspapers announced the inaugural arrival of the *Hindenburg*— "The German dirigible *Hindenburg*, 803 feet of majestic beauty arrived today on the first commercial airship flight between Europe and the United States."[23]

"In a velvet smooth, almost noiseless flight of 3,600 miles from Friedrichshafen, Germany, the *Hindenburg* lopped nearly a day and a half from the westward airship record set by its veteran sister ship, Graf Zeppelin."[24] The *Hindenburg* had made the flight in 61 hours, 50 minutes—33 hours and 32 minutes faster than the *Graf Zeppelin*.

A throng of 150,000 people had gathered to witness the arrival and landing of the giant Zeppelin. Dr. Eckener was the first to leave the ship, and he was greeted by Rosendahl. They got into a car and drove for the mile ride to the hangar. The *Hindenburg* was in the hangar by 0725, with just 11 inches of clearance from end-to-end for the ship.[25] The new Zeppelin was so large that ten feet had been lopped off the nose in Fried-richshafen before the flight to make the ship 803 feet long. The 2,200 pounds of mail the ship delivered from Europe was taken by plane to Newark airport. The Zeppelin had delivered fifty-one passengers and a crew of fifty-six.[26]

To service the Zeppelin following her flight to the NAS, she received 1,500,000 cubic feet of hydrogen gas, 15,000 gallons of fuel oil, and a ton of lubricating oil.[27] Rosendahl celebrated this great day as he privately entertained Dr. Eckener, Ernst Lehmann, and other officers that evening in his home.[28] In an interview, Eckener admitted that the primary purpose of the *Hindenburg*'s cruises to the U.S. in 1936 was to win financial backing for a German-American transatlantic transport service. Such a plan had been laid out in 1928, but it was frustrated by the Depression.[29]

In front of the press, Rosendahl, Eckener, and Peck openly discussed issues surrounding the use of helium vs. hydrogen as a lifting gas. Peck summarized the situation perfectly: "With our helium we had to use lighter, and consequently, weaker, materials. With us it was always a battle against weight. With the Germans it was merely a battle against fire. The Germans have won their battle."[30]

From May 8 to October 10, 1936, the *Hindenburg* made ten roundtrip transatlantic flights from Germany to NAS Lakehurst, and all went smoothly without problems. The flights had become so routine that newspaper coverage of each successive flight became shorter and less dramatic. A new routine seemed to have set in—for the Germans, at least—and one that Rosendahl, and a growing number of investors, hoped America would emulate.

On her last landing at Lakehurst, Paul W. Litchfield proclaimed the now-proven worth of LTA craft and urged the government to start building them again.[31] He described the things that needed to happen to make the LTA picture in America look better. First, the science advisory board appointed by Secretary Swanson had to pass favorable judgment on American airship construction. Second, there had to be a popular demonstration of LTA to make people forget the *Macon* disaster. Third, there had to be awakened interest in LTA flight on the part of the government, because the support of the government was essential. Litchfield believed he was seeing awakened interest in the Department of Commerce and in American business.[32] Rosendahl reminded the public that the U.S. had built and operated three naval airships, but it had produced no commercial airship.[33]

Rosendahl had to rely on the commercial airship successes of the Germans to bolster his arguments for LTA ships, and he turned, naturally, to the achievements of the *Graf Zeppelin*. In the eight years between September 1928 and September 1936, she made 555 flights, was in the air for 16,000 hours, traveled more than 1,000,000 miles, made 132 ocean crossings, and carried 13,000 people, 91,000 pounds of mail, and 126,000 pounds of freight.[34]

In January 1937, Dr. Eckener visited Washington, D.C., for a series of conferences with American businessmen and government officials concerning the operation of a transatlantic air service with dirigibles. He was so intent on making this dream a reality that he offered the plans of the *Hindenburg* and her sister ship, the LZ-130, then under construction to the American Zeppelin Company, for its use in planning American passenger airships. Eckener was seeking cooperation rather than competition, and he believed that the most efficient service could be achieved by four dirigibles—two American and two German.[35] Eckener's new airship would be an improved version of the *Hindenburg*—more powerful engines, accommodations for seventy-five passengers instead of fifty, and at an estimated cost of $2,700,000.

Eckener also announced that he expected to make ten flights during the spring and summer with departures every fortnight, as before. The successes of *Hindenburg* had awakened a growing audience in the U.S. Journalist Betty Wallace of *The Californian* newspaper wrote a lengthy tribute to LTA flight that was rational and enthusiastic. Her article began with a question for her readers: "Did you know that only 157 rigid airships ever have been built? That the first passenger has yet to be killed in one of them?"[36]

As if echoing the words of Admiral Moffett himself, Wallace added, "Whenever a pioneer field is opened, the way is paved by men who were not afraid to lose their lives. This is a sad but very necessary fact. . . . The men who went down with our airships sacrificed their lives to advance an art. Their sacrifice will have been useless only if the world does not utilize the knowledge for which they gave their lives."[37] Rosendahl could not have asked for a more avid and articulate advocate for LTA flight.

Riding the successes of the 1936 transatlantic flights, it was announced that the *Hindenburg* would initiate its intercontinental "shuttle service" in 1937 on May 3. Nine flights were scheduled with the following departure dates from Germany: May 3, 11, and 21; June 1, 11, and 22; July 2 and 13; and August 3.[38]

Captain Lehmann stated that the type of airship represented by the *Hindenburg* had proven itself so airworthy that it would be used as the model for future airship constructions. By 1940, Germany planned to have four modern *Hindenburg*-type dirigibles flying regularly between Germany and the United States, South America, the Dutch East Indies, and the Far East.[39]

On May 3, 1937, the American press informed readers that the *Hindenburg* was scheduled to sail that evening from Germany to the U.S. for the first of its trips scheduled for the current year. The ship would be under the command of dirigible veteran Captain Max Pruss, who had been schooled by Count Ferdinand Zeppelin, Dr. Hugo Eckener, and Ludwig Duerr, the airship designer. These were the best of credentials.[40]

At 2000 (EST) on May 4, the ship was between 1,000 and 1,200 miles off the coast of France, heading west, encountering strong headwinds, which were slowing her sufficiently to prevent her from setting a new transatlantic speed record but not interfering with her anticipated arrival of May 6.[41]

Of all the journalists, photographers, and curious spectators, no observer of the *Hindenburg* was as expert as Rosendahl.

> Around the Press room and the offices in the large hangar was gathered an inaugural or "first nightery" crowd such as had never been seen at any airport. Customs, Immigration and Public Health officials were at hand. Diplomats, foreign officials and friends awaiting passengers on the airship sought the latest information. Personnel of the Naval Air Station hurried to and fro on last-minute activities of many kinds. Reporters checked their recollections and the records of airship "past performances," and scanned the ship's position reports. Alert newsreel crews and photographers, forgetting their keen rivalry for the moment, talked good naturedly as they checked their equipment. Last but not least were several thousand other onlookers, the general public. The whole air was one of happy expectancy.[42]

Successive position reports eventually placed the *Hindenburg* over Nova Scotia, Boston, Providence, and New York City and, eventually, the quiet excitement at the NAS was broken by cries of "There she is!" The majestic airship sailed over the NAS ahead of her designated landing time. It had been headwinds, not storms, over the North Atlantic that reduced the ship's groundspeed over the ocean, and Captain Max Pruss realized he could not reach Lakehurst by the originally scheduled hour of 0600 on May 6. Realizing how many people and agencies were involved in the flight plan—especially for the first trip of the season—Pruss sent a radio message to the NAS to arrange a new landing time that was sufficiently advanced to ensure his timely arrival. As the *Hindenburg* crossed the field of the NAS shortly after 1600, the weather conditions were entirely suitable for a landing, but Pruss did not land—he continued southward, marking time until the newly appointed landing hour of 1800 (EST).

There were few spectators on the broad sandy field to greet the ship because, after her ten previous trips, her arrival was considered as routine as the docking of an ocean liner.[43]

Rosendahl continued his narrative for his memoir:

> General weather conditions in the northwestern part of the United States were unsettled and now began to make themselves felt at Lakehurst. A cold front, with conditions favorable for the development of thunderstorms, was moving across from westward at a moderate rate, accompanied by a well-defined but mild squall line and cumulus and cumulo-nimbus clouds. It passed Lakehurst shortly after 4:30 accompanied by heavy showers and thundershowers which lasted until about 5:45. I had sent the Hindenburg a dispatch recommending that the landing be delayed until further word from us. Quick acknowledgement and concurrence were received from the ship. The ceiling soon was down to between 500 and 600 feet.
>
> At five o'clock, I had sounded the ground crew signal of three groups of three blasts each on the deep-throated station siren, to put in motion our last step in receiving the ship. Ground crew personnel marched to the landing site. Waiting photographers and newsmen sallied forth. During the intermittent downpours, the 92 naval personnel and the 138 civilians recruited for the landing party

scampered from their positions into the dubious shelter of the open lower structure of the mooring mast in the center of the airship landing field.

At intervals, in the clear skies to the south and southeast we caught glimpses of the Hindenburg cruising there peacefully and unconcerned. Soon our weather began to improve, and at 6:12 the ceiling had become 2000 feet, the visibility five miles, wind westnorhtwest [sic] eight knots, and the thunderstorm was practically clear of the station. I sent the ship another message reporting that we were [ready] to receive him and that conditions were considered suitable for landing, as it was apparent that they surely would be by the time the ship could return from the southeast. In another ten minutes there was more improvement. Just after seven, conditions were decidedly better, so I recommended landing at the earliest possible moment, in order that we could lose no time in getting the ship ready for her return trip.

Soon the Hindenburg appeared over the station on a northerly course, almost directly over the mooring mast and at between 500 and 600 feet altitude, to have a look at surface conditions and the disposition of the ground crew, preliminary to swinging into the approach for landing. Local weather conditions then included a sky seven-tenths filled with stratus clouds, a ceiling of between 2000 and 3000 feet, and an almost imperceptibly light rainfall. The surface wind was southeast and variable at two knots, and at 200 feet the wind was west at six knots. The thunderstorms had passed completely. It was not our practice to permit women or general spectators to be near the mooring mast during a landing. But this time, we had an elderly distinguished guest, Mrs. von Meister, who knew many of the Hindenburg officers, and so I had weakened and allowed Mrs. Meister and my wife Jean, to be at the mast to greet the new arrivals.

Aboard the Hindenburg, happy passengers got ready for the arrival. They checked customs declarations, made sure their passports were handy, and redeemed their wine chits from the Chief Steward. Members of the airship crew speculated as to which of them would get ashore for a visit and which would have to stay aboard to reservice the ship.

It was essential to prepare quickly and get off on schedule, since all return trip passenger accommodations were completely sold out, due to the pending coronation of the new King of England, George VI, the Paris Exposition, and the well-merited popularity the airship had established during the 1936 season. On the ground, the landing crew shifted the mooring gear to meet the directional variations in the light fitful breeze. Through my own mind, as Commanding Officer of the station, ran the many items to be discussed with Captain Lehmann, Captain Pruss and others, relating to the new season's operations.

Under normal full control, the ship now swung in a wide circle for the landing approach into the wind. In the ship's control car, the officers checked the ship's static buoyant condition by their instruments and adjusted the trim and buoyancy by valving lifting gas and/ or dropping water ballast. At slow speed and at a height of about 200 feet above the landing field, pointed into the wind, Captain Pruss backed down on all engines to check her headway, some 700 feet from the mooring mast.

At 7:21, the coil of the first landing rope, quickly followed by the second, thumped on to the ground from the bow of the airship, making the first 1937 contact with American soil. On the ground, the landing party hastened to connect the ship's lines to corresponding ones on the ground for steadying the ship into the wind. From the very nose of the ship, the steel cable for pulling the ship to the ground inched out—but it never reached the surface. A light gust of wind from the port side moved the ship very slowly over to starboard, but the port landing rope tautened and checked the movement.

In imposing, majestic silence, the vast silvery, 804-ft. hulk of the Hindenburg floated there motionless like a framed populated cloud. Everything within and without the ship was proceeding in a wholly normal manner. In a few minutes the ship would reach the ground and her mooring mast, safely and smoothly. But at 7:25, just four minutes after the first landing rope touched the ground, there occurred one of the most terrific and harrowing surprises man has ever witnessed.

Without the slightest warning, on top of the motionless ship, just ahead of where the front edge of the upper fin sloped into the hull, there occurred a brilliant burst of flame resembling a mushroom-shaped flower exploding into bloom. To me, the meaning was instantly clear. Nothing short of a miracle could prevent the rapid spread of fire to that whole vast volume of voracious hydrogen with which the ship was inflated. There could be no such thing as a small fire. It was horrifying. The Hindenburg was doomed. In the wink of an eye that graceful, comfortable, luxurious, ocean-going skyliner was transformed into a blazing inferno. All of us beneath and near the flaming ship ran for our lives.

Following the first burst of flame, there was a muffled report and the moving flame spread rearward. Instantly the whole after quarter of the ship was ablaze. As the rear portion of the craft settled to the ground almost on an even keel, the huge remaining forward portion of the hull still retained its buoyancy and inclined nose upward at a sharp angle, breaking the ship's back at about the point where the initial burst of fire had appeared. Aided by the "chimney" or draft action through the corridor of the upward-pointing section of the craft, fire shot rapidly forward and upward, belching flame and smoke out of the ship's bow and igniting one gas cell after another in its forward travel. This catastrophe could not correctly be termed an "explosion"; there were a few muffled reports but nothing violent. Rather it was a progressive, extremely rapid burning of the ship's hydrogen and the combustible materials on board. In a matter of seconds, the peaceful quiet scene had been transformed into blazing terror and turmoil.

As the tail section settled to the ground, the upward-inclined main part telescoped slightly as it pivoted slowly through a fiery arc to the ground. When it struck the resiliency in the still faithful landing wheel under the car caused a slight rebound upward. Then the blazing hull, shooting pillars of flame and heavy smoke into the sky as fuel oil also ignited, settled to the ground. In places, it flattened out elliptically as the metallic structure writhed and yielded in death embrace with the intense white heat of the hottest flame man knows. In less than a minute this admirable example of man's creative ability had become a shapeless, twisted skeleton.

As soon as it was realized that the ship was on fire, the ground crew had been ordered to run for their lives to avoid being caught under that gigantic falling firebrand. But they retreated only enough to insure their not being trapped, and even before the blazing hulk had completely settled to the ground, the men dashed back. Many of them were fully familiar with the ship and knew where crew and passengers would probably be for the landing. On board were fellow airship pioneers with whom we were acquainted. Hopeless as the situation appeared at first, it might still be possible to save some of those in the burning ship. As I stood off to the side, after having to clear of the falling craft, I wondered for an instant if this were not just a horrible dream or nightmare. But quickly the heat and the rapid progress of the fire defined it as an irrevocable, tragic reality. As the flames traveled forward they wiped out, like a huge eraser, letter by letter, the illustrious name HINDENBURG that had been inscribed on the cover of this mightiest of airships.

Tragedy had struck so swiftly that there was little time on board for help or even warning. Some, caught in their cabins or at their duty stations, probably never knew what happened. However, there were those who heeded shouts from the ground and from alert persons within the ship, to jump through the open windows along the passenger spaces. At first it seemed unbelievable that more than a few might escape with their lives.[44]

Rosendahl noted a marked difference in the wind directions at the surface and at the high point of the ship's approach for landing. Consequently, when the burning ship reached the ground, the ground wind, blowing from the port beam, forced flames and smoke to the starboard side. This was fortunate for some but fatal for others, because most of the passengers were gathered in the starboard lounges and promenade, ready for passport examinations. Either they were unaware that a safer exit lay on the port side, or they could not make their way through the crumbling ship to that side.[45]

Amid the ghastly death of the *Hindenburg*, Rosendahl was witness to some miraculous escapes from death. Scarcely believing his eyes, he saw Chief Steward Heinrich Kubis and Watch Officers Walter Zeigler and Max Zable, along with several others, emerge from the wall of fire into the safety of the open air—"as though stepping out from behind a stage curtain, totally unscathed—while others jumped to safety through open windows into the arms of members of the ground crew."[46]

George Grant, a passenger from London, escaped by jumping from a window and landing in the sand beneath the wreck without a scratch or burn, but before he could get to his feet, another passenger leaped through the same window and landed squarely on Grant's back. A Navy ground crewman witnessed the event and helped Grant to get clear of the wreck, but once clear, he did not know what to do with the injured man. The bluejacket ground crewman recognized Jean Rosendahl standing near the mooring mast, and he took Grant to her, thinking she would know what to do with him. "An alert photographer snapped a picture which in my opinion, is an outstanding example of candid camera work. It reveals Mr. Grant's relief and gratitude that he is safe. It clearly depicts the sailor's thought: 'Someone take this man off my hands so I can go back for another.'"[47]

Rosendahl recalled other tales of individual survival. Walter Zeigler was the watch officer on duty in the control car at the time of the crash. After leaping from the car, he tried to escape to starboard, but that direction was blocked. Later, he told Rosendahl that he had recalled reading an account of a wartime Zeppelin that was burning and two of the men on board escaped serious injury by lying flat on the bottom of the control car. This recollection prompted Zeigler to get back into the car and flatten out on the deck, but he realized quickly this was not a good solution to his predicament and he jumped from the car again, this time making a good escape to the port side, where he walked out safely.[48]

The radio officer on watch jumped from the radio room to find the heat to be intolerable. He fell to the ground and covered his feet, hands, and head with wet sand and lay there, waiting for the ship's cover above him to burn off. He then made his way through the red-hot open skeleton of the ship to emerge with no more than minor burns. Werner Franz was a fourteen-year-old cabin boy who jumped to the ground through an open hatch in the bottom of the ship, where he began to choke from the scorching flames and fumes. He was saved when a full water tank above him opened, drenching him. He then worked his way through openings in the wreckage to emerge into open air—wet, but unharmed. Rosendahl overheard the boy telling his shipmates about his escape and heard him conclude his tale with, "You know, I think I was lucky."[49, 50]

"As did every member of the Hindenburg crew, those in the control car stuck to their posts in accordance with the highest traditions of all who go down in ships. Only after the forward section of the ship had settled to the ground following its rebound did the order come: 'Now! Everybody out!'"[51]

Rosendahl recorded that, in the first few seconds following the initial burst of flames, there was "plenty of fast thinking" in the control car. He highlighted the skillful handling of water ballast. When the burning stern section began to settle—even before the forward sections of the ship caught fire—it might have seemed obvious to drop water ballast from the stern section to ease the ground impact, but "in a flash of clear thinking," those in the control car decided to retain the weight of the water in the stern in order to hasten the fall of the burning section to the ground to afford the men in that section their best chance of escaping the fire.[52]

Captain Anton Wittemann, of the *Graf Zeppelin*, was on board the *Hindenburg* as a passenger. He escaped from the control car without the slightest injury. Others who came out of the control car with Wittemann were not as fortunate. Captain Lehmann was burned severely and died in hospital the following day. Captain Pruss was severely burned but survived.

Rosendahl wrote that the many deeds of heroism performed in the emergency by members of the armed services and civilians were too numerous to recount. In the aftermath, he appointed a board to investigate the acts of heroism, but the board concluded that "in view of the high standard displayed by all hands, it was impossible to single out any individuals above others for recognition."[53]

After the ship settled to the ground, Rosendahl found it unnecessary to issue many orders because military and civilian individuals moved about instinctively in attempts to save people and property. He was touched by one incident that came to light that he deemed a tribute to the man involved. John Pannes, a passenger returning from a visit abroad, had been an official of the Hamburg American-North German Lloyd Steamship organization for many years. Mrs. Pannes was with him. As the ship neared the ground, someone shouted to Pannes, encouraging him to jump through an open window. He looked about for his wife but could not find her, and he refused to leave the ship without her. Rosendahl claimed, "They went to their last reward together."[54]

The fire raged for more than three hours, with huge pillars of smoke rising skyward as the flames fed on the tons of fuel oil that remained inside the ship. Assistance streamed into the NAS within minutes after the great airship took fire. Rosendahl felt that one of the most helpful elements was a group of soldiers from nearby Camp Dix who were at the NAS as spectators, awaiting the arrival of the *Hindenburg*. The Army officers offered the assistance of their men immediately and they launched themselves into the "many gruesome and trying tasks."[55]

When the airship burst into flame, some reporters and photographers scattered, while others remained close to capture as much detail as they could. Rosendahl felt there was one observer that day who had a more trying task than the photographers. Radio commentator Herbert Morrison had been sent to Lakehurst along with technician Charley Nehlson by WLS in Chicago for what was expected to be a routine broadcast of the landing of the *Hindenburg*. Because the *Hindenburg* had made ten trips to Lakehurst previously, this trip was not considered important enough to warrant a direct, live broadcast. Morrison was recording his commentary for a delayed broadcast to be aired the following day.

As the Hindenburg approached, Morrison was speaking calmly into his microphone:

> Toward us, like a great feather . . . is the Hindenburg. The members of the crew are looking down on the field ahead of them getting their glimpses of the mooring mast. . . .

It is practically standing still now. The ropes have been dropped and they have been taken hold of by a number of men on the field. It is starting to rain again. The rain has slacked up a little bit. The back motors of the ship are holding it just enough to keep it—[56]

IT'S BURST INTO FLAME! Get out of the way—Charley, get out of the way, please. It is bursting into flames. This is terrible! This is one of the worst catastrophes in the world! The flames are 500 feet into the sky. It is a terrific crash, ladies and gentlemen. It is in smoke and flames now. Oh, the humanity! Those passengers! I can't talk ladies and gentlemen! Honest, it is a mass of smoking wreckage. Lady, I am sorry. Honestly, I can hardly—I am going to step inside where I can't see it. Charley, this is terrible. Listen, folks, I am going to stop for a minute because I have lost my voice.[57]

Morrison recovered his voice within moments and continued his transcription, "But by that time," according to *Time* magazine, "the worst and most completely witnessed disaster in the history of commercial aviation was over, the 803-foot Hindenburg was gone, destroyed in precisely 32 seconds before 1,000 appalled spectators."[58]

Rosendahl kept his press officer, Lieutenant George F. Watson, busy making calls to Washington with situation reports. The international interest in airships was so great that, at about midnight, Rosendahl had to forego many of the things demanding his attention to personally answer telephone calls from newspapers and personnel in Germany, England, South America, and Japan. Rosendahl was keenly aware that there were families and friends of *Hindenburg* crewmen in Frankfurt and Friedrichshafen, who eagerly awaited news of their loved ones. Multiple dispatches were sent to Germany as the casualty and survivor figures were known.[59]

Even as Rosendahl and his men dealt with the vital issues of firefighting and assisting survivors, a seamy side of humanity showed itself. Rosendahl and his men found it impossible to prevent wholesale pilfering that set in even before darkness while the ship was burning fiercely.

Some had the audacity to try to leave through our main gate, carrying whole sections of metal, outer cover, instruments and other items,

even water and fuel tanks they had removed from the smouldering
[*sic*] wreck. Some cars resembled "covered wagons" of yore, so heavily
laden were they with airship parts. How much material disappeared
over and through the station fence it would be impossible to estimate.
No one in the crowds seemed to have any notion that, if undisturbed,
the wreckage might yield helpful clues to the cause of the disaster. The
public's craze for souvenirs over-ruled every other consideration.[60]

For Rosendahl, the looting situation was reminiscent of the aftermath
of the *Shenandoah* disaster. "One might think that a place filled with
injured and dying would be immune to the greedy fingers of souvenir
hunters, but, alas, such was not the case."[61]

The medical staff at the NAS was modest in size, consisting of three
physicians and a few medical corpsmen. The station did not have a hospital but merely a dispensary with limited bed capacity. Additionally,
there was a small family hospital staffed by Navy doctors as additional
duty and two private nurses who were paid for out of the pockets of the
men stationed there.

On the day of the crash of the *Hindenburg*, the dispensary was filled
quickly to overflowing with emergency cases. A number of civilian doctors arrived from nearby vicinities to lend assistance. Some brought their
own instruments and medical supplies.

> Clothing, watches, wallets, and other valuables were taken from
> the seriously injured and piled up in what was thought to be a safe
> place. Later we learned that some of the injured never recovered their
> cigarette cases, wallets, watches, and the like. The next day, the Se-
> nior Medical Officer reported that there had disappeared from our
> Dispensary during those hectic hours, not only a very considerable
> quantity of medical supplies and instruments, but, believe it or [not],
> even the huge king-size, official naval medical text and reference
> book assigned to the Dispensary.[62]

In a garage behind the naval hospital, corpses mounted. One observer claimed there were forty dead in the garage. A group entered the
garage later, attempting to identify the bodies.[63]

The day after the crash, when all seemed to be in hand at NAS Lakehurst, Rosendahl drove to the area hospitals where the overflow injured had been taken and, specifically to visit some of the *Hindenburg* men he knew. He entered a ward in one of the hospitals to find many injured crewmen lying in beds packed closely along both sides of the room. He heard some of them moaning while others were ominously silent. Most of the men recognized Rosendahl and chatted with him briefly.[64]

Shortly after Captain Anton Wittemann had escaped from the burning ship, he sought out Rosendahl on the field and asked to speak with him privately. Wittemann told him that prior to the ship's departure from Frankfurt, the German government had received information that an attempt would be made to sabotage the *Hindenburg* on this trip. Consequently, everything taken on board the ship was examined thoroughly. Wittemann told Rosendahl that to avoid alarming the crew, only he and Captain Lehmann were told of the threat—not even Captain Pruss was aware. On hearing this from Wittemann, Rosendahl asked the New York City Police Department to send experts from their bomb squad to examine the ship's wreckage for any clues that would support a claim of sabotage.[65]

Before Rosendahl could collect his thoughts about the dead and injured, his wife, Jean, sprang into action to assist. In his commanding officer's quarters, the dining room table had been fully extended and set up for a dinner that had been planned for the captain and officers of the *Hindenburg*. As fast as she could, Jean contacted survivors and invited them to their quarters for food and drink. The table remained set and the kitchen active all that night and the next day. The bachelor officer quarters were made ready for the *Hindenburg* survivors who were still ambulatory. Jean had their quarters operating on an emergency basis for days thereafter as numerous people arrived.[66]

As soon as the Rosendahl's "open house" was functioning, Jean made the rounds to the base dispensary and area hospitals, visiting the injured. She found Captain Pruss in a private hospital room and Captain Lehmann in another. Both were burned badly and suffering terribly. When she learned that the hospitals could not provide private nurses that night for the critical cases, she hurried back to the NAS and made arrangements for two civilian nurses from the family hospital to stand watch over Pruss and Lehmann until other nurses could be found. Both Pruss and Lehmann were spiritually uplifted by Jean's visit along with her assurance that they would get the best of care. Captain Pruss was suffering so badly he could hardly speak, and Captain Lehmann kept repeating to her, "My God, Jean. What could have happened to the ship?"[67]

Captain Lehmann's last hours were described best by Rosendahl:

> Needless to say, I did not rest all that long night or the following day. I wanted to visit Pruss and Lehmann particularly, but sometime after midnight my mind was set at ease a bit by learning that Jean had been out to see them. Early the next day, I got a message that Lehmann wished to see me at once. I dashed the ten miles to the hospital as fast as my skillful Marine driver could get me there. In a private room by himself lay Ernst Lehmann swathed in bandages, even over his eyes. His own condition seemed to give him little concern. His mind was crystal clear. Our conversation for a time was concerned with personal matters. Then, his mind turned to airships. It is clear that he then realized his life's work was drawing to an end. Just as one may experience the longest dream in only a few seconds, so, as he had lain there for hours trying to puzzle out the almost unbelievable loss of the Hindenburg, there must have paraded through his mind the great panorama of airship history in which he himself had figured so outstandingly. Together we discussed the probable causes of the disaster, but each one led onto a blind alley. Still a champion of airships, he said to me in his usual calm manner and in his excellent English: "But of course, regardless of the cause in this case, the next ship must use helium. Airships will go on."
>
> Surely, had he been able to throw light on anything that might have helped explain this perplexing catastrophe that was slowly sapping his very life, he would have passed it on to me for the sake of the cause which had been so near and dear to him. With an air of finality, as if to summarize his judgment, he said to me soberly, not with rancor but as if sick at heart that humanity could be so cruel, "It must have been an infernal machine."

The medical pronouncements had been that his chances for survival were about even and that the crisis would not be reached for a least three days. Our conversation had been rather extensive, and to permit him to conserve his strength I departed, promising to return that afternoon. Lehmann himself then asked for oxygen. His injuries were worse than had been diagnosed, for he died only about two hours after my leaving him. . . . I have often thought since that it was a broken heart as much as his injuries to which he succumbed.[68]

Several weeks after the tragic loss of the *Hindenburg*, Rosendahl received a telephone call from the German Consul General in New York City, advising him that his office had received an official package from Berlin with orders for it to be delivered formally to Mrs. Jean Rosendahl. On the appointed day, the consul presented himself to the Rosendahls' quarters and presented Jean with a package. She opened it to find "a handsomely framed, autographed photograph of Reichsmarshal [Hermann Göring] in resplendent white uniform and full regalia."[69] The photograph was accompanied by a letter—in German—from Göring to Jean, which the consul translated. As the consul looked over the letter, he said to the Rosendahls, "Please permit me to first read it in its entirety. It is the most touching letter of its kind that I have ever read."[70] As translated in future years:

The Reich Minister of Aviation   *Berlin W8, June 1937*
and supreme commander of the Air Force   *Leipzigerstr. 8*
                                           Phone: A 2, 6451

Dear Madam!

Because of the report of the German investigation commission of the dirigible accident in Lakehurst and through numerous appreciative reports of German crewmembers of the dirigible, I learned, deeply moved, about your wonderful help, which you bestowed on the injured German passengers and crewmembers, when the "Hindenburg" caught on fire.

With infinite kindness and love, you looked after my fellow countrymen. Through which you not only did help them in the first difficult hours, to get over the terrible experience, but also, time and time again,

through your visits and exemplary selfless act of kindness, to ease the
endurance of their pains and sufferings. With that, dear Madam, you
admirably fulfilled in the most beautiful way the work of human charity.
You may rest assured that your self-sacrificing act and care is not only felt
with indelible gratitude by the immediate befallen passengers and crew;
far beyond it, the entire German people will always honestly be grateful
for your outstandingly good relief, which you bestowed on its people.

I personally would like to express to you my most sincere gratitude and
I respectfully ask you if you would accept, as a small sign of my gratitude,
my enclosed photograph.

In sincere reverence, I remain most obediently
your
                    (signed)   Hermann Göring[71]

Of the translated letter, Rosendahl wrote, "It was indeed a truly sen-
timental expression of gratitude for the kindness and consideration Jean
had shown the shipwrecked sailors of the Hindenburg. It was a touching
composition of which the world would scarcely believe such a person as
[Göring] had ever been capable."[72]

There had been ninety-seven people on board the *Hindenburg*. Thirty-
six of them were passengers, of whom thirteen died in the crash or from
injuries. Normally, the ship had a crew of forty, but on this trip, there
were extra men on board for training purposes, bringing the number to
sixty-one, twenty-two of whom died. One civilian in the ground crew
died. Rosendahl offered the observation that for anyone who witnessed
the tragedy, it was a miracle that out of ninety-seven people on board,
nearly two-thirds—sixty-two of them—survived. For reasons that are
unclear, Rosendahl felt the need to make the distinction that the thirty-
five who lost their lives died of a fire—not a crash.[73]

The charred remains of the *Hindenburg* lay on the landing field for
weeks. Each time Rosendahl saw it, the thought ran through his mind
about the terrific price that had been paid in the loss of the ship and
"thirty-five blameless human souls, just to make the world truly con-
scious of an inert, invisible gas called helium."[74]

AFTERMATH OF THE *HINDENBURG* CRASH

Rosendahl had a full appreciation of the audio and visual record that Morrison and Nehlson produced of the final moments of the *Hindenburg*, but his feelings were ambivalent regarding the impact of that record on the LTA world. "Strange to say, the excellent photography of the burning of the *Hindenburg* dealt the airship one of its worst blows. This dramatic photography, both still and movie, has left in the minds of many people only the stark story of destruction, revealing none of the lessons of the tragedy."[1] With some resentment, he added, "Because the picture record of the *Hindenburg*'s end is so spectacular, it is a popular item with those who get up thrillers for the public. On the slightest provocation, the tale of the end of the *Hindenburg* is retold with pictures, and the public is informed that this accident spelled the end of all airships for all time."[2]

Putting his own spin on things, Rosendahl granted that the crash of the *Hindenburg* had marked the end of an era, but as he saw it, it was the *hydrogen* era that had ended.[3]

It was not surprising that Nehlsen and Morrison received an award for their coverage of the tragic crash. The citation that appeared in newspapers read:

> A special Medal of Merit has been awarded to Engineer Charles Nehlsen and Announcer Herbert Morrison of State WLS in Chicago, by Radio Guide, for their courageous work in the recent Hindenburg disaster.
>
> Sent by their station to Lakehurst, N. J., to make a recording for later broadcast of the arrival of the giant dirigible, Nehlsen and Morrison anticipated only routine duties. Fate ruled otherwise, however,

and these two men recorded history under the most trying circumstances any human being ever experienced. When the Hindenburg
burst into flame, Morrison, who had been speaking into the recording microphone of the beauty of the skyship, of the wisdom of the
officers who were waiting for calm weather to land, and of the crowd
gathered to witness the landing, almost lost control of himself at
sight of the crumpling mass of red-hot steel that was crushing human
life in its fiery grip. But Engineer Nehlsen kept his wits, calmed the
shaken announcer at his side, and from then on began the most horrible yet most wonderful achievement radio has ever accomplished.

Morrison and Nehlsen kept their posts and onto the recording
was graven aviation's unhappiest story. A story that will live for many
years to come. For this remarkable reporting job, under the most terrific strain ever endured by a broadcaster, Radio Guide has awarded
these two men its special Medal of Merit, so that people all over the
country will know of their heroic deed![4]

Ferdinand Lammot "Peter" Belin, Jr. was an American passenger
on board the *Hindenburg*'s last flight. Using his Leica camera, he docu-
mented some of the ship's last happy moments. He captured the entire
silhouette of the ship cast as a shadow on the surface below. Knowing
what was awaiting her soon thereafter, the shadow is a spine-chilling
apparition of the dirigible moving toward her death. Approaching the
landing field at Lakehurst, Belin captured an image of the giant airship
hangar, and getting closer, he photographed members of the ground crew
collecting at the landing flag in the mooring circle, awaiting the dropping of handling lines from the ship. He then unloaded his film from
the camera and stored it in a pocket. Moments later, the great ship was
going down in flames. Belin's camera was destroyed, but his life—and
film—were saved when he jumped from a window, landing safely on the
loamy soil of the NAS.

In the wake of this hydrogen-related disaster, reports emerged that
officials at the NAS had long feared the possibility of a hydrogen explosion when German airships were visiting Lakehurst. This was true
particularly when one of the Navy's helium-filled airships was docked

at the station and sharing the hangar with the hydrogen-filled German vessel. Whenever the *Graf Zeppelin* landed at the NAS, the *Los Angeles*—whether by design or coincidence—was usually off on a training flight, but on one occasion, both ships found themselves in the hangar at the same time. Rosendahl was in command of the *Los Angeles* at that time and he was growing increasingly nervous about the hydrogen-filled ship sharing the hangar with his ship, as the Germans tarried making their departure while awaiting ideal weather. As the story was told, when the departure delay for the *Graf* became too long, Rosendahl called an officer on the Zeppelin and said emphatically, "If you don't take that ship out tomorrow, I'll take her out myself." The *Graf* left the next day.[5]

Eckener received word of the disaster while in a hotel in Graz, Austria. His first words to the press were, "One thing this accident appears to have shown clearly is the necessity, which I have always urged, of using helium in preference to hydrogen in airships. The difficulty has been that we in Germany have no helium supplies of our own. Apart from that I cannot say anything as I have not heard details of the accident so far."[6]

There was a mixed response from Germany to the disaster. Eckener said the *Graf Zeppelin* service would be halted pending inquiry into the *Hindenburg* disaster while Reichminister of air, Colonel General Hermann Wilhelm Göring, ordered the builders at Friedrichshafen to rush completion of the LZ-130, sister ship to the *Hindenburg*. While Eckener was aware of the sabotage theory as the cause of the disaster, he thought there was a small likelihood of that because of the American security precautions. He thought it was far more likely that some electrical phenomenon, likely connected in some way to the weather, had played a role. Eckener offered three possible causes of the crash: hydrogen released while the ship was making ready for landing might have been ignited by a spark or by lightning; water ballast that had been released might have conducted a spark from the earth to the flammable gas-filled ship; or, less likely, a cigarette lighter might have set off the explosion.[7]

The Navy—and the world—needed to know what happened to the *Hindenburg*. The Secretary of Commerce appointed an investigating board consisting of three officials from that department who were experienced investigators: solicitor of the department South Trimble, Jr,

Colonel Denis Mulligan, and Major R. W. ("Shorty") Schroeder. The German government sent a technical commission composed of six distinguished aeronautical experts headed by Dr. Hugo Eckener. To avoid needless repetition and duplication of effort, the two investigating bodies met in joint session to hear testimony from numerous witnesses and survivors, and to question a variety of scientific experts.[8]

Newspapers reported that Rosendahl was only one of several lighter-than-air authorities who saw the burst of flames in the tale of the dirigible, the spread of the fire through the ship, and the explosions which tore her apart.[9] At the exact moment that the *Hindenburg* exploded, Associated Press photographer Murray Becker had his camera focused on the ship. He was capturing images as the ship dropped her lines to be hauled into the mooring mast, and "his camera, in a series of more than fifteen pictures recorded one of the most shocking air disasters in recent years from the moment of the explosion to the rescue of survivors."[10] In later years, Rosendahl wrote that a wealth of motion and still pictures had come from both professional and amateur photographers, but "unfortunately, not a single such picture revealed the initial appearance of the fire. This can probably be explained by the fact that cameras were focused on the forward part of the ship, whereas the fire first appeared near the stern. Furthermore the mooring operation was a routine subject that had been repeatedly photographed during the 1936 season, and now most picture men—and editors—were more interested in persons and personalities than in the airship itself."[11]

Uncertainties surrounding the cause of the *Hindenburg* disaster haunted Rosendahl for the remainder of his life. From the moment Wittemann planted the idea of sabotage in his mind, Rosendahl found it impossible to shake it. In his unpublished memoir, Rosendahl wrote:

> I was not only a witness to the complete sequence of the fire and destruction of the ship, but also a technical adviser to the investigating board, and therefore aware of all the testimony and evidence presented. It is my considered opinion that certain things, such as the following, were definitely established.
>
> After an uneventful ocean passage that involved no weather or other factors that could in any way have severely strained or damaged

her, the Hindenburg arrived at Lakehurst in perfectly normal condition, made a skillful and normal approach, and was being landed in a perfectly normal way. Three widely experienced airship captains on board had considered conditions entirely satisfactory for landing, as had we on the ground.

The loss of the ship was not due to any weakness or defect in the airship as a type. There was no evidence that warranted any belief that there was anything wrong within the ship before the fire broke out. The ship clearly fell prey to fire, and fire alone, of its own hydrogen. To ignite or explode the hydrogen within such an airship from other than premeditated or deliberate causes would require two factors: first, the escape of hydrogen, or a mixture of hydrogen and air outside the gas cells themselves; and second, an igniting agent such as a spark or a flame, at exactly the right place. The airship was not the victim of an explosion, but rather of a progressive burning after ignition.

Search for each of these two primary factors—a proper mixture of hydrogen and air plus an ignition agency, led in many directions, all blind alleys but one. I studied, and heard thoroughly discussed by experts, the many things that might have been contributory factors. The investigating board 'concluded' that the cause of the accident was the ignition of a mixture of free hydrogen and air in the after portion of the ship and that the "theory" of electrostatic "brush discharge" as the ignition agency appeared "most probable." The investigators merit high praise for their thorough work, having delved into every suggestion or possibility advanced. I do not see how they could have been more thorough.[12]

The cause of the crash of the *Hindenburg* became the subject of much speculation for many years after the event. Even after the experts had rendered their judgments, there was always room for conspiracy theory. That Rosendahl's mind was not put at peace on the matter was reflected in his memoir, written two decades after the crash. He emphasized that the investigating board did not intend to present their stated factors finally and definitively as the cause of the fire, but the report stated that "from the observations made, it appears that there was a quantity of free hydrogen present in the after part of the ship when the fire originated." The board stated also that "the theory that a brush discharge ignited such a mixture appears most probable."[13]

Rosendahl agreed to the extent that "if the origin of the fire within the ship was, in fact, accidental in nature, then the combination of these two remote possibilities, namely free hydrogen and St. Elmo's fire (or brush discharge), is, of all the theories or solutions advanced, the least improbable."[14]

"Turning now to the theory of sabotage or premeditated and deliberate origin of the fire, there is hardly any more speculation involved in support of it than in the support of the theory of accidental cause. We do know that, just prior to departure from Germany, there had been official warnings of threatened sabotage to the ship."[15] While not frequent, threats of sabotage of airships were far from unknown. Rosendahl had received several such threats during the 1936 season, and he dealt with it by having operatives mingle in the crowds to spot potential perpetrators. Further, he had received two allegedly "firm reports" that the *Hindenburg* actually had been sabotaged.

"We do not have any concrete, tangible evidence of sabotage, I admit. I saw the whole accident and heard all the testimony and discussion. I was familiar with the ship and with German standards of operation. In the absence of established accidental causes, in the light of circumstantial factors, and after a great deal of thought on the subject, I come to the conclusion that the Hindenburg fire resulted from sabotage."[16]

It was not difficult for Rosendahl to identify a motive for sabotage. Germany was then under the control of the Nazis—a movement not widely admired around the world and with dissidents inside Germany herself. The *Graf Zeppelin* and *Hindenburg* were bringing great prestige to Germany through their successes in the air. The ships were required to display the Nazi swastika painted in huge bold colors on their sides. Rosendahl thought the airships made good targets for sabotage by those wanting to damage the prestige of Germany, and that their destruction would not be an act of revenge against the passengers or crews but against the airships themselves and the Nazis.[17]

As for the method of such sabotage, Rosendahl thought the surest and easiest means was a timed incendiary planted inside the ship. Scientists had stated that the use of such an instrument would be a relatively simple matter and that the device itself would not need to be much larger than a fountain pen. The incendiary device would need to open only a small hole in the fabric gas cell to start a leak, and provide but a small spark to ignite the mixture of escaping hydrogen and air.[18]

Rosendahl went to great lengths to develop his sabotage theory in detail. He pointed out that there was an exhaust trunk between each two gas cells that led to the top of the ship that was large enough to allow a man to crawl through it. It would be very difficult to detect a small incendiary device if placed in such a location. The device's timer could have been armed either before departure or during flight.[19]

He speculated that a change in flight schedule may have interfered with the saboteur's use of a timing device. The *Hindenburg*'s planned arrival was originally set around sunrise on May 6, but the time had been postponed to 1800, followed by a further delay to permit the passing of a thunderstorm. Rosendahl speculated that if events had progressed as scheduled—at 1925—the time the fire originated, the ship would have been secured to her mooring mast with no passengers on board and with a small crew. Because the ship was then in the custody of NAS Lakehurst and, had anything untoward happened, suspicion would have been directed at the American Navy. The loss of life would have been small.[20]

Rosendahl closed out his treatise by giving heavy weight to observations made by crew members who were in the stern of the airship and in positions of vantage. They first saw fire within the fourth gas cell from the stern, and they saw it spread in both directions to adjacent cells. Simultaneously, one of the crew heard a muffled detonation "of the puffing kind one hears sometimes when lighting or turning off the burner of a kitchen gas stove."[21] Another man saw pieces of metal thrown upward.

> It is significant that they definitely saw the first fire within the ship, and at such a location as to agree with that at which the appearance of flames on top of the ship was first observed. That the first sign of fire was inside the ship and well away from the tip of the fin where

brush discharge could logically be expected, argues against the theory of St. Elmo's fire. Furthermore, as viewed from the ground, the first burst of fire was upward as from within the ship.[22]

On hearing of the loss of the *Hindenburg*, Dr. Eckener said that he believed the ship was the victim of sabotage. However, before leaving for the U.S. to participate in the investigation, Air Minister Göring instructed Eckener to give a radio presentation in which he discounted the sabotage theory and ascribed the fire to "natural causes," such as a hydrogen leak combined with a static spark. Further, it was the thinking of some Germans that the investigators who had been sent to Lakehurst went with instructions from the government to find "natural causes" and negate the sabotage theory. To the government, it was a matter of national prestige. The Nazi government needed to hold to the opinion that it was unthinkable that it could be vulnerable to sabotage.[23]

Although a body of highly qualified scientists had come to a consensus as to the cause of the *Hindenburg* fire, it would remain the object of conjecture and conspiracy theories for many years to come. According to Rosendahl, the loss of the *Hindenburg* plunged the Germans into a mood of gloom and mourning. "They devoured stories written about it."[24]

On June 1, 1937, at NAS Lakehurst, Americans and Germans joined in a memorial tribute to those who had lost their lives in the crash of the *Hindenburg*. Rosendahl participated as a representative of the U.S. along with Lieutenant Colonel Joachin Breithaupt, the official representative of the German Air Ministry who was on the Nazi government's commission participating in the investigation of the crash. The two men placed floral wreaths against the ruins of the airship. Standing at the ship's bow, Breithaupt gave a brief speech and the Nazi salute accompanied by "Heil Hitler." The other German members of the commission joined him in the salute. His brief remarks consisted of, "In the names of the German commission and the survivors, I place this wreath in memory of our brave comrades and friends. Your living and your departure has [sic] not been in vain. You have died for the honor and greatness of Germany, and the Fatherland will never forget you. Good-bye, comrades, Heil Hitler."[25]

Rosendahl remained silent as he placed the Navy's wreath beside that of the Germans'. After the ceremony, the American and German groups drove to the memorial chapel on the naval reservation, where Breithaupt placed a wreath at the door to honor the men of the U.S. Navy who had lost their lives in the Navy's three airship disasters.

———

In the normal course of things, Rosendahl's tour at Lakehurst would have ended in the summer of 1937 to return to sea duty, but because the fate of airships was now hanging in the balance, he remained in command of the NAS for another year to help determine the future of the LTA service. Dr. Eckener had made repeated requests to the American government to allow the sale of helium to Germany for their airship program, but the governing board had never given its approval, considering that helium might have military applications. While his latest request was under consideration in Washington, there remained hope that LZ-130 would follow up the successes of the *Graf Zeppelin* and *Hindenburg*.

In July 1938, Rosendahl and Jean were in Germany for the celebration of Count Ferdinand von Zeppelin's one-hundredth birthday. Mayor Captain Schiller presented Rosendahl with the large iron key to Zeppelinheim Village near Frankfurt Airport. The Germans regarded this village as the future world dirigible base, and the key symbolized the close ties between German and American airship men—"a friendship which flourishes despite Germany's lack of American helium supplies."[26]

Schiller asked Rosendahl if he wished to meet Air Minister Hermann Göring, with whom he had exchanged messages at the time of the *Hindenburg* tragedy. Rosendahl expressed his gratitude but said that he did not want to take up the air minister's time unless his airship friends thought it important for him to do so. It was not considered necessary.[27]

Since the crash of the *Hindenburg*, Eckener had changed his thinking about helium altogether. The disadvantages of helium—heavier, less lifting power, and very expensive—were outweighed by its single greatest advantage—safety. Use of helium was attended also by another advantage over hydrogen—airships using helium required only one and a half times their capacity to be replenished annually while hydrogen had to be replaced five to ten times per year.

The U.S. had ample helium supplies to satisfy domestic and foreign appetites. The Amarillo, Texas, helium facility could produce 24 million cubic feet of helium annually, but stepping up production beyond that amount could be achieved easily if required. The director of the U.S. Bureau of Mines estimated that large quantities of the gas could be produced for about $5 per cubic foot. Thus, it was calculated that the 7,063,000-cubic-feet capacity of the *Hindenburg* could have been provided for approximately $35,315.

Wanting to prevent the export of helium to foreign powers for potential military purposes, the U.S. required that sales of helium obtain the approval of the national munitions board and the secretary of the interior. The national munitions board was composed of the secretaries of state, treasury, war, navy, and commerce. Sale of helium to a foreign country required the unanimous approval of these five board members and the secretary of the interior, who, at this time was Harold Ickes.[28] Interestingly, Ickes sat on the board only when there were issues related to the sale of helium.

There had been an informal understanding that Eckener's company could purchase nearly 17,900,000 cubic feet of helium for the LZ-130.[29] Thinking that a personal appearance might sway the president, Eckener traveled to Washington to implore Roosevelt to approve the sale. The board, however, required a guarantee that helium sold to Germany would not be used for military purposes, and because a guarantee had not been received, Ickes blocked Germany's request.[30] Ickes and his staff claimed that the changing political conditions in Europe made it impossible to arrive at a formula that would provide the required guarantees.

The American Army and Navy had given assurances that there were no good reasons to withhold helium from Germany, and Ickes stood alone in his opposition. Ickes apparently was unwilling to acknowledge what American military men knew: There would be no place for dirigibles in the skies over Europe in a modern war, especially given the rapid advances being made with airplanes.

The Rosendahls returned to the U.S. on July 18, 1938, after having been hosted royally by the German people. As they crossed the Atlantic on the steamer *Bremen*, Rosendahl realized it was going to be anticlimactic "to return to the depressing airship situation in the United States. Even so, I was unprepared for the form of greeting that awaited me."[31] Ickes attacked Rosendahl, claiming he had changed his mind regarding helium after having been "wined and dined" in Germany. Rosendahl's words were a matter of record, and he had not changed his views at all on helium. The situation devolved into a petty war of words that eventually ran its course.

Writing of this time, Rosendahl claimed, "The years 1934 to 1938 had been happy ones in spots, and hectic in others. Whatever lay ahead at sea would be welcome relief from the turbulent airship scene I had lived with for four years."[32]

On July 10, 1938, Rosendahl was ordered to duty as executive officer of the USS *Milwaukee*, then in dock at the Pearl Harbor Navy Yard.

Eckener's dreams for his commercial airship enterprise came to a halt on September 1, 1939, when Germany invaded Poland. LZ-130 was grounded immediately and her hydrogen cells were emptied prior to her being suspended from the ceiling of her hangar for the duration of the war. LZ-131 never progressed beyond the earliest stages of construction and, thus, was never completed.

WASHINGTON NIGHTMARE

Following the *Hindenburg*'s successful 1936 season, Rosendahl felt no assurance that he would ever return to airships—"I was not even sure I wanted to, in view of the Navy's inability or unwillingness to meet the airship issue squarely."[1] The crashes of the *Macon* and the *Hindenburg* left him facing the biggest void in his career since the early days when he looked to Fate to guide him.

Admittedly, Rosendahl liked going to sea, and, at least for a brief while, it provided an escape from the travails of the LTA program—but not for long. The morning after New Year's Day 1939, as he stood on the deck of the *Milwaukee*, then in San Diego Harbor, his mind was on anything but airships. Glancing up the harbor, he sighted a three-star admiral's barge approaching the *Milwaukee*'s gangway. It was Admiral King bringing a copy of correspondence he had just received.[2]

King was then a vice admiral serving as the commander of Aircraft Battle Force.

> In characteristically strong, letter-perfect penmanship, which mirrored his clear mental processes and determination, Admiral King had inscribed a note to me on the face of the correspondence which related to an airship matter. Like the innocent bystander on the corner minding his own business, here I was, at sea, undergoing my periodic professional cleansing by salt water, and almost completely insulated from Departmental airship matters. This evidence of King's continued and sincere attitude quickly revived my dormant interest, but it didn't enter my mind that I was going to be "in the middle"

of a situation wherein King and other far-sighted officers would be countered by an anti-airship group within the Navy itself.[3]

After Rosendahl read the correspondence, he sent a signal to the admiral's flagship, asking permission to see him, to which he received a prompt "affirmative." Rosendahl was in King's office without delay, where they embarked on a conversation that turned the pages of history back to 1934 when the LTA service at Lakehurst was trying to get blimps into some activity whereby the rest of the Navy could appreciate their capabilities.

As Rosendahl interpreted things, the Navy was proceeding on a bare-bones existence at Lakehurst with blimp experimentation while training limited numbers of personnel. The airship officers could only wonder what it was all about, conducting this basic activity without apparent thought or plan. "It was amazing how a proud Service that had often been faced with tremendous problems of many kinds, seemed unable or unwilling to cope with airship problems." Any way Rosendahl looked at it, this was a peculiar situation—"the Navy was conducting an activity without telling those in the activity what its basic purpose was, and without a plan for service use of the activity."[4]

When Rosendahl went to sea in 1938, his successor at Lakehurst was Commander J. L. Kenworthy. With the backing of Commander Garland Fulton in the Bureau of Aeronautics, Kenworthy revived the effort to get blimps operating with some part of the fleet to develop wartime uses of airships. Rosendahl's efforts at this had met with limited interest among a few admirals who supported the use of blimps at some Southern California base, but every time his proposal reached the commander-in-chief's staff, it was rejected.[5]

There was a glimmer of new hope, however, when a small former airship shed at NAS San Diego was being vacated. With urging from NAS Lakehurst, the Bureau of Aeronautics addressed a letter to the chief of naval operations, recommending that, about June 1939, two blimps be transferred from Lakehurst to San Diego to "afford opportunity for appraising the value of this type of aircraft for work in proximity of the Fleet."[6]

It was at this point that Admiral King brought Rosendahl back into the picture. Chief of the Bureau of Aeronautics, Rear Admiral Arthur B. Cook, sent copies of pertinent letters relating to blimps to King, asking for his support. King forwarded the letters to Rosendahl with a note stating, "My dear Rosendahl—Herewith copies of letters that explain themselves. I will, of course, back up the ideas when they are presented to me. EJK."[7]

About mid-March, while in the Caribbean, Rosendahl received copies of the somewhat startling correspondence that had resulted from the blimp proposal. The simple proposal had called for two small blimps to be based at San Diego, using an old balloon hangar as a dock and operating from a mooring mast on an isolated North Island and another on the distant San Clemente Island in the fleet operating area.

Once again, the proposal died at the feet of the commander-in-chief, who stated that the presence of two blimps "would disrupt flight operations of the aircraft units of the Fleet based at San Diego . . . would interfere with the overhaul and repair services of the Fleet," and that "their presence would decrease the efficiency of the operations of important units of the Fleet."[8] According to Rosendahl, the chief of naval operations "swallowed this and called the whole thing off."[9]

Rosendahl was aware that a young airplane officer on the commander-in-chief's staff[10] had put forward these unfounded criticisms, yet Rosendahl "marveled that a mature flag officer could affix his signature to such farfetched stuff."[11]

Commander Kenworthy once again earned Rosendahl's admiration for his handling of the correspondence relating to the blimp matter. He had received the correspondence as "for information" but not for "comment." Disregarding these "flags," Kenworthy strongly pointed out the absurdity of conducting an airship training and development program while at the same time denying the craft the opportunity to develop their wartime uses for which they were intended.

Kenworthy expanded his argument to offer specific recommendations for the immediate location of facilities in areas where blimps would be needed in wartime "in view of a rapidly changing international situation and its implications which bear on the problem of national defense."[12] These "sensible recommendations" went into a file and were forgotten.[13]

The departmental rejection of the blimp proposal—viewed as a rejection of airships in general—came as bitter news to Rosendahl, but he was counting on his seagoing duties on board the *Milwaukee* to keep him occupied.

———

During an intermission from fleet exercises, Admiral H. R. Stark left his flagship, the USS *Concord*, to attend a smoker hosted by the *Milwaukee*. He was the center of conversation because of his impending appointment as chief of naval operations. Later, as he was leaving to return to his ship, he paused at the head of the *Milwaukee*'s gangway to ask Rosendahl about airships. A few days later, Stark invited Rosendahl to dinner on board his flagship to discuss these matters further. Rosendahl presumed Stark's interest resulted from the fact that, as the Navy's top uniformed official in Washington, airships would be one of the issues confronting him. Their discussion was capped off with Stark asking Rosendahl to write up some factual matters "in a perfectly frank way" for him.[14]

The *Milwaukee* had participated in a fleet exercise in which one side had drawn high praise for their successes with the use of submarines. Rosendahl viewed this as an inadequacy in the Navy's antisubmarine capabilities. "Heartened by the belief of such officers as King and Stark that airships should be given a chance to demonstrate their abilities, I felt the situation presented an opportunity to strike a blow for blimps. In fact, General Order Number Nine urged officers to submit ideas and suggestions for improvements relative to naval efficiency, especially suggestions based on practical experience."[15]

At King's suggestion, Rosendahl submitted a plan for the establishment of a tactical unit of blimps using such craft as were already available, despite their primitive nature. The plan called for blimps to be based primarily at Lakehurst to operate with seagoing forces in a manner similar to what the flying boats had done. The plan was laid out in a letter to the secretary of the Navy but, as it made its way through channels, Rosendahl found those channels to have been "mined" against airships.[16]

Admiral Stark commented that it had occurred to him that it would be good to explore blimps as antisubmarine and observation craft in U.S.

coastal lanes, but because King's interest in LTA craft was well known, the letter was forwarded to him for comment. King acknowledged the existing evidence indicating the potential usefulness of nonrigid airships and concluded that Rosendahl's proposal was not only feasible but necessary, and he recommended carrying it out.

Rosendahl had reason to be pleased over the prospects for his proposal when it reached the Battle Force commander, "a four-star non-aviator" who endorsed it "beyond question" and promoted expanding the use of nonrigids in defense forces and as valuable adjuncts to the surface fleet.[17]

Rosendahl's unpublished memoir contained the following non-documentable account of what happened next to his proposal.

> On the C-in-C's staff was an aviation commander who had a record of bitter opposition to airships. While at the Naval War College a few years earlier, he had written a denunciation of airships which Admiral Pratt, the head of the College, had passed on to his friend Admiral Moffett. Moffett was distressed by the commander's paper and passed it on to me for refutation. This I did in vigorous terms, to Moffett's satisfaction, and he passed my rebuttal on to the commander. It was admittedly strong stuff. The net result, of course, was that anything favorable to airships, particularly if it came from me, was sure to rouse this particular commander. On the C-in-C staff he had another opportunity when my proposal reached the Fleet flagship for endorsement. One weighty factor in the commander's mind was that airplanes weren't yet getting all the support he felt they should; so he was opposed to spending money on airships if there was a chance that it might otherwise go to planes. Disregarding what had been said by endorsing admirals, the C-in-C wrote an endorsement that spelled the end to my proposal.[18]

The commander-in-chief's official endorsement effectively blocked Rosendahl's proposal. Years later, Rosendahl wrote of this decision and its impact on the LTA program at what he considered a critical time in history.

> Less than two years later, World War II descended upon us and we were desperate for blimps. Those two years, of course, should have

been spent not only in the procurement of blimps, but, even more important, in training for their use with other naval forces and in developing an organization for them. The war caught us without an airship organization, even on paper . . . and at a time when the world was once more becoming seriously worried about submarines.[19]

The ships of the fleet were back in the Pacific in their designated positions when, on September 1, 1939, word of German-Poland hostilities reached the U.S. The White House received word by telephone at 0250 (EST) from Ambassador Biddle in Warsaw and from Ambassador Bullitt in Paris that Germany had invaded Poland and bombed four cities.

On September 27, 1939, it was announced that the Navy was prepared for the immediate transfer of up to one-third of the Pacific Fleet from the West Coast to Hawaii to engage in intensive antisubmarine training and combat drills "in the peaceful privacy of the mid-Pacific." The decision to dispatch a segment of the fleet to Hawaii came within twenty-four hours of a closed conference between the president and Admiral Harold R. Stark, now chief of naval operations.[20]

The experience with submarines in the First World War prompted the fleet movement, and most of the vessels involved were destroyers— "the ablest adversaries of submarines."[21] Apparently, most of the Navy's senior leadership, while remembering the experience with submarines, had forgotten the important and highly effective role of blimps for hunting U-boats.

The president had not put the nation on a war footing, but inside the Navy, there was a palpable sense that war was inevitable—"All signs were ominous."[22]

Rosendahl's preoccupation with seagoing duties made any airship news of mere academic interest to him, but he was gratified to learn that in October 1939, the general board had reaffirmed the favorable airship policy which it had handed down two and a half years previously.

On January 2, 1940, Charles Edison, after serving three years as assistant secretary of the Navy, became the secretary of the Navy, succeeding the late Claude A. Swanson. Rosendahl had prior contact with Edison while in command of NAS Lakehurst, and he was aware that Edison had formed the opinion that airships had never had an adequate opportunity for development.

Edison selected King to accompany him on a tour of naval facilities, and while in Hawaii, he asked for an audience with Rosendahl which resulted in an agreement that Rosendahl should return to airship duty. While his belief in airships was as strong as ever, he suspected that any airship proponent as zealous as he would be most unwelcomed in the Bureau of Aeronautics, dominated as it was by airplane men—many of whom were ardently opposed to airships.

Because Rosendahl was only a commander, he thought it hopeless for him to take on the airship struggle without higher-placed backing—any real hope for airships had to come from the top.[23] Edison suggested that Rosendahl be attached to his office and try to make changes from there.[24] With King's approval, Rosendahl reported to the secretary of the Navy on May 23, 1940. He was now hopeful that the airship impasse would be broken at last.[25]

Heading into his new position, Rosendahl was thinking, "With the prestige of the office of the Secretary of the Navy in support, together with the active help of such a highly regarded officer as Admiral King, a wholly new situation had been created for airships."[26] Yet, he still had obstacles to overcome and he found cooperation a difficult thing to get.

The secretary of the Navy's directive to Rosendahl had stated that the General Board's lighter-than-air report of February 17, 1937, had been approved by him. Following Secretary Swanson's death, a reaffirmation letter was found in his desk. The "Special Report on the Lighter-than-Air Situation" dated February 12, 1940, had been approved by him also. These documents set them up clearly as Navy policy. The contribution of the General Board was:

> To build and maintain nonrigid airships in numbers and classes adequate for coastal patrol and other essential naval purposes. . . . To explore the possibilities of developing rigid airships to meet naval requirements, to cooperate with other agencies in developing large commercial airships, and to continue training personnel.[27]

The special report had been made by Rear Admiral King and Captain Garland Fulton at the direction of Secretary Edison. Rosendahl knew that King never attached his name to any project or idea without being satisfied with its merits. Fulton had grown up with the naval airship program and possessed more technical knowledge of airships—large and small—than anyone in the U.S. He was the Navy's leading expert on the technical aspects of airships.

As summarized by Rosendahl, the "King-Fulton report was an exhaustive survey, concluding with a recommended program for clear-cut recognition of airships, and a naval airship construction program for immediate building of a training rigid airship of 3,000,000 cu. ft. volume, and annual building of two to four nonrigid airships per year. . . . Altogether, it was a solid, common-sense program, consistent in every respect with the Navy's long-continued official interest."[28]

Secretary Edison heard through the "grapevine" that his tenure in office was drawing short because of some political reorganizations by the president. On June 24, 1940, Edison's "resignation was accepted." It was unknown who would become the next secretary of the Navy and how he would react to having Rosendahl in his organization. Subsequently, Rosendahl was shifted to the office of the assistant secretary of the Navy.

The Navy's airship program was in a highly uncertain state, and Rosendahl found himself alone, surrounded by hostile forces. He described what his situation was like during this time.

I soon learned what it meant to be alone and furthering a project against the wishes of "the organization." Their countermeasures were directed not only at the airship project, but also at me personally. As but one example, even while in the office of the Assistant Secretary, it was difficult for me to get office space and typing assistance. During this tour in the Department, I had at least six different typists, often on only a part-time basis, and at times returned to find my desk and file unexpectedly moved to some other cubby hole. The double-barreled attack produced one clear result. It succeeded in stealing a lot of very valuable time from the effort to achieve adequate airship readiness and strength. As for its effects on me, it was, of course, irritating and discouraging, but in the long run, I did not suffer from it professionally or personally. It didn't even give me an ulcer.[29]

On June 4, 1940, the U.S. Senate approved legislation authorizing expansion of the Navy's air force to 10,000 planes and providing for the establishment of a defensive ring of naval air bases around the U.S.[30] Part of the "10,000 Plane Program" called for the addition of forty-eight blimps. A multitude of problems had to be worked out, the largest of which was the provision of an airship organization. The responsibility fell to Rosendahl to head up boards to make recommendations for solutions.

While he had not succeeded in overcoming the Navy's opposition to building more rigid airships, he had won a victory for blimps as Congress authorized more of them to be built. He had convinced the Navy and Congress of the economy of blimps compared to rigid airships. The *Akron* had a capacity of 6,500,000 cubic feet, while that of the *K-2*, then the only modern airship in service, was only 400,000 cubic feet. Four new combat blimps and two training blimps would cost but $1,300,000, and this was just the beginning for the new blimp program.[31]

Rosendahl remained clear in his thinking about blimps—it was his belief that blimps would be useful in coastal patrol work, patrolling America's harbors and over sea lanes guarding convoys. In addition to speeds of 68 miles per hour, the blimps had the advantage over airplanes of being able to fly slowly to allow greater scrutiny of surface and sub-surface waters in the task of detecting mines and submarines, which constituted the chief contribution of blimps in the First World War. He believed this would be the chief value of blimps in all future wars. At a normal cruising speed of 40 miles per hour, blimps could carry enough fuel to cover 2,000 miles and stay aloft for slightly more than two days.[32]

The blimp program required bases in addition to Lakehurst. Following extensive study of maps, the special board visited candidate sites. This involved a tremendous amount of work, covering the coasts from Maine to the tip of Florida, from the Straits of Juan de Fuca to the Mexican border. These surveys were the first steps toward acquiring Naval airship bases at South Weymouth, Massachusetts; Elizabeth City,

North Carolina; Glynco, Georgia; Richmond, Florida; Houma, Louisiana; Hitchcock, Texas; Santa Ana, California; and Tillamook, Oregon.[33] Rosendahl envisioned a base in the Miami area capable of housing six 250-foot blimps.

On the West Coast, the Navy needed a blimp base in the San Francisco area, but the base at Sunnyvale had been transferred to the Army, which was using it for basic air training. While everyone recognized the wisdom of the Navy's using Sunnyvale as a blimp base and relocating the Army's training base, the issue was politically sensitive. The issue was resolved in a meeting that included Admiral Stark, General George C. Marshall, and several other high-ranking Army figures. Marshall grasped the situation immediately and directed General H. H. ("Hap") Arnold to agree to the move and Congress appropriated $7,000,000 for the new Army base.

Issues surrounding a blimp base in Florida were not so simple. Because of the numerous shipping lanes to and from Central and South America, the Caribbean was an area that presented U-boats with rich targets. The density of shipping traffic was along the Florida coast, through the Florida Straits, through the passages between the islands of the West Indies, and in other critical areas in the Caribbean and Gulf of Mexico.

The original blimp program called for a base in Southern Florida comparable to NAS Lakehurst, from which the Navy could extend blimp operations into the entire Caribbean area. Rosendahl's board set out to find a suitable site for a base in September 1940, and after an extensive search, it filed its report and recommendations. "Not long thereafter, the Chief of the Bureau of Aeronautics sent for me. He was in a burning rage. 'I am not going to approve an airship base for Southern Florida. In the first place, our naval airplanes will take care of any submarines in that area, and what's more, no submarines would ever attempt to get through the Straits of Florida into the Gulf of Mexico.'" The chief was aware also that there was some noise from D.C. that too many military installations were going to Florida.[34]

> As the bloody pages of history show, the Caribbean and its swarming trade routes became one of the earliest and most lucrative hunting grounds the U-boats had. Unaware of the BUAER Chief's angry

interdiction, they did pass through the Straits of Florida and they did operate in the Gulf of Mexico. Not only was the Bureau Chief's action contrary to the recommendations of other officers and agencies at least as well qualified to judge, but it ran afoul of the recommendations of the Commander of the Atlantic Fleet.[35]

In mid-1940, Congressional figures, backed by the Navy, exhibited a growing concern over the vulnerability of American naval forces in the Atlantic. While discussions centered on the need to replace battleships with newly designed, smaller ships, the major sentiment surrounded strengthening the Atlantic Fleet. In a broadcast on June 16, 1940, Rear Admiral King of the Navy's general board told his audience that the country might need a two-ocean navy in the future—defined as one strong enough in the Pacific to meet any threat and simultaneously strong enough to meet any situation in the Atlantic.

King proclaimed, "We may need such a navy for the future. For the present, however, we must concentrate on building up the navy now authorized. When we get along with that building we can consider the advisability of a two-ocean navy," adding that as long as the Panama Canal was secure, and the fleet could move quickly from one ocean to the other, the U.S. could get along "with what you might call a one and one-half ocean navy."[36]

In December 1940, the Navy Department announced a change of command of "its steadily increasing patrol force in the Atlantic," ordering nineteen organized reserve fleet divisions to report for active duty within thirty days. The fleet divisions comprised sixty-five officers and 1,540 men and came under the command of Rear Admiral King. Captain Oscar C. Badger was assigned as chief of staff and King's aide.[37] This force inevitably developed into a growing Atlantic Fleet.[38]

A few months later, Admiral King, accompanied by Captain Badger, went to Washington and asked Rosendahl to meet with them. They explained that the limited number of patrol vessels and antisubmarine forces that had been assigned to them were needed urgently for convoy duty, which left extremely few available for area patrols. They were convinced that the Caribbean, fanning out from the coast of Southern

Florida, would be an irresistible target for U-boats and that blimps could provide a useful reconnaissance function, summoning prompt counter-measures by airplanes and patrol craft once enemy vessels were sighted.

Rosendahl took the ideas put forth by King and Badger and trans-lated them into a plan for blimp operations and facilities in the Florida-Caribbean area. When he set the proposal into motion through official channels, he discovered quickly that the Bureau of Aeronautics barrier against a blimp base in Florida stood firm. Time dragged on with no action until, five days after the attack on Pearl Harbor, the president directed the full blimp program to be executed.

Admiral King was called to Washington in preparation for taking over higher command, and not long after arriving, he asked Rosendahl for a memorandum that he had prepared and submitted at King's direc-tion. Subsequently, on December 20, Rosendahl met with Admiral Stark concerning the blimp program and showed him King's initials, indicat-ing his approval of yet another memorandum that called for the Carib-bean blimp program and the Southern Florida airship base. Stark told Rosendahl that if King wanted them, he would get them.[39]

As an official memorandum was prepared and routed through official channels, Stark directed Rosendahl to tell Secretary of the Navy Frank Knox about the desirability of the Caribbean program. With Rosendahl still in his office, Stark telephoned Secretary Knox to advise him of the authorized but yet-to-be-implemented blimp program and to inform him that the president had said, "Hell, I've wanted that for the last year."[40]

When Secretary Knox returned from an inspection tour of the dam-age done at Pearl Harbor, he met with Rosendahl, greeting him with, "Well, I see you got your program through while I was away," to which Rosendahl replied that it was Admiral Stark who had finally been able to discuss it with the president, and added that Stark had advised him to go ahead with the program. Knox advised Rosendahl not to proceed too fast as the program would have to be approved by him or the president, and he would discuss it with the president. The meeting ended.[41]

The Bureau of Aeronautics continued to oppose the blimp base in Florida, but once Admiral King was installed as Commander-in-Chief of the U.S. Fleet and Chief of Naval Operations, the Florida base became a reality, but it was not until three months after the bombing of Pearl Harbor that the Navy got a board to Florida to select a site. When Rosendahl finally got blimps to Florida, the worst U-boat activity had subsided, and he felt it would be a matter of speculation as to what they could have achieved if they had been in place earlier.[42]

While Rosendahl was in a position that should have allowed him to engineer great advances for LTA craft, he was actually in a hostile environment, surrounded and outnumbered by airplane advocates who held strong anti-airship sentiments. He felt like a "marked man" who was the target of unabated "sniping," both overtly and covertly.

Rosendahl felt that airship men detailed directly to airship duty in the Navy Department had never had an easy time of it, but this was particularly true just prior to and during World War II. "Some yielded to expediency, submerged as they were in a scene dominated by airplanes and airplane men who had little or no time for or interest in airships. As for non-aviation officers and personnel in the Department and elsewhere throughout the service, they were generally sympathetic, cooperative and easy to work with in airship matters."[43]

On June 8, 1940, it was announced publicly that the House of Representatives had received a conference report on the Navy expansion bill, which authorized the Navy to build its LTA strength to forty-eight non-rigid airships to be used for coastal scouting and patrol. These airships were to be added to the already existing authorization for one rigid airship to be used for training purposes. The swiftness of this construction was dependent upon the president's approval of the emergency defense funds to construct airships, and Secretary Edison, soon to retire from his position, urged the quick availability of funds to build the airships.[44]

When the president did speak out on the matter, it required further clarification and discussion, and Rosendahl was called to testify before the Senate Appropriations Committee. While the House had approved a $200,000 blimp in the defense appropriation measure, it failed to make available the initial $300,000 appropriation for rigid airships after the president made a last-minute recommendation that the proposed 3,000,000-cubic-feet training airship be split into three smaller ships.[45]

When the Senate Appropriations Committee brought the defense bill to the floor for action, it was missing the requested funds for the rigid training airship, ending expectations that the Navy would get this ship in 1940.[46]

As Rosendahl explained the issue, "In those days, every national defense project needed a priority rating. They varied from 'A' to 'AAA,' in many combinations of letters and numbers, but the saying around Washington was that only one priority meant anything and that was 'FDR.' The President took an interest in every defense project, it seemed."[47]

"A blimp program had been included . . . in the Act which became law on 15 June 1940, but Admiral Stark did not feel we should proceed with its full execution until we had those three magic initials on a piece of paper."[48]

To exemplify his frustrations in matters surrounding LTA craft, Rosendahl recalled a day in early 1941 when Admiral Stark sent for him. Stark asked him to sit down and Rosendahl wondered what was coming. "Rosendahl," he said, "You have worked hard for the airship program and I am satisfied no one could have done more. But I have not yet been able to get the President to make a decision on it, and it doesn't seem that I can jar it loose. I know it would be a great disappointment to you as well as to me, but perhaps we should now drop the whole matter."[49]

This suggestion came as a terrific blow to Rosendahl, but he asked Stark if they might try one more time. Stark unhesitatingly agreed to try again. This time, a memorandum was prepared for the secretary of the Navy to send to the president, which cited that the proposed blimp program was in accord with approved naval policy; that belief in the value of blimps had been expressed by every chief of the Bureau of Aeronautics; that district commandants in San Francisco and in the Canal Zone had requested blimps; that the program had the approval of Admiral King, then commanding the Atlantic Fleet; and that the general board had recommended action.[50]

The memorandum was effective. On April 22, 1941, the president approved the go-ahead for the first year's increment. Rosendahl found the president's response to be interesting in light of the history of the issue:

I approve your memo of April 18th in regard to the additional patrol blimps and authorization for three temporary stations.

This whole thing amuses me a little, and I see no reason why you should not tell the Navy so. After construction of our last big dirigible, the Navy first wanted no more big dirigibles built and then turned around and recommended the construction of one or two big ones.

All through these several years I took the position that the Navy ought to experiment with one or two small dirigibles 250 or 300 feet long, or with an enlarged form of blimp, both of which types could be used for near-shore patrol purposes.

The Navy's attitude was that it was not interested in the medium-sized patrol ship and so many reasons were advanced against building a medium-sized lighter-than-air craft that nothing was done about it.

I am heartily in favor of what I have been heartily in favor of all this time.[51]

Rosendahl found the last sentence of the president's memorandum somewhat enigmatic because no one who had spoken with the president ever related the idea that he was heartily in favor of airships. "In any event, we now had something in writing."[52]

After Admiral Stark received presidential approval, he once again called for Rosendahl and said, "Read this, Rosendahl. Congratulations. Now you can move ahead."[53] By that time, there was a huge backlog of things to put in motion that had accumulated by the summer of 1941. Rosendahl was called upon to make repeated appearances before Congressional committees and attend numerous sessions with airship boards in addition to a heavy administrative load within the department. "Weekends and office hours became only a myth; they ran continuously with timeout only to eat and sleep. But the airship program now stood on firmer ground."[54]

By early September 1941, the first year's program was well underway, and Rosendahl turned his attention to planning for the second year by drawing up a memorandum for the secretary to send to the president for approval. This plan asked for twenty-seven more blimps and three more airship bases in the continental U.S. Further, Stark directed Rosendahl to include a request for five airship bases outside the continental U.S. Rosendahl got no action from his proposal until five days after Pearl Harbor had been attacked.

When Stark sent for Rosendahl again, Admirals King and Ingersoll were in his office. Stark handed Rosendahl a memorandum to read—it was the president's approval for the full program.

On April 23, 1942, Rosendahl was moved from the office of the chief of naval operations to the Bureau of Aeronautics. Just prior to this move, Rosendahl had discussed with King the possibility of getting another airship officer into the department when he left for sea duty. Captain Thomas "Tex" Settle's name was suggested. He was at sea at the time and not eager for any shore duty, but Secretary Knox knew Settle and, thus, he and King selected Settle to fill the position.[55] Settle was quite capable, and the decision proved to be a good one.

Rosendahl was able to see the start of the full implementation of the expanded blimp program, with the full weight of Admiral King's prestige behind it, before he set off to sea. Rosendahl witnessed some of the sweeping changes that were being made in the Aeronautical Organization. Material matters became the chief function of the Bureau of Aeronautics, while operational and administrative functions were put under the chief of naval operations. The entire Navy Department was being reorganized, but before all of the changes were made, Rosendahl's "Washington nightmare" was behind him, and he was out in the Pacific Ocean where "one at least knew who was shooting at him."[56]

The world stage was changing rapidly, and as things evolved, Rosendahl had to leave the LTA program behind in the hands of others as he headed to the Pacific to the surface fleet. He was with his mother when she died on November 6, 1941, and a month later, the U.S. was at war with Japan.

—•—

When Pearl Harbor was attacked on December 7, 1941, the USS *Minneapolis* (CA-36) was at sea, operating several miles outside the harbor, steaming toward Pearl as the attack was taking place. The smoke and fires resulting from the attack were visible over the horizon, and the initial impression from the *Minneapolis* was that the smoke was from burning sugar cane fields—such as happened regularly at harvest time—but all became clear at 0823 when the ship received the message, "The Japanese are attacking Pearl Harbor; this is no drill."[57] From that moment, the source of the smoke was apparent.

Months later, Rosendahl received orders to assume command of the *Minneapolis*. With tight security regarding the names and locations of warships, finding the *Minneapolis* and joining her became an adventure of its own. His orders required him to report to the Commander-in-Chief of the Pacific Fleet, Admiral Chester W. Nimitz. Nimitz greeted Rosendahl and then promptly turned him over to members of his staff for a briefing on strategy and the situation in the Pacific. "Never before had the expanses of the Pacific seemed so tremendous to me. The briefing impressed upon me the magnitude of the task confronting us."[58]

An account of Rosendahl's wartime command of the *Minneapolis* is beyond the scope of this book, which focuses on the history of the LTA program. Rosendahl performed brilliantly as he waged an epic battle to save his ship after she was struck simultaneously by two Japanese torpedoes. He succeeded in nursing the ship back to Pearl Harbor, where his time with the *Minneapolis* came to an end. Commander McCool was given command of the ship as Rosendahl returned to Washington, D.C., where he was promoted to rear admiral and given command of the Navy's expanding LTA program.

RETURN TO AIRSHIPS AND RETIREMENT

When Rosendahl left Washington, D.C., to take command of the *Minneapolis*, Admiral King told him—off the record—that he intended to bring him back to airship duty once he completed his combat command tour. With that in mind, Rosendahl went to see Admiral Nimitz and learned that Nimitz was fully aware of King's intentions, and with Nimitz's approval, Rosendahl wrote an informal letter to King as a gentle reminder of the plan.

In his reply, King informed Rosendahl that he had created an Airship Training Command with headquarters at NAS Lakehurst and that he, Rosendahl, would be given the new command while simultaneously being nominated for flag rank.

While Rosendahl was resting and recovering from some health issues encountered in the Pacific, he had administrative plans to make, such as selecting a staff and exploring general aviation training.

> Lakehurst in mid-May 1943 was a beehive of activity such as that station had never seen. The U-boat threat had long since become stark reality. Almost in a frenzy, we were reaping the bitter fruits of our long, peacetime indifference to airships. We found ourselves in a "crash program" of enormous proportions. We needed more of everything, not today, but day before yesterday. Ships, bases, material things comprised but one basic part of our needs. Trained airship crews made up another, but the need that transcended all others should have been the simplest and easiest to fill. That was the need for a logical, workable administrative integration of airships into the naval establishment, both afloat and ashore. In general, the forces

afloat and in the field had accepted airships on a sound working basis. But the Washington situation was still a mess.[1]

An airship training command was not organized until a year and a half after the attack on Pearl Harbor. Airship training was an "added on" function at Lakehurst and Moffett Field, but the Navy did an excellent job with its airplane training and facilities.[2]

For Rosendahl, who had participated in life-and-death combat in the South Pacific, the political battles in Washington were often frustrating.

> In the Pacific, you knew who the enemy was and where he was. Once an enemy destroyer was sighted, you could fire a salvo of 8-inch rounds and pretty quickly learn the result of your effort as the enemy ship either exploded or shells landed in water. In Washington, however, the "enemy" was often buried in layers of bureaucracy, unseen, and when one fired a round—a letter or memo—you often did not know where it landed or what its impact was, and the result was often long in coming.
>
> Every time I tried to get more authority over airship matters into the hands of qualified men by training and experience in airships, I was told that since airships were aircraft, they simply had to be integrated into the "aeronautical" organization. This view, of course, utterly fails to recognize the fundamental differences between airships and airplanes.[3]

Rosendahl did not expect what he called the "firmly entrenched heavier-than-air organization" to permit itself to be integrated into the larger Navy, but he held some hope that "someone in authority might recognize the plight of airships under airplane domination," but he realized that "integration" and "airship autonomy" ideas would be regarded by the airplane fraternity as "aeronautical heresy."[4]

Returning to the world of airships as the undisputed senior airship officer, Rosendahl thought it logical that he should be placed somewhere in the commander-in-chief, chief of naval operations organization headed by Admiral King in Washington, but he realized that because of his "heretical ideas," the airplane crowd was strongly opposed to his being in Washington anywhere in King's organization. Thus, he was relegated to Lakehurst. It is uncertain exactly what King meant at the time, but he told Rosendahl informally that he expected him to run the airship show. Rosendahl's orders were modified later, designating him as "Special Assistant (Lighter-than-Air)" to the Deputy Chief of Naval Operations (Air) (DNCO [Air]). This made Rosendahl the principal advisor on LTA policy—theoretically.[5]

In mid-1943, the press announced that the necessity of sinking Hitler's U-boats had led to the creation of a special training command for LTA personnel. The Navy had admitted that the contribution of blimps to their current system of escorting merchant vessels had resulted in a sharp expansion of their procurement and training since the early days of the war. Congress had authorized a fleet of two hundred blimps to be placed into convoy service as soon as completed. Referring to Rosendahl, the newspaper article concluded, "His technical knowledge and experience should be turned to great practical service as head of the blimp patrol in waters free from enemy air attack."[6] Rosendahl informed the public that "blimps are carrying their weight in this war" and that not a single ship under blimp escort had been attacked successfully by the enemy.[7]

Rosendahl's new title sounded good, but he discovered quickly that it meant very little. "I went to Washington frequently on business, and found this 'Special Assistant' title was not worth much in practice."[8] Such was the atmosphere in which Rosendahl assumed his new duties as chief of naval airship training on May 15, 1943—his fifty-first birthday. When it became apparent that there was much at Lakehurst that needed supervision and guidance, his title was expanded to chief of naval airship training and experimentation—CNATE.[9]

In the post-World War II years, meaningful LTA activities and advances steadily slowed, and while Rosendahl was still regarded with respect as the senior LTA officer in the Navy, his meaningful role was diminishing, and it was increasingly difficult to find a place to land within Naval aeronautics. LTA activities were assimilated into the general category of aeronautics controlled by the larger airplane faction.

When, before the war, King had asked for a blimp program in the Caribbean, Rosendahl had begun recommending a considerably larger blimp to afford the performance needed in the higher tropical temperatures, but it was not until October 27, 1943, when the XM-1—the first of its type—was ready for christening. This airship was 294 feet long with a maximum diameter of 71 feet, and it displaced 647,500 cubic feet—about 50 percent greater in volume than the K-class. Twenty of the M-type ships had been ordered initially, but due to late delivery, the number was cut to four. Jean Rosendahl, "spruced out in a borrowed mink coat and a new, one-feathered hat" her husband had purchased for her, did the honor of christening the XM-1 in the large hangar at Akron. The ceremony included breaking a bottle of liquid air against the ship's structure.[10] Unlike the giant rigid airships that had gone before, the newspaper mention of the XM-1 did not receive front-page attention, and it was brief: "Mrs. Jean Rosendahl, wife of Rear Admiral C. E. Rosendahl, christens the Navy's newest and largest airship here today, in a ceremony coinciding with America's celebration of Navy Day."[11]

As the war began to wind down, Rosendahl had to reduce his personnel accordingly. Gradually, during the war, he had built up a group of excellent young men, most of whom were Naval Reservists. It hurt him to lose such men, but he made it his policy never to stand in the way of their early return home and to their chosen civilian pursuits. Rosendahl believed that at least 50 percent of his time and efforts as CNATE was spent on developmental work that should have been done before the war, while the other 50 percent was spent on "political" chores—trying to get and keep for the airship organization the same considerations afforded other wartime activities.[12]

During his time in the Pacific, Rosendahl had injured his back and required spinal surgery in 1942. Although he had a satisfactory recovery, it left him with a stiff back for which he had to be careful at all times. On his return from the South Pacific, Admiral King had promised him a flag command at sea whenever he felt the airship situation was well in hand. Rosendahl kept this promise in mind, but he knew that for his own well-being—and his back—it was probably best that he did not get back to sea.[13]

"Up to the end of World War II, I had given almost no thought to retirement and the future. Suddenly it was decided for me. In the service, one sees other officers reaching retirement but always it seems to be the other fellow, and most officers are startled when their own names come up. So it was with me."[14]

With the end of the war, the Navy needed to cut down its list of officers, and to facilitate the process, the Navy Department ordered an unusually rigid physical examination to be conducted by a special board of medical examiners for all officers aged fifty and above. "In due time I came before that board. To my surprise this board found that I required hospitalization for hypertension and further observation. During that period, the medicos checked further into the condition of my back and told me that I would have been foolish ever to have undertaken vigorous sea duty again. The net result was my retirement for physical disability as of 1 November 1946."[15]

Rosendahl and Jean purchased a home in Toms River, which Jean named "Flag Point," and they resided there for the remainder of their lives.

The Second World War was over and Rosendahl was in full retirement following a long and distinguished career in the Navy, yet hardly a day passed when his mind was not occupied by thoughts of LTA technology and the grand promises he envisioned for it—both military and commercial. He developed an intense interest in the attack on Pearl Harbor—a level of interest bordering on obsession. He read everything he could find about the planning and execution of the attack. At the heart of this interest was his belief that if the Navy had had airships—even if only a few—the attack on Pearl Harbor probably would not have happened.

He never forgot a meeting he attended about a year before the attack on Pearl Harbor with Secretary of the Navy Frank Knox and Rear Admiral Walter R. Sexton, Chairman of the Navy's general board. Sexton had asked Rosendahl to accompany him, along with a group of other high-ranking officers, to meet the secretary with the intent to make a strong push for the Navy's blimp program. The meeting's focus was the blimps to be used for coastal patrol and antisubmarine surveillance, but Sexton added some remarks about the large rigid airships, as well.

Sexton stated without reservation, "Mr. Secretary, if the Commander in Chief had a dozen rigid airships out in the Pacific, he would be finding abundant and valuable use for all of them."[16] Indeed, the Navy's original interest in having a fleet of airships was born of the need for craft capable of ranging far into the Pacific Ocean to conduct reconnaissance against an attacking fleet, presumptively from Japan.

Rosendahl considered Sexton's "almost prophetic remark about rigids in the Pacific" many times, and it came to mind automatically with every anniversary of the attack.

After the war, the details of the planning and execution of the attack on Pearl Harbor became known. On November 25, 1941, Admiral Yamamoto gave the order for the Japanese fleet to get underway the following day.[17] The armada consisted of over thirty vessels, including battleships, cruisers, destroyers, tankers, submarines, and six aircraft carriers carrying 360 combat planes. Rosendahl considered this to be "a pretty fair sized group to conceal, even at sea. Yet the success of Nagumo's mission depended wholly on concealment, followed by maximum surprise to us. . . . From a point about 200 miles north, the Japs caught us like sitting ducks at Pearl Harbor that Sunday sunrise."[18] Rosendahl's accounts of the attack were not first-hand—he was not there—but his research revealed that the Japanese destroyed 188 American planes and sank four battleships and two other men of war. They damaged four other battleships, three cruisers, three destroyers, and two other vessels. There were 2,334 Americans killed and another 1,347 wounded. The Japanese losses were "unbelievably low," consisting of five midget submarines, twenty-eight aircraft, and less than one hundred men.[19]

As if he had heard already some whispers of conspiracy theories, Rosendahl wrote, "Whether official Washington kept our Pearl Harbor military adequately informed will be debated and discussed for many more years to come. There will also always be varying opinions as to our faults and deficiencies out in the Pacific that fateful day."[20]

"But there is one thing that is crystal clear. The awful trouncing that we took on that Sunday morn might have been at least mitigated, had we possessed, and utilized, an effective long-range service of information at sea, call it scouting, patrol or whatever you like. The fact is that such a service might even have deflected the raid altogether, and without having had to fire a single shot."[21] Of course, Rosendahl knew that a combination of surface ships and airplanes would not be capable of doing such a scouting job, but his airships, if available, might have succeeded. He borrowed from other historians to build his case.

Having read Walter Lord's book, *Day of Infamy*, published in 1957, Rosendahl learned some details of the orders under which Admiral Nagumo was operating, and like pieces of a puzzle, they fit nicely into his treatise. Nagumo's armada left home stations on November 26, making for Pearl Harbor under orders that if his fleet were sighted by the Americans any time before December 6, he was to turn around and return home. If sighted on the sixth, he was to use his own judgment, but even if sighted on the seventh, he was committed to the attack.[22]

The last message to the Japanese fleet before its attack on Pearl Harbor was relayed from Honolulu by Tokyo: "December 6 (Local Time) Vessels moored in Harbor: 9 Battleships; 3 Class-B Cruisers; 3 Seaplane Tenders; 17 Destroyers. Entering Harbor are 4 Class-B Cruisers; 3 Destroyers. All Aircraft Carriers and Heavy Cruisers have departed Harbor. . . . No indication of any changes in U.S. Fleet or anything else unusual."[23]

According to Rosendahl, "Lady Luck" had smiled on Nagumo. Nagumo's route over the Pacific was well northward of the usually traveled shipping lanes and he remained unseen during the entire twelve-day journey.

On the 10th day, he was within a thousand miles of Hawaii. This was a distance within the scouting ability of a rigid airship such as we could have had at that time. Had Nagumo's force knowingly been sighted that day, or before, by just one airship, or even by one plane from an airship, that planned attack on Pearl Harbor would not have come about. Had such a sighting of his force occurred on even the next day, December 6th, Nagumo's orders permitted him still to turn back. And in addition, in surmising what his decision might then have been, consideration must be given to Nagumo's now known, basic lack of confidence in the success of his task.

But to speculate a bit further, suppose Nagumo had been discovered on the 6th and nevertheless decided to go ahead with the attack. Or, suppose the sighting had not occurred until even as late as the dawn patrol of the 7th of December. The prospects for success of Nagumo's mission would have been greatly impaired, to say the least, for we could have at least some semblance of readiness to meet the oncoming attack. For such timely information, no cost in scouts—one airship or several even, together with radar, planes and all, would have been too great. An off-duty Army operator at a shore radar did observe and try to report what turned out to be the approaching Japanese aircraft. However, his information was lightly brushed off that fateful December 7th. But had there been a contact report coming in from a scout at sea, it definitely would have been given far greater credence.[24]

Rosendahl revisited an argument about airships that had been around since the days of the *Akron* and the *Macon*—that these large rigid airships were easily sighted from surface ships and were vulnerable to being destroyed. Although it might be argued that a Japanese task force would have sent out planes to shoot down any airships that came into sight, Rosendahl seriously disputed it on the grounds that up to December 5, at least, Nagumo had orders to remain undetected or abandon his mission. Nagumo's armada was a sizeable force, and if he saw an airship, he could be certain that he had been seen and reported by the airship.[25]

Rosendahl cautioned believers of this line of thought that if a large rigid airship or a balloon ranging out over the Pacific Ocean sighted the Japanese fleet and was, in turn, sighted from below, the U.S. and Japan were not yet at war with each other. He doubted, further, that Nagumo would risk opening hostilities in turn for shooting down an airship or two.

So, to me, it does not seem at all out of order to speculate on what airships might have contributed in those hectic days. Our possession and utilization of long-range scouting airships, such as we could have had, might have led to the calling off of the Pearl Harbor attack altogether, or at least to some softening of the blow by our being at least somewhat prepared for it. In the same vein of speculation, one might go further and ponder how differently Japan might have planned or looked upon a raid on Pearl Harbor, knowing we possessed and used effective long-range airship scouts.[26]

Realizing that the American Navy had no far-ranging ships of any type at the time of the attack on Pearl Harbor, Rosendahl was aware that his analysis might be regarded as no more than speculative hindsight—conjecture—but "I will not agree that my idea of what airships might have been and might have done in those days is at all fantastic."[27]

As late as November 3, 1941, Admiral William V. Pratt had given his assessment of naval assets to *Newsweek* magazine.

The Pacific is a vast sea area to search, yet an offensive strategy even there is better than sticking strictly to a defensive one. . . .

The situation is one in which the dirigible—that neglected stepchild of aviation—could be very useful in conducting an efficient but not too costly offensive operation against raiders.

If we had a few lighter-than-air craft which, forming a task force with a cruiser or two, could comb the Pacific from one end to the other, they ought to pay for themselves.[28]

As things happened, there was no long-range air or surface reconnaissance at the time of the attack.[29]

A detailed account of the blimp service during the war is beyond the scope of this book. However, from an exhaustive examination of logbooks and war diaries of U-boats, and from interviews with U-boat captains and documents of the American Navy, Rosendahl was able to amass a record that indicated U-boat activities were highest during times when airship activity was lowest, and when airships were most active, U-boat activity was diminished greatly or ceased altogether in some geographic areas. The results of his investigations resulted in the indisputable conclusion that the Navy's blimp program had been a huge success. Only one Navy blimp was lost to enemy action during the war.

———

At the age of seventy-nine, Dr. Eckener, health and stamina fading, made a final trip to the U.S. at the invitation of Paul Litchfield of the Goodyear Zeppelin Corporation. Eckener visited President Herbert Hoover in Washington and made a return trip to NAS Lakehurst, where he found the bay of the iconic Hangar No. 1, which had once housed the *Graf Zeppelin* and the *Hindenburg*, filled with airplanes.

As related by Nielsen, Eckener spent his final hours reminiscing about the glory days of the airships and how, crossing continents and oceans, they brought people closer together.[30] "He was disillusioned and tired, too tired to remain in this world. He died on the 14th August 1954 at the age of 86."[31]

In the summer of 1955, Germany began transoceanic commercial flights with its Lufthansa airline. Rosendahl and Jean were invited to fly as guests on the first flight from New York. Rosendahl's old airship friends and their families greeted them on their arrival in Frankfurt, the start of a tour of sightseeing and entertainment hosted by Baron Studnitz of Lufthansa and a number of other German officials. In Munich, Rosendahl and Jean broke from the group and traveled by train to Friedrichshafen, where they met Dr. Durr and two former Goodyear airship engineers, Karl Hurtle and Erich Hilligardt. They then went to the city cemetery to place a wreath on the grave of Dr. Eckener.

On June 26, 1961, the American Navy decided officially to deflate the blimps at NAS Lakehurst. Eight of its ten blimps were to go into storage by November 30, 1961. The remaining two blimps were to be used for research and development until the middle of 1962, and it was expected that these would no longer require the level of maintenance or repair that was normally provided by the NAS Overhaul and Repair department. The Navy cited two reasons for this move: a shortage of funds and personnel, and the fact that helicopters and airplanes had become better for hunting submarines.[32]

In March 1962, the NAS service information officer informed the press that the two blimps, which had not been deflated and stored, were still contributing to the Navy's operations. One of these was being used as a flying wind tunnel, testing factors affecting low-speed aircraft. The other blimp, dubbed "Rudolf the Red Nosed" because of its brightly painted red nose, was involved in secret research involving antisubmarine warfare. It was airborne only occasionally and its activities were top secret. The plan was for these last two blimps to remain in service until June 1962, but if no additional funds were appropriated, they would follow their brothers into war reserve storage.[33]

Finally, on September 1, 1962, it was announced that the last airship flight from NAS Lakehurst had taken place. "A big white airship ghosted up from its moorings Friday and loomed in the sky for two hours. With its descent the era of the Navy blimp was over."[34] Captain Ronald F. Stultz, commanding the NAS, described the flight as just a bit of nostalgia.

While the airship program ended officially in November 1961, the last flight marked the actual closing. Previous flights by the large rigid airships had attracted crowds of untold thousands, but this final "nostalgic" flight attracted slightly over one hundred spectators, largely interested in taking photographs. There was no ceremony attendant to this event—no speeches or fanfare of any kind.

The blimp that made the final flight was the one that had been used for the wind tunnel experiments. On board with Captain Stultz were Vice Admiral Rosendahl and Captain Frederick N. Klein, former commanding officer of the NAS. Deflation of the two final blimps was slated for November 4.

One day after his final blimp flight at the NAS, seventy-year-old Rosendahl lashed out publicly at the Navy for its handling of the LTA program. He claimed there were "three practically new early warning blimps 'boxed-up in solitary confinement' at the Naval Air Station that [had] demonstrated marked superiority in both efficiency and economy and should right now be out at sea on station."[35]

Rosendahl launched a diatribe against the Navy's "almost scandalous" neglect of airships. He predicted a return of the blimps to active duty, claiming, "It is inevitable that despite this indefensible interruption and its attendant needless waste of time and taxpayers' money, airships before long will be reinvented or re-discovered. . . . When the whole story is written—as it is sure to be—the tale of airships will not be one of the most flattering chapters in the history of our navy."[36]

In the 1970s, Rosendahl and a small group of airship enthusiasts embarked on an effort to create a museum to preserve the history of airships and balloons. The prospective site for the museum was a 13.5-acre tract on the property of the NAS about mid-way between the Cathedral of the Air and the main gate. Rosendahl and his nonprofit organization, The Airship Association, hoped to receive the land title before the end of 1975. Transfer of the land required congressional action and a lobbying campaign was begun among New Jersey's congressional delegation. The museum would serve as an information and research center on airships and balloons and to collect airship ephemera to be displayed to the public and researchers.[37]

The entire New Jersey congressional delegation sponsored a bill that allowed the secretary of the Navy to convey about 13 acres of excess land at the NAS in the proposed museum location, with the recipient of the land being The Airship Association. In 1971, as the NAS celebrated its fiftieth year of active service, the iconic Hangar No. 1 was designated a national shrine. Navy officials pointed out that the problem of establishing an airship museum was not political but a matter of funding.[38]

On October 27, 1976, with the trustees of The Airship Association present, the deed to the land was presented to Rosendahl, who recognized that acquiring the tract was but the first step in a complicated project. When Congress gave the land, it was with the condition that The Airship Association had five years to build its proposed museum, or the land would revert to the government.

———

Rosendahl's health began a slow but steady decline shortly after the end of the Second World War, almost paralleling that of the LTA program itself. His problems began in 1946, when he was diagnosed with hypertension, followed fifteen years later by a diagnosis of congestive heart failure—an incurable cardiac condition requiring life-long management. In addition to insulin-dependent diabetes mellitus, he had a host of problems related to atherosclerotic cardiovascular disease (hardening of the arteries). In May 1977, he was admitted to hospital with fever, hypotension, mental status changes, and leukopenia (low white blood cell count). His clinical picture was consistent with sepsis (a bacterial bloodstream infection), and his blood cultures confirmed the clinical suspicion. Despite antibiotic treatment, he went into cardiopulmonary arrest on the third hospital day and died on May 14, 1977, at the Philadelphia Naval Hospital at the age of eighty-five.[39]

A couple of weeks after his death, Navy spokesmen gathered at Lakehurst to eulogize Rosendahl. The chief speaker was Admiral Carl Seiberlich, deputy chief of Naval operations for air warfare. He claimed, "There are few truly great men in the history of aviation and all of them are household names because of their contributions. Lighter-than-air or naval airships, as he liked to call them, and Admiral Charles E. Rosendahl are really synonymous."[40]

Jack Glickstein Wildwood, who was stationed at Lakehurst in 1943, offered that the thing he would always remember about Rosendahl was that "no matter what, no matter how low-ranking the man was, the admiral would greet him and say, 'glad to see a fellow shipmate.'"[41]

On November 18, 1977, Jean announced that her husband's lighter-than-air aviation collection, once intended to be housed in a museum at NAS Lakehurst, had been donated to the University of Texas at Dallas.[42] Jean told the press, "It was the admiral's express desire to have me place his collection where it would be displayed for use by lighter-than-air scholars and proponents of the airship."[43]

The History of Aviation Collection, which had been housed on the Austin campus, had outgrown its space, but there were about 10,000 square feet of space at the Dallas campus. President of the University of Texas at Dallas, Dr. Bryce Jordon, said that the acquisition of the History of Aviation Collection and the incorporation of the Admiral Charles E. Rosendahl Collection of lighter-than-air aviation would create one of the major aeronautical libraries in the U.S. Rosendahl had been in communication with George Haddaway, who started the University of Texas aviation history collection in 1963, and he asked Jean to investigate the facilities at Dallas to make certain they were suitable. The facilities, combined with President Jordan's enthusiasm and sincerity, convinced Jean that this was the proper place for her husband's LTA materials.[44]

Fundraising efforts for a museum at Lakehurst ended with Rosendahl's death. Jean Rosendahl told the press that she did not believe the airship museum would ever be built at Lakehurst, but the University of Texas at Dallas was building a $6 million addition to house its aviation collection, and her husband's material had been promised "first place." She felt confident in her decision to select a brand-new museum with plenty of space and plenty of money behind it.[45]

Rosendahl's memorabilia and manuscripts lie in rest in Dallas, Texas, about fifty miles from his boyhood home of Cleburne, available to historians and authors interested in LTA flight.

Jean Rosendahl remained in Toms River, New Jersey, for the remainder of her life, dying there on October 26, 1981, at the age of seventy-nine.

———

Although Dr. Eckener had died nearly a quarter century before Rosendahl, the two men shared a common ending—bitterness and disappointment at the apparent failure of their shared vision for LTA flight.

RENAISSANCE OF AIRSHIPS

It appeared to many that the crash of the *Macon* followed by that of the *Hindenburg* signaled the end of the era of large rigid airships, but such was not the case. The American program was stalled by a lack of government funding combined with strong anti-airship sentiment in Congress and the Navy's Bureau of Aeronautics. While the American focus was on airships for military use, the Germans continued to pursue commercial interests. The loss of the *Hindenburg* did not bring an end to Zeppelin developments. The Germans were already in the earliest stages of construction of LZ-131, but work on this airship came to a halt with Germany's invasion of Poland in 1939, and the ship was never completed.

Men like Eckener, Rosendahl, and Pruss never lost their faith in LTA technology. Max Pruss had survived Zeppelin raids over London in the First World War, the crash of the *Hindenburg*, and the Second World War to die on November 18, 1960, at the age of sixty-nine. He never abandoned his belief in rigid airships, insisting that they offered comfort unmatched by airplanes, and he maintained a vision of airships carrying one hundred passengers across the Atlantic in two days.

While the American Navy of necessity had to abandon any program involving the large rigid airships, the Second World War saw extensive development, construction, and use of those LTA craft, known as blimps, which were used extensively by the Navy for coastal and convoy patrol and antisubmarine reconnaissance.

Following the disruption of rigid airship development caused by the Second World War, there has been a slow but steady renaissance of interest in such vessels.

The advantages of airships over airplanes are noted once again—long range of operation, variable speeds including hovering, greater comfort to passengers and crew, and new uses are emerging.

Technological advances for modern airships include newer, lighter, stronger materials for construction. It remains to be seen if helium will be sought as a lifting gas or whether the cheaper hydrogen could be used when combined with modern materials and technology to make it safer. The concept of lighter-than-air flight is not dead but merely struggling, once again, to find its place.

As with all things, developments in LTA flight are limited only by the human imagination combined with ample funding.

There are men of devotion whose beliefs are practical—they realize that everything has its time and then is replaced by whatever follows—but Eckener and Rosendahl were from a special breed of believers—they were dreamers. They could see things others could not, and in the face of overwhelming evidence to the contrary, they could see a future for their cause. For such men, the dream never dies, but unfortunately, the dreamer does.

One man cannot always understand the unflagging devotion that another man has for his dream and, therefore, perhaps such dreamers are understood better by poets than historians.

❧

"WE FIGHT FOR LOST CAUSES BECAUSE WE KNOW THAT OUR DEFEAT AND DISMAY MAY BE THE PREFACE TO OUR SUCCESSORS' VICTORY, THOUGH THAT VICTORY ITSELF WILL BE TEMPORARY; WE FIGHT RATHER TO KEEP SOMETHING ALIVE THAN IN THE EXPECTATION THAT ANYTHING WILL TRIUMPH."

—T. S. ELIOT IN "ESSAYS ANCIENT AND MODERN"

THE FUTURE FOR AIRSHIPS

By Dan Grossman
Aviation Historian and Author

The airship has a future, but despite the dreams of many airship lovers, it will not look like the glory days of the 1920s and early 1930s, when airships were the most capable aircraft in the world, providing fast and luxurious transportation that outclassed all other means of travel, and people imagined a future with fleets of airships crossing the globe.

The twenty-first century will see a limited number of airships used for specialized applications that take advantage of their essential qualities: a true LTA craft—one that can fly solely with aerostatic lift, without requiring airspeed to generate dynamic lift—does not need to burn fuel to simply remain in the air and can take off and land vertically, operate without downwash, and fly slowly, quietly, and close to the ground.

Airships have already been used for aerial advertising for almost a hundred years and could also perform new niche tasks, such as aerial surveillance of remote pipelines and power transmission lines. Small airships, such as the Zeppelin NT, are currently being used for short passenger sightseeing flights, and large airships could provide longer flights as private yachts of the air, and perhaps ultra-luxury cruise ships, to wealthy individuals. Even more important than providing pleasure flights to a select few, airships could perform humanitarian missions that could never be accomplished by helicopters or fixed-wing airplanes; their long range, endurance, payload capacity, and ability to operate without paved runways could allow large airships to deliver relief supplies to areas of the world lacking surface infrastructure, or where surface conditions have been disrupted by hurricane, earthquake, or other disaster, and to remain over a devastated area providing internet or cellular connectivity, command-and-control, and other services.

Much attention has been given to the airship's potential ability to deliver cargo to remote areas that require service too infrequently to justify the construction of infrastructure such as airports, highways, railway lines, or ports, but this concept requires a solution to the difficult problem of load exchange. An airship becomes heavier or lighter when it takes on or discharges a load and, unless compensated, the release of a heavy payload of cargo could cause an airship to rapidly rise into the air. Many of the proposed solutions to this problem have been impractical; for example, suggestions about exchanging the weight of cargo for ballast water taken from a nearby body of water limits cargo delivery to areas near water, and taking water from one place and discharging it elsewhere presents serious environmental concerns; proposals requiring the construction of infrastructure at landing areas would reduce the key benefit of being able to deliver cargo to locations without ground infrastructure and personnel; and the age-old idea of compressing and decompressing lifting gas has confounded engineers for decades due to issues including the weight of storage tanks, the weight and energy required for equipment that can rapidly compress gas, and the heat created by that process.

While airships may perform several new tasks in the future, we are not likely to see the widespread use of airships for basic passenger transportation. It is difficult for airships to compete with high-speed trains or fixed-wing airliners in cost, efficiency, speed, or reliability of service in almost all weather conditions, and so airships will not be used to transport large numbers of paying passengers who simply want to travel from one place to another.

We will also not see airships replace the world's airplanes solely for their potential environmental advantages. Emerging technologies for "green" airplanes will likely outpace the concept of using airships to reduce carbon emissions. One such technology—Sustainable Aviation Fuel—already exists and has been used in jet aircraft, and new powerplant technologies, such as electric and hydrogen-powered engines, will continue to evolve. Tens of thousands of airplanes currently exist, and billions of dollars of airplanes will not simply be scrapped in favor of airships. If the demand for environmentally destructive air transport reaches a point where additional money will be spent, it will be spent operating conventional airplanes in a cleaner way rather than replacing thousands of airplanes with thousands of airships.

Safety concerns will also preclude the widespread replacement of the world's airplanes with airships. It has taken decades of operational experience and many accidents to create the level of safety we see in today's transport airplanes, and the world is unlikely to set those advances aside to adopt a completely new form of transportation on a large scale. This is not to say airships are unsafe—to the contrary, a small number of airships can be operated very safely and have been for many years—but a rapid shift to the use of airships on a vast scale would carry risks that do not apply to the operation of a small number of airships, including the need to maintain strict schedules. Hugo Eckener's impressive safety record derived, in part, from his willingness to alter or cancel a flight in the interest of safety, and a similar safety culture can exist around a small number of airships, but when aircraft are used for routine transportation of passengers and cargo, and when the world becomes dependent on the reliability of those services, maintaining schedule becomes an indispensable part of their mission.

Finally, despite the dreams of airship enthusiasts, the future will not see any of the fanciful airship concepts that somehow receive attention in the news media, which regularly publish stories about "proposed airships" that defy the laws of physics. The outlets publishing these fanciful stories either do not realize that beautiful computer renderings have nothing to do with the physical realities of aviation—interior design has never made an aircraft fly—or they do not realize that fact but know airship fantasies captivate people and will drive clicks, views, and online engagement.

Airships have always had a hold on the public's imagination, and people have an appetite for airship stories that allow them to dream, even when those "airships" are physically impossible. This was the case as early as the nineteenth century, with futuristic images of imaginary airships; continued through the twentieth century, with stories about atomic and iron-hulled airships; and has persisted into the twenty-first century with ostensibly-serious media outlets publishing images of airships with open-air swimming pools floating over mountain ranges, amphibious air yachts that would lack sufficient life to leave the ground, and alluring passenger accommodations aboard airships that defy the realities of physics and engineering.

Unlike the dreams of computer artists who never venture from their keyboards, and even some airship adventurers in the real world whose love of the airship has sometimes blinded them to unpleasant realities, the successful airships of the future will be designed and built by people with solid backgrounds in engineering and project management, who focus on technological and economic realities. But I strongly suspect that even the most hard-nosed and practical engineers who find their way into lighter-than-air will, before too long, inherit the feelings of Rosendahl, Moffett, and Wiley toward the romance of the great rigids and become captivated by the beauty and magic of ships that float in the air.

—D. G.

ENDNOTES

CHAPTER 1: THE LONG JOURNEY TO LAKEHURST

1. Charles E. Rosendahl, "Annapolis and the Early Years," unpublished memoir: Rosendahl Collection, Special Collections and Archives Division, History of Aviation Archives, The University of Texas at Dallas, Box 042, Folder 5 (undated), p. 1.

Following his retirement from the Navy, friends encouraged Rosendahl to write an autobiography. He undertook the project with sincerity using the working title *Far Away Places*. The manuscript was never completed and, thus, never submitted for publication. Consequently, his efforts came to represent a personal memoir. He produced a number of rewrites, labeling most with the date of the edit. While incomplete, the manuscript provides bridges to gaps in his military record and offers numerous insights into his thoughts at various times of his life and career. Material extracted from Rosendahl's drafts used here will be referenced as, "Rosendahl, Charles E., unpublished memoir," followed by the date of the revision, if revised, and page number.

2. Ibid.

3. *The Lucky Bag, 1914, Vol. XXI, Being the Annual of The Brigade of Midshipmen*. Published by the Graduating Class of 1914, Printed by The Wm. H. Hoskins Company, Philadelphia, 1914, p. 117.

4. Lemuel F. Parton, "Who's News Today," *Evening Sun* (Baltimore, MD), May 13, 1932, p. 30.

5. "Middies In Mimic War," *Baltimore (MD) Sun*, June 3, 1914, p. 2.

6. Rosendahl, "Annapolis and the Navy," unpublished memoir, revised April 1959, p. 4.

7. Ibid., p. 5.

8. Ibid., p. 7.

9. "Americans Lauded—Pres. Wilson Addresses Graduating Class at Annapolis," *Roseburg (OR) Review*, June 5, 1914, p. 1.

10. "Navy For Humanity, Not for Conquest, President Tells Midshipmen," *Washington Post*, June 6, 1914, p. 5.

11. Rosendahl, "'A' Is For Airships," unpublished memoir, revised April 1959, Box 041, Folder 5, p. 4.

12. Rosendahl, "'A' Is For Airships," unpublished memoir, revised July 19, 1956, p. 8.

13. Ibid., p. 8(a).

14. Ibid.

15. Ibid.

16. Ibid., p. 9

17. Ibid., p. 10.

18. Ibid.

19. Ibid.

20. Ibid., p. 13.

21. Ibid., p. 10.

22. Ibid., p. 13.

23. Ibid., p. 12.

24. Ibid.

CHAPTER 2: THE LIGHTER-THAN-AIR PROGRAM AND ZR-1

1. "Secretary Daniels Discusses the Need of Zeppelins," *State Journal* (Raleigh, NC), September 29, 1916, p. 16.

2. Rene Bache, "'Flocks of Blimps' to Defend Coasts; Is a New Type of 'Wingless' Airplane," *El Paso (TX) Herald*, May 5, 1917, p. 27.

3. "Rigid Airships For Navy Vital, Sims Declares," *Chicago (IL) Tribune*, February 24, 1919, p. 5.

4. W. F. Althoff, *Sky Ships: A History of the Airship in the United States Navy* (Orion Books: New York, 1990), p. 3.

5. Rosendahl, unpublished memoir, revised April 1959, p. 1.

6. Ibid.

7. Ibid.

8. Ibid.

9. Ibid., p. 6.

10. Personnel File, Frank R. McCrary, Report of Compliance with Orders, National Personnel Records Center, National Archives and Records Administration, St. Louis, MO, November 22, 1922.

11. Rosendahl, "Daughter of the Stars," unpublished memoir, p. 8(a).

12. Ibid.

13. Ibid.

14. Ibid., p. 8(b).

15. Rosendahl, "A Spartan Start," unpublished memoir, revised May 1958, p. 6.

16. Rosendahl, "Daughter of the Stars," unpublished memoir, revised May 1958, Box 041, Folder 5, p. 3.

17. Althoff, *Sky Ships*, p. 26.

18. Rosendahl, "Daughter of the Stars," unpublished memoir, p. 4.

19. Ibid.

20. Ibid., p. 5.

21. Ibid.

22. Douglas H. Robinson, *The Zeppelin in Combat: A History of the German Naval Airship Division – 1912–1918* (Atglen, PA: Schiffer Military/Aviation History, 1994, p. 230.

23. "Work Started On Big U.S. Dirigible – Cradle to Hold 700-Ft. ZR-1 Is Begun at Lakehurst Naval Station," *Asbury Park (NJ) Press*, June 27, 1922, p. 1.

24. Richard J. Beamish, "U.S. Building First Dirigible in Phila. – Constructors at Local Navy Yard Being Guided by Past Disasters," *Philadelphia Inquirer*, June 29, 1922, p. 10.

25. Ibid.

26. "Airship ZR-1 Being Built – Two Million Cattle Contribute to Construction of the Gigantic Dirigible," *Salt Lake (UT) Tribune*, June 25, 1922, p. 37.

27. Ibid.

28. Althoff, *Sky Ships*, p. 28.

29. Lieutenant Clifford A. Tinker, "To the Top of the World in the Navy's Huge Rigid Airship," *Boston Globe*, July 1, 1923, p. 72.

30. Ibid.

31. Ibid.

32. Rosendahl, "Daughter of the Stars," unpublished memoir, revised May 1958, p. 2.

33. "Big Airship Trial Flight," *Pottsville (PA) Republican*, September 5, 1923, p. 5.

34. "Navy Airship ZR-1," p. 37.

35. Ibid., p. 2.

36. Frederic J. Haskins, "Navy's Giant Dirigible Ready for Trial Flights," *Ithaca (NY) Journal*, September 4, 1923, p. 12.

37. "Navy Airship ZR-1, Largest of Kind, Flies Perfectly," *St. Louis Post-Dispatch*, September 5, 1923, p. 1.

38. Oliver H. P. Garrett, "ZR-1 Flies Half Day – Successful in Great Test," *Boston Globe*, September 12, 1923, p. 1.

39. "Lighter Than Air Lines Safe, Comfortable, Swift," *Buffalo (NY) Times*, September 30, 1923, p. 71.

40. "2,200-Mile Flight by ZR-1 Completed," *Baltimore (MD) Sun*, October 4, 1923, p. 2.

41. "ZR-1 A Triumph Of American Effort, Navy Expert Says," *St. Louis Post-Dispatch*, October 3, 1923, p. 2.

42. Ibid.

43. Letter from: Bureau of Navigation. To: Commander Frank R. McCrary, U.S.N., Commanding Officer, Naval Air Station, Lakehurst, N. J. Subject: To additional duty in command of USS Shenandoah, October 5, 1923. (NARA, St. Louis, MO.)

CHAPTER 3: USS *SHENANDOAH* (ZR-1)

1. "ZR-1 Christened Shenandoah On Way To Capital," *Brooklyn (NY) Citizen*, October 10, 1923, p. 2.
2. Ibid.
3. Logbook, USS Shenandoah (ZR-1), October 10, 1923. National Archives and Research Administration (NARA), Box 1 of 2, R.G. 118-8, USS Shenandoah, Washington, D.C., p. 3.
4. Ibid.
5. Ibid.
6. Rosendahl, "Daughter of the Stars," unpublished memoir, revised May 1958, p. 6.
7. Althoff, *Sky Ships*, p. 32.
8. Logbook, USS Shenandoah (ZR-1), October 27, 1923, p. 43.
9. Logbook, USS Shenandoah (ZR-1), January 12, 1924.
10. "Navy Pole Flight Details," *Elizabethville (PA) Echo*, January 3, 1924, p. 2.
11. Logbook, USS Shenandoah, January 16, 1924.
12. Rosendahl, "Daughter of the Stars," unpublished memoir, revised May 1958, p. 8.
13. "Shenandoah Safe After Battle With Big Gale," *News-Herald* (Franklin, PA), January 17, 1924, p. 1.
14. "Gale Blowing 70 Miles An Hour Hits New York; Six Dead, 3 Ships In Distress," *News-Herald* (Franklin, PA), January 17, 1924, p. 1.
15. Logbook, USS Shenandoah, January 16, 1924, p. 51.
16. "Skeptics Converted by Dirigible's Gallant Flight," *Asbury Park (NJ) Press*, January 18, 1924, p. 4.
17. Logbook, USS Shenandoah, January 16, 1924.
18. "Shenandoah Safe After Battle With Big Gale," p. 1.
19. Logbook, USS Shenandoah, January 17, 1924.
20. "Shenandoah Safe After Battle With Big Gale," p. 6.
21. Ibid.
22. Ibid., p. 8.
23. In his article, Butman misspelled Robertson's last name. The Shenandoah's logbook listed him as Gunner Robertson.
24. Carl H. Butman, "No SOS from NERK – 'Shenandoah' Radios 'Under Control,'" *Radio World*, February 2, 1924, p. 4.
25. Ibid.
26. "Navy Heads Elated at Dirigible's Victorious Battle Against Storm," *Tampa (FL) Tribune*, January 18, 1924, p. 1.
27. "Shenandoah Repairs Are to Cost $78,000," *Atlanta (GA) Constitution*, February 21, 1924, p. 16.
28. "Shenandoah Crew Wary On Skipper For Trip To Pole," *Brooklyn (NY) Daily Eagle*, January 19, 1924, p. 1.
29. "Shenandoah Crew On Arctic Jaunt to be Volunteers," *Janesville (WI) Daily Gazette*, January 26, 1924, p. 9.
30. Ibid.
31. William F. Trimble, *Admiral William A. Moffett – Architect of Naval Aviation* (Washington: Smithsonian Institution Press, 1994), p. 130.
32. Rosendahl, "Daughter of the Stars," unpublished memoir, revised May 1958, p. 9.
33. Logbook, USS Shenandoah, February 15, 1924.
34. Rosendahl, Charles E., "Daughter of the Stars," May 1958 edit, p. 9.
35. Ibid.
36. Aaron J. Keirns, *America's Forgotten Airship Disaster: The Crash of the USS Shenandoah* (Howard, Ohio: Little River Publishing, 2010), p. 28.
37. Trimble, p. 130.
38. Ibid.
39. "Pigeonhole Plans for Shenandoah's Flight to Pole," *Buffalo Courier*, February 24, 1924, p. 72.
40. Junius B. Wood, "Seeing America From The 'Shenandoah' – An Account of the Record-making 9,000-mile Flight from the Atlantic to the Pacific Coast and Return in the Navy's American-built, American-manned airship," *National Geographic Magazine* (January 1925): p. 1.
41. Logbook, USS Shenandoah, September 3, 1924.
42. Wood, p. 1.

43. Ibid., p. 2.

44. Ibid., p. 1.

45. Ibid., p. 6.

46. Ibid., p. 7.

47. Ibid., p. 7-10.

48. Ibid., p. 18

49. Ibid.

50. Ibid., p. 23.

51. Logbook, USS Shenandoah, October 8, 1924.

52. Logbook, USS Shenandoah, October 9, 1924.

53. Logbook, USS Shenandoah, October 10, 1924.

54. Rosendahl, "Daughter of the Stars," unpublished memoir, revised May 1958, p. 11.

55. Ibid.

56. Logbook, USS Shenandoah., October 21, 1924.

57. Logbook, USS Shenandoah, October 22, 1924.

58. Wood, p. 45.

59. Rosendahl, "Daughter of the Stars," unpublished memoir, revised May 1958, p. 11.

CHAPTER 4: ZR-3

1. 1 Ernst A. Lehmann, *Zeppelin: The Story of Lighter-Than-Air Craft* (United Kingdom: Foothill Media Limited, 1937), p. 196.

2. Construction of L-72 was completed after the war, and it was surrendered to France as part of the war reparations.

3. Karl H. von Wiegand, "Zeppelin Fleet is 'Sunk' by Young Naval Officer," *Times Dispatch* (Richmond, VA), August 31, 1919, p. 6.

4. Wiegand, "Zeppelin Fleet is 'Sunk,'" p. 6.

5. Ibid.

6. Robert Barry, "American Naval Personnel Will Fly Zeppelin from Germany to United States," *Dayton (OH) Herald*, December 29, 1921, p. 13.

7. Ibid.

8. Cyril Brown, "Huge Zeppelin Claimed for U.S.," *Philadelphia Inquirer*, April 6, 1920, p. 2.

9. Ibid.

10. "Make Zeppelins in America," *Daily Gate City and Constitution-Democrat* (Keokuk, IA), June 17, 1920, p. 6.

11. "Germans to Build New Zeppelin for Uncle Sam; Council of Ambassadors Gives Its Permission, Ending Negotiations for Dirigible Replacement," *Salt Lake City (UT) Tribune*, December 18, 1921, p. 1.

12. Lehmann, p. 205.

13. "U.S. to Order Giant Zeppelin From Germany," *New York Tribune*, December 18, 1921, p. 1.

14. "Germany to Build 'Zepp' for America," *San Francisco (CA) Examiner*, December 18, 1921, p. 86.

15. "American Zeppelin Germany's Last One," *New York Herald*, January 17, 1922, p. 5.

16. S. B. Conger, "Giant Zeppelin for U.S. to be Delivered During 1923," *Brooklyn (NY) Daily Eagle*, June 8, 1922, p. 22.

17. "Build Big Zeppelin for U.S.," *Greeley County Republican* (Tribune, KS), June 29, 1922, p. 3.

18. "World's Largest Airships to Have Latest in Radio," *Oakland (CA) Tribune*, July 31, 1922, p. 22.

19. Ibid.

20. "Navy Yard Notes," *Boston Globe*, December 27, 1922, p. 20.

21. "ZR-3, Erected in Germany, Is 985 Feet Long," *Miami (FL) News*, May 17, 1923, p. 1.

22. "Zeppelin Town Stalls Completion of ZR-3," *Philadelphia Inquirer*, October 6, 1923, p. 3.

23. Minot Saunders, "Bavarians Plot to Commandeer ZR-3," *Bristol (PA) Daily Carrier*, November 8, 1923, p. 1.

24. "Zeppelin Plant For U.S. If ZR-3 Proves Success," *Minneapolis (MN) Star*, October 9, 1923, p. 9.

25. "Germans Will Bring New Zeppelin to U.S.," *Asbury Park (NJ) Press*, November 22, 1923, p. 7.

26. Oscar K. Goll, "New Dirigible ZR-3 May Be White Elephant for America," *Altoona (PA) Tribune*, August 12, 1924, p. 13.

27. "Crew of ZR-3 All Officers," *Times* (Shreveport, LA), October 16, 1924, p. 14.

28. William J. Mevoy, "ZR-3 Zeppelin Shun Ceremony When U.S. Gets," *Herald-Press* (St. Joseph, MI), September 11, 1924, p. 3.

29. Ibid.

30. W.F. Althoff, *USS Los Angeles: The Navy's Venerable Airship and Aviation Technology* (Washington, D.C.: Potomac Books, Inc., 2004), p. 30.

31. G. K. Spencer, "German Crew That Was Trained to Bomb New York and Would Have Done So If War Had Lasted to Be in Charge of Great Dirigible," *St. Louis (MO) Post-Dispatch*, October 5, 1924, p. 6.

32. Ibid.

33. Ibid.

34. Ibid.

35. Ernest A. Zadig, "Great Zeppelin Guided to U.S.A. by Radio," *Dayton (OH) Daily News*, October 12, 1924, p. 77.

36. Samuel Spewack, "Gasoline and Baggage Unloaded – Would Be Passenger With Rifle Arrested Near Hangar," *St. Louis (MO) Post-Dispatch*, October 12, 1924, p.1

37. Ibid.

38. "ZR-3 Speeds Out To Sea On Trip To U. S.," *Oakland (CA) Tribune*, October 12, 1924, p. 1.

39. "ZR-3 Speeds Past Azores Headed For Bermuda; May Reach Coast Today," *Philadelphia Inquirer*, October 14, 1924, p. 1.

40. "Friedrichshafen Bids Adieu," Ibid.

41. "Arrangements Completed for Lakehurst Reception," *Philadelphia Inquirer*, October 13, 1924, p. 2.

42. "ZR-3 Arrival Set at Tomorrow Noon," *Philadelphia Inquirer*, October 14, 1924, p. 2.

43. "Bid Dirigible In Record Voyage Across Atlantic," *Times Herald* (Olean, NY), October 15, 1924, p. 13.

44. Frank Getty, "Giant Zeppelin ZR-3 Arrives Safely at Lakehurst Ending 80-Hour Trip Over Atlantic," *Mount Carmel (PA) Item*, October 15, 1924, p. 1.

45. Ibid.

46. "ZR-3 Deflation to take 14 Hours," *Brooklyn (NY) Times Union*, October 15, 1924, p. 2.

47. "Air Liners to Sail on Schedule Soon, Says ZR-3 Officer," *Philadelphia Inquirer*, October 16, 1924, p. 2.

48. "German Crew on the ZR-3 Catching Up On Smoking," *Boston Globe*, October 16, 1924, p. 14.

49. Ibid.

50. "Los Angeles Name Selected for ZR-3," *Morning Call* (Allentown, PA), October 17, 1924, p. 1.

51. "ZR-3 Tests Next Week," *Morning News* (Wilmington, DE), November 14, 1924, p. 5.

52. S. D. Weyer, "Germany Surrenders Zep Wizard to U.S.," *Birmingham (AL) News*, November 15, 1924, p. 11.

CHAPTER 5: USS *LOS ANGELES* (ZR-3)

1. Rosendahl, "The Shenandoah Goes West," unpublished memoir, revised May 1958, p. 1.

2. Ibid.

3. Ibid.

4. P. W. Litchfield, "Mammoth Airship, Twice as Large as 'Los Angeles,' Will Be Built in the U.S.," *Tampa Bay (FL) Times*, December 23, 1924, p. 27.

5. Ibid.

6. Ibid.

7. Ibid.

8. Ibid.

9. Ibid.

10. M. Ernest Marshall, *Rear Admiral Herbert V. Wiley: A Career in Airships and Battleships* (Annapolis, MD: Naval Institute Press, 2019), p. 55.

11. Lieutenant H. V. Wiley, U.S.N., "A Celestial Cruise," *United States Naval Institute Proceedings*, Vol. 81, No. 266, April 1925, p. 604.

12. Rosendahl, "U.S.S. 'Los Angeles,'" *United States Naval Institute Proceedings*, Vol. 57, No. 340, June 1931, p. 752.

13. Wiley, "A Celestial Cruise," p. 608.

14. Logbook, USS Los Angeles, January 24, 1925.

15. Wiley, "A Celestial Cruise," Ibid.

16. Logbook, USS Los Angeles, Ibid.

17. Logbook, USS Los Angeles, February 4, 1925.

18. Logbook, USS Shenandoah, February 17, 1925.

19. "Will Fly To The Bermudas," *Evening Journal* (Wilmington, DE), February 20, 1925, p. 10.

20. Rosendahl, "The Shenandoah Goes West," unpublished memoir, revised May 1958, p. 5.

21. Rosendahl, "U.S.S. 'Los Angeles," Ibid.

22. "Plan Flight to England," *Evening Journal* (Wilmington, DE), February 23, 1925, p. 3.

23. Logbook, USS Los Angeles, April 22, 1925.

24. Ibid., May 5, 1925.

25. Ibid., May 7, 1925.

26. "Los Angeles on Unique Tour Today," *Daily Times* (New Philadelphia, OH), May 15, 1925, p. 1.

27. The passenger list included: Graham McNamee, a renowned pioneering sports radio broadcaster with WEAF in New York City; a representative from Pathé News in New York City; and three rear admirals, including Rear Admiral C. F. Hughes, Rear Admiral C. C Bloch, and Rear Admiral H. P. Jones. Jones was a senior admiral serving on the highly influential general board of the U.S. Navy. Hughes served as president of the American Society of Naval Engineering (ASNE). Captain J. T. Tomkins had been the president of the ASNE from 1923–1924. The world of industry was represented by Irenee DuPont, president of the DuPont Company; Major K. K. V. Casey, manager of military sales, DuPont Company; J. W. Rawls, vice president and general manager of the J. G. Brill Company, a manufacturing firm specializing in transportation; a Mr. Stumble from Bethlehem Steel Corporation; Dr. William Elgin from the Franklin Institute in Philadelphia; George Horace Lorimar and Churchill Williams, the editor and assistant editor, respectively, of the *Saturday Evening Post*; Eldridge Johnson, founder and president of the Victor Talking Machine Company; John C. Jones, chief of the Philadelphia District Ordnance Office; Major J. K. Crane from the Bureau of Ordnance and the War Department; Major General Dennis Nolan, acting chief of staff; Atwater Kent, president of the Atwater Kent Company which, in 1925, was the largest maker of radios in the U.S.; A. C. Dinkey, president of Midvale Steel Company, Philadelphia; Dwight F. Davis, assistant secretary of war; and a few lesser military figures.

28. Rosendahl, "The Shenandoah Goes West," unpublished memoir, Ibid.

29. Letter from: Commanding Officer, To: Chief of Naval Operations, Washington, D.C., Subject: Minneapolis – Landing of USS Los Angeles, 13 May 1925. (Courtesy NARA, Washington, D.C.).

30. "Border to See U.S. Dirigible Sunday," *Windsor (ON) Star*, June 6, 1925, p. 1.

31. Logbook, USS Los Angeles, June 7, 1925.

32. Althoff, *USS Los Angeles: The Navy's Venerable Airship and Aviation Technology* (Washington, D.C.: Potomac Books, Inc., 2004), p.63.

33. Rosendahl, "The Shenandoah Goes West," unpublished memoir, Ibid.

34. Logbook, USS Shenandoah, July 16, 1925.

35. Rosendahl, "The Shenandoah Goes West," unpublished memoir, Ibid.

36. Rosendahl, "The Shenandoah Goes West," unpublished memoir, p. 7.

37. Ibid.

CHAPTER 6: THE *SHENANDOAH* DISASTER

1. Letter from: Commanding Officer; To: Bureau of Navigation; Subject: Travel Orders, 29 June 1925.

2. Rosendahl, "The Shenandoah Goes West," unpublished memoir, p, 7.

3. Ibid., p. 8.

4. Ibid.

5. Ibid.

6. Ibid.

7. Ibid.

8. "Big Dirigible Shenandoah Leaves Her Moorings Late Today and Heads Westward," *Des Moines (IA) Tribune*, September 2, 1925, p. 1.

9. "Thousands Will See Shenandoah Here Saturday," *Minneapolis (MN) Star*, September 1, 1925, p. 1.

10. "15 Perish as Shenandoah Breaks in 3 Parts During Electric Storm Over Ohio; Many Hurt," *Brooklyn (NY) Daily Eagle*, September 3, 1925, p. 1.

11. "Technical Aspects of the Loss of the U.S.S. Shenandoah," *Journal of the American Society of Naval Engineers*, August 1926, p. 488–505.

N.B., Because Rosendahl was the senior surviving officer of the ship and gave a lucid account of the events that led to the crash, his statement will be presented here nearly intact as he gave it. Any differences in accounts among individuals will be dealt with separately.

12. Rosendahl, "The Shenandoah Goes West," p. 13.

13. Ibid., p. 14.

14. Ibid.

15. The fourteen dead in the control cabin were: Lieutenant Commander Zachary Lansdowne; Lieutenant Commander Louis Hancock, Jr.; Lieutenant J. B. Lawrence; Lieutenant A. B. Houghton; Chief Petty Officer George C. Schnitzer; Machinist's Mate James A. Moore; Chief Rigger E. P. Allen. Others killed were: Lieutenant E. W. Sheppard, Rigger Ralph G. Joffray; Machinist's Mate B. B. O'Sullivan; Machinist's Mate W. A. Sprattley; Chief Machinist Charles H. Broom; Machinist's Mate C. P. Mazzuco; Machinist's Mate James W. Cullinan. (*Philadelphia Inquirer*, September 4, 1925, p. 1.)

16. "15 Perish," Ibid.

17. "Navy Airship Wrecked; 14 Killed," *Albuquerque (NM) Journal*, September 4, 1925, p. 2.

18. Ibid

19. "Dead Man's Log Bares Air Fight," *Oakland (CA) Tribune*, September 5, 1925, p. 1.

20. Ibid., p. 7.

21. Ibid.

22. "Mrs. Lansdowne Retracts Charge," *Kingston (NY) Daily Freeman*, September 4, 1925, p. 1.

23. Ibid.

24. Ibid

25. "Begin Probe of Air Disaster, Gave Lives to Save Helium, Heinen Says," *News-Herald* (Franklin, PA), September 4, 1925, p. 11.

26. Ibid

27. H. W. Sharpe, "Survivors Return to Lakehurst While Board Visits Scene," *News-Herald* (Franklin, PA), September 4, 1925, p. 1.

28. "Moffett Declares Disaster Will Not Affect Air Policy," *Brooklyn (NY) Daily Eagle*, September 3, 1925, p. 1.

29. "Plans Drawn for Dirigible Bigger Than Shenandoah," *St. Louis (MO) Post-Dispatch*, September 9, 1925, p. 2.

30. "Removal of Gas Valves," Ibid.

31. Ibid. p. 79.

32. Ibid., p. 120.

33. Record of Proceedings, pp. 217–224.

34. Rosendahl, "Uproar," unpublished memoir, edited June 1958, p. 3.

35. Record of Proceedings, Technical Argument by Professor William Hovgaard, Technical Adviser to the Judge Advocate, p. 2133.

36. Ibid., p. 2175.

37. Ibid.

CHAPTER 7: ROSENDAHL AND THE *GRAF ZEPPELIN*

1. Logbook, USS Los Angeles, March 15, 1926.

2. Logbook, USS Los Angeles, May 10, 1926.

3. Logbook, USS Los Angeles, June 8, 1926.

4. Althoff, *USS Los Angeles*, p. 90.

5. G. W. Settle, Oral History Given to William Althoff, July 12, 1976, p. 64; recorded in William F. Althoff Oral History Library, Smithsonian Libraries/Nartional Air and Space Museum, Washington, D.C.

6. Logbook, USS Los Angeles, May 10, 1926.

7. Althoff, *USS Los Angeles*, p. 92.

8. Logbook, USS Los Angeles, August 25, 1927.

9. Ibid.

10. Ibid.

11. G. W. Settle, Oral history given to W. F. Althoff, transcript p. 47.

12. Rosendahl, "Uproar," unpublished memoir, p. 19.

13. Ibid.

14. Ibid., p. 20.

15. Logbook, USS Los Angeles, January 20, 1928.

16. "Landing of Los Angeles on Aircraft Carrier Is Considered Real Success," *Dayton (OH) Daily News*, January 29, 1928, p. 34.

17. Logbook, USS Los Angeles, Ibid.

18. Letter from: the Commanding Officer, U.S.S. Los Angeles, To: The Chief of the Bureau of Navigation, March 15, 1928. (Courtesy of the National Archives, St. Louis, Missouri.)

19. "Los Angeles Flies Toward Canal Zone," *Emporia (KS) Gazette*, February 27, 1928, p. 7.

20. "Dirigible Leaves Panama for Cuba After Record Trip," *Shreveport (LA) Journal*, February 28, 1928, p. 1.

21. Letter from: Bureau of Navigation; To: Charles E. Rosendahl, U.S.N.; Subject: Temporary Additional Duty, Personnel File, NARA, St. Louis, MO, June 26, 1928.

22. Wiegand, "Giant Airship Is Christened," *Times* (Shreveport, LA), July 10, 1928, p. 13.

23. "Huge Zeppelin in First Flight," *Burlington (VT) Free Press*, September 20, 1928, p. 7.

24. "Graf Zeppelin, Damage Repaired, Flies On," *Evening Journal* (Wilmington, DE), October 13, 1928, p. 1.

25. "Zeppelin Under Control in Blow, Rosendahl Says," *Asbury Park (NJ) Press*, October 18, 1928, p. 1.

26. Ibid.

27. Ibid.

28. "Graf Zeppelin Is Safe Over U. S.," *News-Herald* (Franklin, TN), October 15, 1928, p. 1.

29. "Graf Zeppelin Is Landed Safely at Lakehurst; Flight from Germany Is Made in 111 Hours," *Cincinnati (OH) Enquirer*, October 16, 1928, p. 1.

30. Marvin Murphy, "Graf Zeppelin Reaches Goal," *Baltimore (MD) Sun*, October 16, 1928, p. 2.

31. "Storm Shuts Off Radio Contact," *Boston Globe*, October 30, 1928, p. 1.

32. "Feasibility of Air Passage Over Atlantic Tested," *Austin (TX) American*, March 30, 1929, p. 6.

33. "New Navy Dirigibles Will Carry Airplanes," *Honolulu (HI) Advertiser*, February 13, 1929, p. 14.

34. Ibid.

35. "New Commander for Los Angeles," *Daily News* (New York, NY), May 5, 1929, p. 241.

36. From: Lieutenant Commander C. E. Rosendahl; To: Bureau of Navigation; Re: Report of Compliance with Orders, May 9, 1929.

37. "Graf Zeppelin Plans Cruise Around World," *Pittsburgh (PA) Press*, May 5, 1929, p. 1.

38. "Giant Dirigible to Circle Globe," *Roanoke (AL) Leader*, May 8, 1929, p. 1

39. Rosendahl, "Uproar," unpublished memoir, edited 1958, p. 22.

40. Ibid.

41. "Consider Sites for Air Base on Pacific," *Post-Crescent* (Appleton, WI), May 8, 1929, p. 2.

42. "Site for New Dirigible Base," *Napa Valley (CA) Register*, May 10, 1929, p. 4.

43. "Zeppelin Starts Flight to America," *Boston Globe*, May 16, 1929, p. 1.

44. "Zeppelin Seems Trying for Cuers, In Southern France," *Boston Globe*, May 17, 1929, p. 1.

45. "Zeppelin in World Cruise," *Billings (MT) Gazette*, July 4, 1929, p. 7.

46. Ibid.

47. "Zeppelin All Set to go Tomorrow," *Morning News* (Wilmington, DE), July 31, 1929, p. 3.

48. Ibid.

49. "Graf Zeppelin Lands at Lakehurst After Paying Visit to New York City," *News and Observer* (Raleigh, NC), August 5, 1929, p. 1.

50. "3 Famed Correspondents to Pen Story of Flight," *San Francisco (CA) Examiner*, August 6, 1929, p. 2.

51. "Airship Here to Stay, Says Commander," *San Francisco (CA) Examiner*, August 6, 1929, p. 2.

52. "Zeppelin Off on Around-the-World Flight," *St. Louis (MO) Globe*, August 8, 1929, p. 8.

53. "Zepp Approaching England," *Boston Globe*, August 9, 1929, p. 1.

54. Ibid., p. 8.

55. Wiegand, "Ship Slated at First to Pass London," *San Francisco (CA) Examiner*, August 10, 1929, p. 2.

56. Ibid., p. 13.

57. Ibid.
58. Ibid.
59. Ibid.
60. Ibid.
61. Ibid.
62. Dr. H. Eckener, "'Graf,' After Record Trip to Germany, Starts for Tokio [sic.] Wednesday Night," *Hartford (CT) Courant*, August 11. 1929, p. 1.
63. Wiegand, Ibid.
64. Ibid.
65. Ibid.
66. Ibid.
67. Ibid.
68. Ibid., p. 2.
69. Ibid.
70. "Zepp Waiting for Good Wind," *Indiana (PA) Gazette*, August 13, 1929, p. 2.
71. Wiegand, "'Graf Zeppelin' Starts for Tokio,"p. 1.
72. Lady Drummond-Hay, "Safety Supercedes Glory in Flight Arrangements," *Hartford (CT) Courant*, August 13, 1929, p. 1.
73. Ibid.
74. "Zeppelin Not to Start Tokyo Flight Tonight," *Wilkes-Barre (PA) Record*, August 13, 1929, p. 1.
75. "Wildest Area Known to Man Lies in Path," *Bee* (Danville, VA), August 15, 1929, p. 3.
76. Rosendahl, "Uproar," unpublished memoir, revised June 1958, p. 23.
77. Wiegand, "Record Trip Over Siberia Speeds Time for Landing," *San Francisco (CA) Examiner*, August 18, 1929, p. 1
78. Lady G. D. Hay, "What a Day! Our Radio Has Picked Up Japan!" *San Francisco (CA) Examiner*, August 18, 1929, p. 1.
79. "Expects to Reach Tokio Monday," *Boston Globe*, August 17, 1929, p. 1.
80. "Graf's Radio Picked Up by Jap Station," *San Francisco (CA) Examiner*, August 18, 1929, p. 2.
81. Ibid.
82. Ibid.
83. "Fair Weather Awaits Graf," *San Francisco (CA) Examiner*, August 18, 1929, p. 2.
84. Wiegand, "Million in Japan Greet Graf as King of World Sky," *San Francisco (CA) Examiner*, August 20, 1929, p. 1.
85. Ibid., p. 2.
86. Sir Hubert Wilkins, "Smiles, Flags, Whistles Greet Voyagers at Tokio," *San Francisco (CA) Examiner*, August 20. 1929, p. 5.
87. Ibid.
88. Ibid.
89. James R. Young, "Eckener Will Be Honored by Emperor," *San Francisco (CA) Examiner*, August 20, 1929, p. 4.
90. Lady Drummond Hay, "Gondola Damaged as Great Liner is Leaving Hangar," *San Francisco (CA) Examiner*, August 22, 1929, p. 2.
91. "Zeppelin Leaves Japan and Heads for America on Its Tour of World," *Courier-News* (Bridgewater, NJ), August 23, 1020, p. 1.
92. George H. Beale, "Zep to Sail Tonight from L. A. on Final Lap of World Flight," *Oakland (CA) Tribune*, August 26, 1929, p. 1.
93. Ibid.
94. Ibid.
95. Ibid.
96. "Graf Zeppelin Ready to Hop for Lakehurst," *Tampa (FL) Tribune*, August 27, 1929, p. 1.
97. Lyle C. Wilson, "Zeppelin Ends Globe Record Trip in Jersey," *Brooklyn (NY) Times Union*, August 29, 1929, p. 1.
98. "Hoover is First to Hail Eckener as Flight Ends," *Brooklyn (NY) Times Union*, August 29, 1929, p. 1.
99. Ibid.

100. "Germany Repaying America's Aid to Dr. Hugo Eckener," *News Journal* (Wilmington, DE), August 31, 1929, p. 3.

101. Ibid., p. 12.

102. Ibid.

103. Rear Admiral W. A. Moffett "Two Giant Airships to be Added to Sky Defense," *San Francisco (CA) Examiner*, December 9, 1928, p. 41.

104. "Moffett Tells Need of West Airship Base," *Honolulu (HI) Star-Bulletin*, July 5, 1930, p. 1.

105. "General Board of Navy Supports Secretary Adams in Deciding on Camp Kearny for Naval Air Base," *San Bernardino County (CA) Sun*, December 20, 1929, p. 3.

106. "San Francisco Looming as Center of Aviation," *Clarion-Ledger* (Jackson, MS), June 26, 1930, p. 3.

107. "Navy Zeppelins, Built at Akron, to Dwarf Graf," *Knoxville (TN) News-Sentinel*, August 9, 1929, p. 11.

108. "Plan Expansion Airship Service," *Montana Standard* (Butte, MT), August 25, 1929, p. 44.

CHAPTER 8: USS *AKRON* (ZRS-4)

1. "Contracts for Two Giant Navy Dirigibles Let," *Honolulu (HI) Advertiser*, October 22, 1928, p. 12.

2. Ibid.

3. "Navy's Dirigibles to Carry Powerful Radio Transmitters," *Sacramento (CA) Bee*, November 10, 1928, p. 29.

4. Harold J. Taylor, "Pageantry Is Succeeded by Actual Labor," *Akron (OH) Beacon Journal*, November 8, 1929, p. 1.

5. Ibid., p. 28.

6. Ibid.

7. Harold E. Righter, "Start Work on Giant Dirigible," *Muncie (IN) Evening Press*, November 7, 1929, p. 1.

8. "Start Assembling of New Navy Dirigible in Akron," *News-Journal* (Mansfield, OH), November 8, 1929, p. 1.

9. Harold J. Taylor, Ibid., p. 28.

10. "Ceremonies at Ring Laying of Giant Dirigible," *Times* (Munster, IN), October 31, 1929, p. 19.

11. G. E. Hancock, "Banquet Guests Pay Tribute to Paul Litchfield," *Akron (OH) Beacon Journal*, November 8, 1929, p. 28.

12. "Zeppelin World Flight on Screen at Columbia," *San Francisco (CA) Examiner*, December 8, 1929, p. 64.

13. Ibid.

14. Letter from: Bureau of Navigation; To: Lieutenant Commander Charles E. Rosendahl, June 23, 1930, (NARA, St. Louis, MO).

15. Rosendahl, "Akron Adventure," unpublished memoir, revised June 1958, p. 3.

16. Letter from: Bureau of Navigation; To: Lieutenant Commander Charles E. Rosendahl, U.S.N., Subject: Change of duty, April 6, 1931. (NARA, St. Louis, MO).

17. Oscar Leding, "Lt. Charles E. Rosendahl to Guide Fate of Akron," *Lubbock (TX) Morning Avalanche*, April 9, 1931, p. 7.

18. Laurence M. Benedict, "New Navy Superdirigible Soon to Ride Skyways," *Los Angeles Times*, April 19, 1931, p. 8.

19. Smith, Robert B. "World's Largest Airship Nearly Ready," *Cincinnati (OH) Enquirer*, May 3, 1931, p. 120.

20. Ibid.

21. "First Lady Gets Ovation of Multitude," *Akron (OH) Beacon Journal*, August 8, 1931, p. 1.

22. Ibid.

23. Ibid.

24. Ibid.

25. Ibid.

26. "Calls About Zeppelin Akron Swamp Telephone Operator," *Akron (OH) Beacon Journal*, September 23, 1931, p. 23.

27. Harold J. Taylor, "Craft Taken Up on Fourth Trial Flight," *Akron (OH) Beacon Journal*, September 28, 1931, p. 1.

28. "Akron Heads West on Long Test Cruise," *Akron (OH) Beacon Journal*, October 16, 1931, p. 1.

29. Harold J. Taylor, "Board Approves U. S. S. 'Akron,'" *Akron (OH) Beacon Journal*, October 19, 1931, p. 1.

30. Rosendahl, "Akron Adventure," unpublished memoir, p. 5.

31. Logbook, USS Akron, January 10, 1932.

32. Richard K. Smith, *The Airships Akron & Macon: Flying Aircraft Carriers of the United States Navy* (Annapolis, MD: Naval Institute Press, 1965), p. 49.

33. Logbook, USS Akron, January 11, 1932.

34. Ibid.

35. Smith, *Airships Akron and Macon*, p. 51.

36. "House Naval Committee Votes Probe of Rumored Defects of U. S. S. Akron," *Daily Republican* (Monongahela, PA), January 5, 1921, p. 1.

37. Logbook, USS Akron, February 22, 1932.

38. "Rosendahl to Leave 'Akron' for New Assignment at Sea," *Akron (OH) Beacon Journal*, February 2, 1932, p. 1.

39. "Rosendahl Gets Texas Vacation," *Akron (OH) Beacon Journal*, March 28, 1932, p. 20.

40. Radford E. Mobley, "Bill Provides $1,450,000 for U. S. S. Macon," *Akron (OH) Beacon Journal*, April 19, 1932, p 1.

41. Ibid.

42. "C. E. Rosendahl's Father is Taken," *Akron (OH) Beacon Journal*, April 25, 1932, p. 17.

43. Logbook, USS Akron, April 25, 1932.

44. Logbook, USS Akron, May 2, 1932.

45. Logbook, USS Akron, May 3, 1932.

46. "Electrical Storm Forces Akron to Turn Back," *Pasadena (CA) Post*, May 10, 1932, p. 2.

47. "Forced Back on Reaching San Angelo," *Santa Cruz (CA) Sentinel*, May 10, 1932, p. 1.

48. Ibid.

49. Ibid., p. 2.

50. Rosendahl, "Akron Adventure," unpublished memoir, June 1958, p. 6.

51. Logbook, USS Akron, Ibid.

52. Rosendahl, Ibid., p. 9.

53. "U. S. S. Akron Heads Up Coast; Possibly Over Valley Tonight," *Santa Maria (CA) Daily Times*, May 12, 1932, p. 1.

54. Rosendahl, Ibid.

55. Ibid.

56. Ibid.

57. Ibid., p. 13.

58. Ibid.

59. Lieutenant Commander C. E. Rosendahl, "Rosendahl is Grieved at Tragedy," *Oakland (CA) Tribune*, May 12, 1932, p. 2.

60. Logbook, USS Akron, May 12, 1932.

61. "Airship Base Proved," *Oakland (CA) Tribune*, May 22, 1932, p 44.

62. Ibid.

63. Rosendahl, Ibid. p, 13.

64. "Akron Awaits Call to Battle Maneuvers, 50,000 See Liner," *Press Democrat* (Santa Rosa, CA), May 15, 1932, p. 1.

65. "Bay Visualized as Center of Dirigible Era," *San Francisco (CA) Examiner*, May 15, 1932, p. 7.

66. "Com. Rosendahl Forced Down at S. P. Airport," *Ventura County Star and the Ventura (CA) Daily Post*, May 16, 1932, p. 1.

67. Rosendahl, Ibid.

68. "Akron to 'Spy' on Maneuvers of U. S. Fleet," *San Francisco (CA) Examiner*, June 1, 1932, p. 14.

69. Ibid.

70. "Naval Armada Awaits Akron," *Modesto (CA) News-Herald*, May 31, 1932, p. 1.

71. Logbook, USS Akron, June 1, 1932.

72. Smith, *Akron & Macon*, p. 58.

73. Ibid.

74. Ibid.

75. Logbook, USS Akron, June 3, 1932.

76. Smith, *Akron & Macon*, Ibid.

77. "Akron Tactics Put Navy's Scouting Planes to Test," *Los Angeles (CA) Times*, June 5, 1932, p. 25.

78. Smith, *Akron & Macon*, Ibid.

79. "Akron Leaves for Sunnyvale," *San Pedro (CA) News-Pilot*, June 4, 1932, p. 2.

80. "Akron's Maneuvers in West Complete," *Courier-News* (Bridgewater, NJ), June 4, 1932, p. 6.

81. Rosendahl, Ibid.

82. Smith, *Akron & Macon*, Ibid.

83. Rosendahl, Ibid.

84. "Rosendahl Honor Urged in Congress," *Akron (OH) Beacon Journal*, June 3, 1932, p. 33.

85. Logbook, USS Akron, June 11, 1932.

86. Smith, *Akron & Macon*, p. 61.

87. Logbook, USS Akron, June 12, 1932.

88. Smith, *Akron & Macon*, Ibid.

89. Rosendahl, Ibid., p. 14.

90. Rosendahl, Ibid., p. 15.

91. Logbook, USS Akron, June 22, 1932.

92. Ibid.

93. "Akron Returns Home," *Oakland (CA) Tribune*, June 20, 1932, p. 23.

94. Rosendahl, Ibid., p. 15.

95. "Akron's New Skipper Devises War Program for His Airship," *Pittsburgh (PA) Press*, July 20, 1932, p. 23.

96. Logbook, USS Los Angeles, June 30, 1932.

97. Ibid.

98. "Los Angeles Scrapped, Ending 8-year Career," *Courier-News* (Bridgewater, NJ), June 30, 1932, p. 1.

99. "Pick Robust Sailor-Man to Guide U. S. S. Macon in Test," *Akron(OH) Beacon Journal*, August 25, 1932, p. 15.

100. Rosendahl, "Pacific Cruise," unpublished memoir, June 1958, p. 1.

101. Ibid.

102. Ibid., p. 2.

103. Ibid.

104. Ibid.

105. Ibid.

106. Rosendahl, "Pacific Cruise," unpublished memoir, June 1958, p. 3.

107. Ibid.

108. Ibid.

109. Ibid.

110. Rosendahl, "Pacific Cruise," unpublished memoir, June 1958, p. 4.

111. Ibid.

112. "Rosendahl Declines to Guess at Cause," *Arizona Daily Star* (Tucson, AZ), April 5, 1933, p. 7.

113. Ibid., p. 3.

114. Ibid., p. 1.

115. From: Secretary of the Navy; To: Rear Admiral Henry V. Butler, U. S. Navy, Commandant, U.S. Navy Yard, Washington, D. C., Subject: Court of Inquiry to Inquire into All the Facts and Circumstances Surrounding the Loss of the U. S. S. Akron, 4 April 1933, NARA.

116. A detailed account of the crash of the Akron and details of the subsequent court of inquiry proceedings can be found in: Marshall, *Rear Admiral Herbert V. Wiley*, pp. 142–174.

117. Akron Court of Inquiry, pp. 48-49.

118. "Wreckage of Akron Inspected by Divers But No Bodies Found," *Statesville (NC) Record and Landmark*, April 21, 1933, p. 7.

119. "Entire Wreckage of Big Navy Blimp Located," *Hutchinson (KS) News*, April 27, 1933, p. 1.

120. Smith, *Akron & Macon*, p. 85.

121. Rosendahl, *What About the Airship?* (New York: Charles Scribner's Sons, 1938), pp. 115–116.

122. Ibid., pp. 123–124.

123. Rosendahl, "Pacific Cruise," unpublished memoir, edited June 1958, p. 5.

124. Ibid., p. 6.

125. "Committee Recommends Replacement of Akron for Service in Navy," *Valley Morning Star* (Harlingen, TX), June 16, 1933, p. 3.

CHAPTER 9: THE NAVY'S LAST GREAT RIGID AIRSHIP

1. "Rosendahl Promoted to Commander Rank," *Fort Worth (TX) Star-Telegram*, February 15, 1934, p. 4.

2. Harold J. Taylor "Rosendahl Leaves Cruiser," *Akron (OH) Beacon Journal*, March 24, 1934, p. 1.

3. Ibid., p. 2.

4. Helen S. Waterhous, "Rosendahl, Serving on Battleship, Ready to Take Over Lakehurst, N. J. Command," *Akron (OH) Beacon Journal*, April 10, 1934, p. 11.

5. Rosendahl, "On Trial," unpublished memoir, edited June 1958, p. 1.

6. Waterhouse, "'Good News' to Lighter-Than-Air is Coming, Rosendahl Promises," *Akron (OH) Beacon Journal*, July 28, 1934, p. 13.

7. Ibid.

8. Waterhouse, "Good News," p. 13.

9. Ibid.

10. "Airship Will Hum But Not Go Anywhere," *Daily Record* (Long Branch, NJ), September 4, 1934, p. 1.

11. John Toland, *The Great Dirigibles: Their Triumphs & Disasters* (New York: Dover, 1972), p. 276.

12. Ibid.

13. Logbook, USS Macon, April 21, 1934, RG 24 entry 118-G, NARA.

14. Smith, *Akron & Macon*, p. 117.

15. Logbook, USS Macon, April 22, 1934.

16. Smith, Akron & Macon, p. 119.

17. "Airship's Value to Fleet Will Be Known Soon," *Sedalia (MO) Democrat*, May 10, 1934, p. 3.

18. "Macon's Caribbean Flight to Decide Airship Policy: Fleet Maneuver Will Determine If Government Will Construct More Dirigibles," *Salt Lake (UT) Tribune*, May 7, 1934, p. 1.

19. "Macon Worth for Fleet to Be Discussed," *San Bernardino County (CA) Sun*, May 10, 1934, p. 1.

20. Logbook, USS Macon, May 6, 1934.

21. Ibid.

22. Smith, *Akron & Macon*, p. 121.

23. "Navy Chieftans Debating Giant Airship's Worth," *Scranton (PA) Republican*, May 10, 1934, p. 1.

24. Rosendahl, "On Trial," unpublished memoir, edited June 1958, p. 2.

25. Ibid., p. 3.

26. Ibid.

27. Ibid.

28. A. H. Dresel, USS Macon: Damage to Structure in Flight to Opa-locka, Florida – Report of, U. S. Naval Air Station, Sunnyvale, Mountain View, California, June 8, 1934, NARA.

29. Captain F. R. McCrary, Assistant Chief of Bureau of Aeronautics, to Commanding Officer, USS *Macon*, Subject: Damage to Girders, July 24, 1934, NARA.

30. John T. Mason Jr., "Reminiscences of Rear Admiral Harold B. Miller, U.S. Navy (Retired)," U. S. Naval Institute, Annapolis, Maryland, 1995, p. 73.

31. Letter from: E. J. King To: Lt. Comdr. H. V. Wiley, USN. 18 June 1934, in personnel file, NARA (St. Louis, MO).

32. "Roosevelt to Visit Panama Wednesday," *Bismarck (ND) Tribune*, July 11, 1934, p. 1

33. Smith, *Akron & Macon*, p. 128.

34. Logbook, USS Macon, July 19, 1934.

35. W. O. Boss, "The Macon Mail Drop to FDR on the Houston," *Jack Knight Air Log: The Zeppelin Collector*, July 1997, p. 44 (NARA).

36. Mason, p. 78; Smith, *Akron & Macon*, p. 128.

37. "'Macon' Contacts the President's Cruiser and Delivers Papers," *Santa Cruz (CA) Sentinel*, July 20, 1934, p. 1.

38. Smith, *Akron & Macon*, p. 131.

39. Letter from: Commanding Officer: To: Chief of Naval Operations. Operations of U. S. S. *Macon*, 18–21 July 1934; Contact with U. S. S. Houston, 25 July 1934. (NARA, Washington, D.C.).

40. "Macon Goes on Hunt for 'Foe Craft,'" *San Francisco (CA) Examiner*, October 10. 1934, p. 19.

41. "Rosendahl Agrees," *San Pedro (CA) News-Pilot*, October 16, 1934, p. 9.

42. "Rosendahl Urges 4 New Dirigibles," *Asbury Park (NJ) Press*, October 31, 1934, p. 1.

43. Ibid.

44. Ibid.

45. "France Seeks Military Object in Eckener Visit," *San Francisco (CA) Examiner*, November 1, 1934, p. 2.

46. Ibid.

47. Logbook, USS Macon, November 7 and 8, 1934.

48. Ibid., November 8, 1934.

49. Logbook, USS Macon, November 9, 1934.

50. Smith, *Akron & Macon*, p. 141.

51. "Naval Strategy Will Be Tested," *Billings (MT) Gazette*, December 5, 1934, p. 10.

52. Logbook, USS Macon, December 6, 1934.

53. Ibid.

54. Ibid.

55. Logbook, USS Macon, December 7, 1934.

56. Smith, *Akron & Macon*, p. 145.

57. Rosendahl, Ibid., p. 2.

58. Smith, p. 145.

59. Rosendahl, Ibid., p. 4.

60. Ibid.

61. Ibid., p. 5.

62. Ibid.

63. Ibid., p. 1.

64. Ibid.

65. "Commander Is Married," *Daily Record* (Long Branch, NJ), December 24. 1934, p. 8.

66. Rosendahl, Ibid., p. 2.

67. Ibid., p. 4.

68. "American Fleet Plans Greatest Pacific Maneuvers," *Santa Ana (CA) Register*, December 29, 1934, p. 1.

69. "American Fleet to Encompass Pacific in Spring Maneuver," *Capital Journal* (Salem, OR), December 29, 1934, p. 1.

70. Logbook, USS Macon, February 11, 1935.

71. Campbell, George W., Lt. (jg), USN, Testimony Given During Court of Inquiry Convened by Commander-In-Chief, U. S. Fleet, to Inquire into All the Circumstances Connected with the Loss of the USS Macon Near Point Sur, California, on 12 February 1935, p. 107., Case No. 18580, Box 656, NARA.

72. Lieutenant Commander Herbert V. Wiley, U.S.N., Testimony Given During Court of Inquiry, USS Macon, 12 February 1935, p. 1-2.

73. George W.Campbell, "Five O'Clock off California," *Saturday Evening Post*, May 15, 1937, p. 124.

74. "Chief of Navy Will Oppose New Airship, Swanson Stand Seen as End of Dirigible Ships for U.S.," *Salt Lake (UT) Tribune*, February 21, 1935, p. 1.

75. Rosendahl, "On Trial," p. 16.

CHAPTER 10: THE *HINDENBURG*

1. "81 Saved in Wreck of Macon," *News* (Paterson, NJ), February 13, 1935, p. 1.

2. "Macon Crash Hard Blow to Navy Program," *Journal and Courier* (Lafayette, IN), February 13, 1935, p. 1.

3. "Abandons Bill," *News* (Paterson, NJ), February 13, 1935, p. 25.

4. "Asks 5-Year Trial Given Dirigibles," *Record* (Hackensack, NJ), June 20, 1935, p. 5.

5. "Rosendahl, Believer in Airships," *Akron (OH) Beacon Journal*, June 28, 1935, p. 4.

6. "Macon Crash to be Probed," *Akron (OH) Beacon Journal*, July 2, 1935, p. 1.

7. Harold J. Taylor, "Navy Resents Macon Attack," *Akron (OH) Beacon Journal*, July 27, 11935, p. 2.

8. Ibid.

9. "Plan Zeppelin Trips Between Germany, U. S.," *Dayton (OH) Daily News*, October 20, 1935, p. 6.

10. Ibid.

11. Ibid.

12. "Rosendahl Urges Ocean Dirigibles," *Baltimore (MD) Sun*, October 31, 1935, p. 2.

13. Ibid.

14. "New Dirigible Is Favored for American Navy," *Evening News* (Wilkes-Barre, PA), January 27, 1936, p. 9.

15. Ibid.

16. Ibid.

17. "Rosendahl Urges Dirigible for U. S.," *Philadelphia Inquirer*, March 22, 1936, p. 28.

18. "Zeppelin Due at Lakehurst on May 8 or 9," *Courier-News* (Bridgewater, NJ), April 18, 1936, p. 2.

19. Ibid.

20. H. H. Kroh, "Lakehurst Makes Ready for Visit of Hindenburg," Courier-Post (Camden, NJ), April 20, 1936, p. 10.

21. Gregory Hewlett, "Lakehurst Ground Crew Rehearses Routine for Receiving Hindenburg," *Record* (Hackensack, NJ), May 8, 1936, p. 2.

22. Ibid.

23. Sandor E. Klein, "Crowd Hails Queen of Air at Lakehurst," *Brooklyn (NY) Times Union*, May 9, 1936, p. 1.

24. Ibid.

25. Ibid., p. 3.

26. "Ship Returns Upon Monday," *Charleston (WV) Daily Mail*, May 10, 1936, p. 53.

27. Klein, "Crowd Hails Queen of Air," p. 1.

28. "Ship Returns Upon Monday," p. 53.

29. Ibid.

30. "Hindenburg's Tanks Refilled for Trip Back," *Richmond (VA) Times-Dispatch*, May 10, 1936, p. 2.

31. "Zeppelin Ends Ocean Trips Until Spring," *Asbury Park (NJ) Press*, October 10, 1936, p. 1.

32. Waterhouse, "Zep Comeback Being Staged," *Akron (OH) Beacon Journal*, October 28, 1936, p. 21.

33. "Rosendahl Visions Return of Airships," *Morning Post* (Camden, NJ), November 26, 1936, p. 13.

34. Ibid.

35. "Dr. Eckener Arrives in U. S. for Ocean Air Line Parleys," *Baltimore (MD) Sun*, January 10, 1937, p. 2.

36. "Sky Ship," *Californian* (Salinas, CA), January 16, 1937, p. 20.

37. Ibid.

38. "Nine Flights Scheduled for Hindenburg," *Courier-News* (Bridgewater, NJ), January 23, 1937, p. 9.

39. "Germany Plans for 4 Dirigibles Within 3 Years," *Harrisburg (PA) Telegraph*, March 12, 1937, p. 18.

40. "Hindenburg to Arrive May 6; Lakehurst Prepares a Berth," *Asbury Park (NJ) Press*, May 3, 1937, p. 3.

41. "Hindenburg Combats Headwinds Over Sea," *Morning News* (Wilmington, DE), May 5, 1937, p. 1.

42. Rosendahl, "End of the Hindenburg," unpublished memoir, p. 2.

43. "Few Persons Saw the Hindenburg Destroyed," *Gazette and Daily* (York, PA), May 7, 1937, p. 1.

44. Rosendahl, "End of the Hindenburg," unpublished memoir, pp. 3–8.

45. Ibid., p. 8.

46. Ibid.

47. Ibid.

48. Ibid., p. 9.

49. Ibid.

50. In his memoir, Rosendahl recalled a trip he made to Germany in the summer of 1955, during which he met up with Werner Franz and "a number of other old zeppelin men." Franz had become a Luftwaffe pilot during the Second World War. He was shot down, captured, and interned in Canada. Franz got word that Rosendahl was in Friedrichshafen, and he drove a great distance to see him to introduce his two young sons and tell of his wartime experiences. Rosendahl said Franz was but one of many remaining Zeppelin men who had retained their belief in airships despite their harrowing experiences in the Hindenburg. These men would serve again gladly in airships—if filled with helium.

51. Rosendahl, Ibid., p. 10.

52. Ibid.

53. Ibid., p. 11.

54. Ibid.
55. Ibid., p. 12.
56. "A radio Announcer's Account of the Hindenburg Disaster," *Birmingham (AL) News*, May 22, 1937, p. 4.
57. Ibid.
58. Ibid.
59. Rosendahl, Ibid., p. 12(a).
60. Ibid., p. 13.
61. Ibid., p. 14.
62. Ibid.
63. "Few Persons Saw the Hindenburg Destroyed," p. 1.
64. Rosendahl, Ibid., p 15.
65. Ibid.
66. Ibid., p. 16.
67. Ibid.
68. Ibid., p. 17.
69. Ibid., p. 18.
70. Ibid.
71. Letter from: Hermann Göring; To: Mrs. Jean Rosendahl, Rosendahl Collection, Special Collections and Archives Division, History of Aviation Archives, The University of Texas at Dallas.
72. Ibid.
73. Ibid., p. 11.
74. Ibid., p. 18.

CHAPTER 11: AFTERMATH OF THE *HINDENBURG* CRASH

1. Rosendahl, "End of the Hindenburg," unpublished memoir, Box 041, Folder 6, revised June 1958, p. 1.
2. Ibid.
3. Ibid., p. 2.
4. "Radio Flashes: WKBO," *Harrisburg (PA) Telegraph*, May 31, 1937, p. 10.
5. "Lakehurst Officials Long Feared the Explosion Possibility," *Gazette and Daily* (York, PA), May 7, 1937, p. 16.
6. "Disaster Demonstrates Need of Helium to Lift Dirigibles Says Eckener," *York (PA) Daily Record*, May 7, 1937, p. 16.
7. "Says Motor of Zep Backfired," *La Crosse (WI) Tribune*, May 8, 1937, p. 1.
8. Rosendahl, "Hindenburg Aftermath," unpublished memoir, Box 041, Folder 6, revised June 1958, p. 1.
9. Joe Alex Morris, "Chief Radio Man of Hindenburg is Dead; Fatalities Total 35," *News-Herald* (Franklin, PA), May 8, 1937, p. 1.
10. "A. P. Photographer 'Caught' Explosion with His Camera," *Gazette and Daily* (York, PA), May 7, 1937, p. 16.
11. Rosendahl, "Hindenburg Aftermath," unpublished memoir, p. 2.
12. Rosendahl, "Hindenburg Aftermath," p. 2.
13. Ibid., p. 4.
14. Ibid.
15. Ibid.
16. Ibid., p. 5.
17. Ibid.
18. Ibid., p. 6.
19. Ibid.
20. Ibid., p. 7.
21. Ibid.
22. Ibid.
23. Ibid., p. 7(a).
24. Ibid., p. 11.

25. "Germany, U. S. Join in Tribute," *Asbury Park (NJ) Press*, June 1, 1937, p. 2.

26. "Rosendahl Guest at Zeppelin Fete," *Central New Jersey Home News* (New Brunswick, NJ), July 8, 1938, p. 8.

27. Rosendahl, "Hindenburg Aftermath," unpublished memoir, p. 14.

28. "Ickes and Helium. Why Opposition? Is It Politics?" *Akron (OH) Beacon Journal*, April 27, 1938, p. 13.

29. "Sale of Helium to Germany Delayed Pending Guarantees," *Albuquerque (NM) Journal*, March 24, 1938, p. 1.

30. Ibid.

31. Rosendahl, "Hindenburg Aftermath," unpublished memoir, p. 21.

32. Ibid.

CHAPTER 12: WASHINGTON NIGHTMARE

1. Rosendahl, "The Peaceful Sea," unpublished memoir, revised June 1958, p. 1.

2. Ibid., p. 3.

3. Ibid.

4. Ibid., p. 4.

5. Ibid.

6. Ibid., p. 5.

7. Ibid.

8. Ibid.

9. Ibid.

10. In is memoir, Rosendahl occasionally alluded to specific individuals within the Bureau of Aeronautics who opposed him almost at every step, but he chose not to mention them by name.

11. Ibid., p. 7.

12. Ibid.

13. At this point in his unpublished memoir, Rosendahl made the editorial comment, "Less than two years later, with the advent of WW II, there was genuine reason to regret this."

14. Ibid., p. 8.

15. Ibid., p. 9.

16. Ibid.

17. Ibid.

18. Ibid., p. 11.

19. Ibid., p. 12.

20. "U.S. to Shift Part of Fleet," *El Paso (TX) Times*, September 28, 1939, p. 1.

21. Ibid.

22. Rosendahl, "The Peaceful Sea," p 13.

23. Ibid., p. 2.

24. Ibid., p. 3.

25. Ibid.

26. Rosendahl, "Washington Nightmare," p. 4.

27. Ibid., p. 5.

28. Ibid., p. 6.

29. Ibid., p. 7.

30. "Senate Votes Authority for Navy to Have 10,000 Planes, Ring of Bases," *Blackwell (OK) Daily Journal*, June 4, 1940, p. 1.

31. Mark S. Watson, "18 Ships Increase Navy Fleet 'Train'," *Baltimore (MD) Sun*, October 31. 1940, p. 16.

32. Ibid.

33. Rosendahl, "Washington Nightmare," p. 8.

34. Rosendahl, "Washington Nightmare," p. 11.

35. Ibid.

36. "Report U.S. to Construct Powerful Atlantic Coast Fleet; New Type Warship Hinted," *Daily Press* (Newport News, VA), June 17, 1940, p. 1.

37. "King to Command Atlantic Patrol," *Philadelphia Inquirer*, December 12, 1940, p. 9.

38. Rosendahl, "Washington Nightmare," p. 11.

39. Ibid., p. 12.
40. Ibid.
41. Ibid., p 13.
42. Ibid.
43. Ibid., p. 16.
44. "48 Non-rigid Blimps Approved by Navy," *Akron (OH) Beacon Journal*, June 9, 1940, p. 2.
45. "Rosendahl to Aid in Airship Fight," *Akron (OH) Beacon Journal*, June 17, 1940, p. 3.
46. "Order for Navy Blimps Expected," *Akron (OH) Beacon Journal*, June 21, 1940, p. 13.
47. Rosendahl, "Washington Nightmare," p. 16.
48. Ibid.
49. Ibid., p. 17.
50. Ibid.
51. Ibid., p. 18.
52. Ibid.
53. Ibid., p. 19.
54. Ibid.
55. Ibid., p. 25.
56. Ibid., p. 26.
57. A. T. Luey and H. P. Bruvold, *The "Minnie" or The War Cruise of the USS* Minneapolis (Elkhart, IN: Bell Printing Company, 1946), p. 11.
58. Ibid.

CHAPTER 13: RETURN TO AIRSHIPS AND RETIREMENT

1. Rosendahl, "Back to Airships," unpublished memoir, revised June 1958, p. 2.
2. Ibid.
3. Ibid.
4. Ibid., p. 7.
5. Ibid., p. 8.
6. "Blimps Tracking U-Boats," *Star Press* (Muncie, IN), July 2, 1943, p. 6.
7. "Blimps Praised by Rosendahl," *Asbury Park (NJ) Press*, August 27, 1943, p. 1.
8. Rosendahl, "Back to Airships," unpublished memoir, p. 2.
9. Several years after his retirement, Rosendahl was greatly disappointed to learn what had become of all his efforts at NAS Lakehurst. In connection with an inquiry that he had received relating to an experimental project he had set up, he was told by Lakehurst that all the experimental files had been shipped off to a dead-storage facility.

"It was disheartening that neither the Navy Department nor the Navy at large ever had a clear understanding of airships. The Deputy Chief of Naval Operations for Air was frequently changed. Airplane men with excellent reputations were chosen for this high assignment, but as each new man came to duty as DCNO (Air), he admittedly had but meager, if any, knowledge of blimps or the blimp program. Yet these airplane men had complete authority over airships." Rosendahl, "Back to Airships," p. 10.
10. Ibid.
11. "Rear Admiral's Wife to Christen Blimp," *Daily Times* (Salisbury, MD), October 27, 1943, p. 4.
12. Ibid., p. 13.
13. Ibid.
14. Rosendahl, "Retirement," unpublished memoir, revised August 1958, p. 1.
15. Ibid.
16. Rosendahl, Charles E. Rosendahl, *SNAFU – The Strange Story of the American Airship* (Atlantis Productions: 2004), p. 9.
17. Walter Lord, *Day of Infamy* (New York: Henry Holt and Company, LLC, 1957), p. 16.
18. Rosendahl, "Rejected Opportunity," unpublished memoir, edited December 14, 1956, p. 2. (Rosendahl Collection, Box 041, Folder 3, University of Texas at Dallas).
19. Ibid.
20. Ibid.
21. Ibid., p. 3.

22. Lord, *Day of Infamy*, p. 20.

23. Ibid., p. 23.

24. Rosendahl, "Rejected Opportunity," p. 4.

25. Ibid.

26. Ibid., p. 5.

27. Ibid.

28. Admiral William V. Pratt, "The Naval Job Facing the U.S. in the Pacific," *Newsweek*, November 3, 1941, p. 24.

29. Letter from: Captain Charles E. Dingwell, To: Rear Admiral C. E. Rosendahl, August 12, 1966, p. 1. (Rosendahl Collection, Box 065, Folder34, University of Texas at Dallas).

30. Thor Nielsen, *The Zeppelin Story* (London: Allan Wingate, 1955), p. 239.

31. Ibid.

32. "Navy Dooms Blimp Fleet at Lakehurst," *Asbury Park (NJ) Press*, June 27, 1961, p. 1.

33. "Navy Gets Research Mileage Out of its Last Two Airships," *Asbury Park (NJ) Press*, March 25, 1962, p. 9.

34. "Big White Airship in Last Flight," *Nashua (NH) Telegraph*, September 1, 1962, p. 14.

35. "Blimp Grounding at Lakehurst Stirs Ex-Commandant's Wrath," *Asbury Park (NJ) Press*, September 2, 1962, p. 1.

36. Ibid.

37. "Airship Museum Project at Lakehurst Supported," *Asbury Park (NJ) Press*, July 31, 1975, p. 1.

38. "Lakehurst Site Proposed for Airship Museum," *Asbury Park (NJ) Press*, September 18, 1975, p. 3.

39. "Dirigible Chief of Navy Dies," *Valley News* (Van Nuys, CA), May 15, 1977, p. 33.

40. "Navy, Dirigible Spokesmen Eulogize Adm. Rosendahl," *Asbury Park (NJ) Press*, May 29, 1977, p. 4.

41. Ibid.

42. Edward L. Walsh, "Aviation Collection Will Go to Texas," *Asbury Park (NJ) Press* (Asbury Park, NJ), November 18, 1977, p. 26.

43. Ibid. Following Admiral Rosendahl's death, his wife, Jean, became the guardian of the admiral's unpublished manuscripts. One of these, titled, *SNAFU – The Strange Story of the American Airship*, was considered by Mrs. Rosendahl to contain so much "vindictive" material that she considered destroying it. Fortunately, it was placed in the archives at the University of Texas at Dallas along with Rosendahl's other papers to be rediscovered years later, edited, illustrated, and published by LTA author/historian Richard G. Van Treuren, assisted by David R. Smith, Eric Brothers, and Herman Van Dyk. Hepburn Walker, Jr., a wartime shipmate and friend of Rosendahl's, who had reviewed an early version of the manuscript, provided the foreword.

44. "Aviation Collection Displayed at UTD," *Plano Daily (TX) Star-Courier*, November 16, 1977, p. 8.

45. Ray W. Ollwerther, "Navy Men 'Lied to Rosey,' Widow Declares," *Asbury Park (NJ) Press*, December 11, 1977, p. 27.

SELECTED BIBLIOGRAPHY

Action Report, Commander Airship Squadron 21, ASW-6 Form Report of Action on 18/19 July 1943. Rosendahl Collection, Box 176, Folder 23, University of Texas at Dallas.

Althoff, William E. Oral History Library, Smithsonian Libraries/National Air and Space Museum, Washington, D.C.

————. *Sky Ships: A History of the Airship in the United States Navy.* New York: Orion Books, 1990.

————. *USS Los Angeles: The Navy's Venerable Airship and Aviation Technology.* Washington, D.C.: Potomac Books, Inc., 2004.

Court of Inquiry Convened by Order of the Secretary of the Navy, to Inquire into the Circumstances Connected with the Loss of the USS Akron, off Barnegat Inlet, New Jersey, on April 4, 1933, boxes 614 and 615 (#18069), National Archives and Records Administration, Washington, D.C.

Court of Inquiry Convened by Commander-in-Chief, U.S. Fleet, to Inquire into All the Circumstances Connected with the Loss of the USS Macon near Point Sur, California, on February 12, 1935, box 656 (#18580), National Archives and Records Administration, Washington, D.C.

Court of Inquiry No. 13965 (Shenandoah), Record Group 125, Records of the Office of the Judge Advocate General (Navy), Records of Proceedings of Courts of Inquiry and Boards of Inquiry. May 1866–Dec. 1940, boxes 407–409, National Archives and Records Administration, Washington, D.C.

Crenshaw, R. S., Jr. *The Battle of Tassafaronga.* Baltimore, MD: Naval Institute Press, 2010.

Doenitz, Karl, Admiral. *The Conduct of the War at Sea (essay).* Division of Naval Intelligence, 1946.

Dyer, George C. *On the Treadmill to Pearl Harbor: The Memoirs of Admiral James O. Richardson, USN (Retired).* Washington, D. C.: Naval History Division, Department of the Navy, 1973.

Keirns, Aaron J. *America's Forgotten Airship Disaster: The Crash of the* USS Shenandoah. Howard, OH: Little River, 2010.

Lehmann, Ernst A. *Zeppelin: The Story of Lighter-Than-Air Craft.* Croydon, U. K.: Fonthill Media, Limited, 1937.

Logbook, USS Akron (ZRS-4). National Archives and Research Administration, RG 24 A-1 entry 118-G, box 1, USS Akron, Washington, D.C.

Logbook, USS Los Angeles (ZR-3). National Archives and Research Administration, RG 24, A1, entry 118-G-L boxes 1-7, USS Los Angeles, Washington, D.C.

Logbook USS Macon (ZRS-5). National Archives and Records Administration, Washington, D.C.

Logbook, USS Shenandoah (ZR-1). National Archives and Research Administration, Box 1 of 2, R. G. 118-8, USS Shenandoah, Washington, D.C.

Lord, Walter. *Day of Infamy*. New York: Henry Holt and Company, LLC, 1957.

Lucky Bag. Vol. 21, Class of 1914. Philadelphia: Wm. H. Hoskins, 1914.

Luey, A. T. and H. P. Bruvold. *The "Minnie" or The War Cruise of the* USS Minneapolis. Elkhart, IN: Bell Printing Company, 1946.

Marshall, M. Ernest. *Rear Admiral Herbert V. Wiley. A Career in Airships and Battleships*. Annapolis, MD: Naval Institute Press, 2019.

McCrary, Frank N., Captain. National Personnel Records Center, National Archives, St. Louis, Missouri.

Moffett, William A., Captain, Director of Naval Aviation. *Airships and the Scientist*. Exclusive Release to U.S. Air Services, Press Release 089m June 28, 1921. Nimitz Library, Department of the Navy, U.S. Naval Academy, Annapolis, Maryland.

Nielson, Thor. *The Zeppelin Story: The Life of Hugo Eckener*. London: Allan Wingate, 1955.

Robinson, Douglas H. *The Zeppelin in Combat: A History of the German Naval Airship Division, 1912-1918*. Atglen, PA: Schiffer Military/Aviation History, 1994.

Rosendahl, Charles Emery, Vice Admiral. National Personnel Records Center, National Archives, St. Louis, Missouri.

Rosendahl, Charles Emery. *What About the Airship?* New York: Charles Scribner's Sons, 1938.

Rosendahl, Charles E., VADM. *United States Navy Airships in World War II*. Atlantis Productions, 1977.

Rosendahl, Charles E., Vice Admiral. *SNAFU The Strange Story of the American Airship*. Atlantis Productions, 2004.

Smith, Richard K. *The Airships Akron & Macon: Flying Aircraft Carriers of the United States Navy*. Annapolis, Maryland: Naval Institute Press, 1965.

Stephenson, Charles. *Zeppelins: German Airships 1900-1940*. Oxford, U.K.: Osprey, 2004.

"Technical Aspects of the Loss of the USS *Shenandoah*," *Journal of the American Society of Naval Engineers*, August 1926.

Toland, John. *The Great Dirigibles: Their Triumphs & Disasters*. New York: Dover, 1972.

Trimble, William F. *Admiral William A. Moffett: Architect of Naval Aviation*. Washington, D.C.: Smithsonian Institution Press, 1994.

USS *Minneapolis* (CA-36), Action Report for November 30–December 1, 1942, Serial 0247, RG 38, Records of the Office of the Chief of Naval Operations, World War II War Diaries, Boz 1220, National Archives and Records Administration, College Park, Maryland.

Winchester, Jim. *A Chronology of Aviation: The Ultimate History of a Century of Powered Flight*. New York: Metro Books, 2007.

Wood, Junius B. "Seeing America from the 'Shenandoa*h*': An Account of the Record-
    Making 9,000-Mile Flight from the Atlantic to the Pacific Coast and Return in the
    Navy's American-Built, American-Manned Airship." *National Geographic* 67, no. 1
    (January 1925), 1-47.
Zacharias, Ellis M. *Secret Missions – The Story of an Intelligence Officer*. New York: G. P.
    Putnam's Sons, 1946.

About the Author

M. Ernest Marshall, M.D. is a graduate of the School of Arts & Sciences and School of Medicine of the University of Virginia in Charlottesville, Virginia. A former Professor of Medicine in Hematology/Oncology, he is currently an award-winning author/historian focused on U.S. Navy history during the World Wars and inter-war years. His book, *Rear Admiral Herbert V. Wiley – A Career in Airships and Battleships* was the recipient of the prestigious Rear Admiral Samuel Eliot Morison Award for naval literature given by the New York Commandery of the Naval Order of the United States. He is noted for the depth of his research and his fluid writing style. With an abiding interest in the individuals who lived the history about which he writes, much of his work is biographical and based on oral histories and memoirs. The personal accounts are woven into official archival records from the National Archives and Research Administration. His research philosophy is, "if it can be known, I want to know it." He is a member of a number of historical societies including the Society for Military History, Naval Historical Foundation, Naval Airship Association, Naval War College Foundation, Naval Order of the United States, and Navy Lakehurst Historical Society. He resides in Charlottesville, Virginia, with his wife, Lisa.

www.ingramcontent.com/pod-product-compliance
Lightning Source LLC
Chambersburg PA
CBHW030410100426
42812CB00028B/2895/J